Erect Men
Undulating Women

The Visual Imagery of Gender, "Race" and Progress
in Reconstructive Illustrations of Human Evolution

Erect Men
Undulating Women

The Visual Imagery of Gender, "Race" and Progress
in Reconstructive Illustrations of Human Evolution

Melanie G. Wiber

Wilfrid Laurier University Press

This book has been published with the help of a grant from the Humanities and Social Sciences Federation of Canada, using funds provided by the Social Sciences and Humanities Research Council of Canada.

Canadian Cataloguing in Publication Data

Wiber, Melanie, 1954-
  Erect men/undulating women : the visual imagery of gender, "race" and progress in reconstructive illustrations of human evolution

Includes bibliographical references and index.
ISBN 0-88920-274-5

1. Feminist anthropology. 2. Anthropological illustration – Social aspects. I. Title.

GN799.W66W52 1997   305.40901   C97-930147-5

Cover design by Leslie Macredie using illustrations by H.T. Dignam

Printed in Canada

Table of Contents

List of Figures vii

Acknowledgments ix

ONE
Of Gender, "Race," Progress and Evolution: Human
Evolution Reconstructive Illustration 1

TWO
Contested Knowledge in the Human Evolution Story Field:
Man the Hunter versus Woman the Gatherer 17

THREE
Reconstructive Human Evolution Illustrations: Utilizing
Western Art Conventions in a Contested Story Field 47

FOUR
Gender: The Ubiquitous Story Operator 75

FIVE
Conflation and the Significant Other:
Racism and Codes of the Primitive 105

SIX
Window or Mirror? Primates and Foragers:
Analogies of the Pre-Cultural Life 121

SEVEN
Progress: Inevitable as Moral Rewards–
The Ultimate Story Operator 153

EIGHT
Lucy as Barbie Doll: Eroticism in the
Human Evolution Meta-Narrative 189

NINE
The Commodification of Human Evolution:
Selling a Story Field through Illustrations 203

TEN
Conclusions and Future Directions for Research 227

Figures 241

References Cited 257

Index 279

List of Figures

FIGURE   PAGE

1. The Greco-Roman Classical Male 241

2. Erect Man/Undulating Woman 242

3. The Gothic Nude Encased in Invisible Clothing 243

4. A Typical Dendrogram of Primate Evolution 244

5. A Typical "Progress Ladder" of Human Evolution 245

6. Male Centrality among *Homo erectus* 246

7. *Homo erectus* and the Beginnings of Culture 247

8. The Neandertal as Grotesque Other... 248

9. The Neandertal and the Prehistoric Patriarchal Family 249

10. Neandertal Burial Imagery Showing Male Masters of Ritual 250

11. *Homo sapiens sapiens*–Just Below the Angels 251

12. Archaic Humans Done with Aesthetic Athleticism 252

13. The Male-Sponsored Rise of Religion 253

14. Male Technological Prowess as the
    Inspiration for Art and Ritual 254

15. Anatomically Modern Humans in the
    French Postcard Genre 255

16. The Victorian Trope of Unruly Hair 256

Acknowledgments

RESEARCHING AND WRITING THIS BOOK hardly felt like "work" at all; over the past several years, many people have pondered with me over lunch and laughed with me in the hallways at each discovery of yet another outrageous illustration. Without this enjoyment and encouragement on the part of a number of friends, family, colleagues and students, I know this book would never have been completed. I am grateful to my husband, Darcy Dignam, for listening and offering constructive comments throughout the research and for reading through the various drafts. My brother-in-law Hugh Timothy Dignam stepped into the breach and with a very fuzzy charge and too little lead time, completed important illustrations without which the book would have suffered. The Women's Studies Group at the University of New Brunswick gave me feedback in the early stages of this research; the UNB Arts Faculty Publications Fund as well as the Department of Anthropology and WLU Press assisted with the permission fees for the illustrations. I am indebted to Peter Lovell and David Black of the Department of Anthropology for lending me books, discussing the paleoanthropological readings and being open to the deconstruction of their teaching bailiwick. I need also to thank the undergraduate and graduate students who were involved in one way or another with the research projects, especially Susan Blair who made time to participate while doing her master's degree in archaeology at UNB. Thanks to Sandra Woolfrey at Wilfrid Laurier University Press for seeing the potential in the very shaky first draft of this book and for encouraging a complete rewrite. Finally, I am grateful to the two anonymous reviewers who made important contributions to the final form of the book.

This book is dedicated to June Anne (Olshaski) Wiber and to Ernest Stanley Wiber, my mother and father, both of whom died while it was in production. Their loving encouragement and support were always there for me. I will miss them forever.

CHAPTER ONE

Of Gender, "Race," Progress and Evolution: Human Evolution Reconstructive Illustration

THE RESEARCH FOR THIS BOOK began in 1989 when a volume was published on the problem of integrating gender issues into college anthropology courses. In that volume, Adrienne Zihlman encourages instructors to ask their students to focus attention on "how women have been depicted in evolutionary reconstructions" and to "question the assumptions underlying these depictions" (1989:39). Suggested activities for students include examining the relative numbers of females portrayed in comparison to males, the relative placement of the two genders in the picture (foreground/background), the body posture, activities and demeanour of the two genders, whether a sexual division of labour is implied and whether reconstructions of our evolutionary past might actually reflect our own cultural stereotypes. I took Zihlman's advice by incorporating these questions into the course components of an undergraduate gender course which I have taught for many years. But in investigating the topic myself, I found that Zihlman's questions were incomplete and were addressed to too limited an audience. It is not only university students who are exposed to these sorts of illustrations, nor is it only gender stereotypes which underlie illustration form and content. Investigating the visual field of human evolution led me out into wider and wider circles of critical analyses, and to increasingly diverse fields of study. The results of this investigation embrace not only human evolution illustrations, but also the entire theoretical edifice upon which they are founded, and the process of popularization by which that theory is disseminated to the wider public.

Given the popularity of human evolution as a topic in the educational and quasi-educational publishing world, most people are familiar with the kinds of illustrations to which Zihlman refers. Whether one is reading older introductory textbooks in anthropology, or the latest issue of *National Geographic* or *Natural History*, the imagery often sticks with the reader longer than the text. In the Time-Life series of books on human evolution, the "road to *Homo sapiens*" is portrayed with a line of male figures travelling single file across the page, each looking progressively more human than its predecessor.

In *National Geographic*, an "ape-woman" pauses while crossing a volcanic plain to take an anxious look around. While she clutches her child on one hip, her male companion forges on ahead, fleeing the volcano with primitive weapon in hand. In an academic book on the African evidence for human origins, members of a band of hominids look like the proverbial "missing link." They cluster around the central figure of a male who confronts the viewer with a threatening display of temper. The several females present are all encumbered with offspring and crouch down, peripheral to the main action. In an anthropology textbook on the "emergence of man," several grotesquely robust Neandertal males sight a rhinoceros herd in the distance and prepare for a hunt, while the lone female sits and nurses an infant.

In image after image, the males hunt, make tools, protect their dependents, practise incipient rituals and solve evolutionary problems. Their gender-specific role is written in their upright physical form, marked out for straightforward and determined action. They are masters of their environment. Meanwhile, the females crouch low, nursing children, skinning animals and tending fires—bystanders to male activities. Their gender-specific role in evolution is equally written in the sinuous curves of their lax and grounded bodies. They are only called onto the evolutionary stage to play the role of sexual partner to the male protagonists, and to mother the resulting offspring. But gender turns out to be only one of several questionable themes in these illustrations. In the "road to *Homo sapiens*" image, for example, earlier hominid forms are represented as apelike, hairy and Negroid in features; later representatives on the road to humanity get progressively more hairless and fair skinned. In other examples of this same type of image, earlier hominids have no tools, or crude tools, while more recent hominids heft stone-tipped spears. Primates and modern hunter/gatherer populations are coded as primitive, while Euro-american *whiteness* and explicitly masculine technology act as conventions of progress; these codes are as pervasive an element of reconstructive scientific illustrations as are the androcentric biases. What message is it these illustrations are designed to convey?

As I sought more and more examples of the illustrator's art, another interesting factor emerged. Illustrations have changed in the past twenty years. Indeed, Zihlman discusses several illustrations as examples of a recent improvement in terms of the representation of gender. But other gender analysts examining educational publications are not so optimistic. Sue Rosser (1990) investigated science textbooks for the junior high school curriculum in the United States and found that subtle uses of illustrative material as well as other forms of sexism in textual material replaced many overt forms of sexism such as the use of masculine pronouns and exclusion of females from illustrations. A diachronic approach to investigating human evolution material demonstrates similar problems.

Human evolution publications seem particularly resistant to what some might call "political correctness." While the overt form of androcentric pronouns and language use has become less common in both textbook and quasi-educational publications on topics such as natural history and biology, this is not true in human evolution, particularly among those publications designed for the popular press. Titles, for example, often remain unabashedly androcentric, as with: "New Views of the Origins of Man" (Augereau and Dufour 1994), and "Skull in Ethiopia Is Linked to Earliest Man" (Wilford 1994); even the 1996 computerized version of *Encyclopaedia Britannica* on the World Wide Web is full of such terminology. Where textbooks or articles have been designed to avoid this overt androcentrism, many of the messages that no longer appear explicitly in the text remain embedded in the illustrations.

Several related questions are raised by these patterns. First, what are the motives of the people involved in crafting these illustrations (artist intention)? How do those motives relate to the text in which the illustrations appear and to the intentions of the science authors and publishers of that text? Second, how are these illustrations viewed and interpreted by the reader (readerly autonomy)? Third, how does that interpretation influence the reader (illustrative outcome)? The question of intention is extremely difficult to answer and presents a number of methodological challenges, many of which were beyond the scope of this study. However, the illustrator's training as an artist involves first and foremost developing skills in Western artistic technique. Recently, feminist art criticism has played an important role in exposing the relationship between technique (particularly in the use of Western conventions or "tropes") and the resulting messages contained in the medium. The use of these tropes is very suggestive of artist intentions. Elements of composition also serve as important clues. The rigorous realism employed as a stylistic convention in human evolution illustrations is now recognized as part of a larger science illustration pattern that Gifford-Gonzalez (1993:28) has called the "drive for credibility through visual realism." This need for credibility is suggestive of author and publisher intent, as well. Finally, another indirect source of information is found in the choice of what has been called the rhetorical mode of visual argument, wherein "the elements of pictures can individually encode or represent the premises of a verbal argument ... [and] then imply a conclusion of which the viewer is to be convinced" (Shelley 1996). Thus the rhetorical context of academic debates and the sociopolitical milieu of the day are also vital to explore. All of these sources of information have been employed in this book to look into the question of intention. In the future, however, it will be important to expand on these indirect sources with more direct ones, such as interviews conducted among the illustrators who make these images, scientists and editors who commission them, and publishers who get them into print.

This book also begins the investigation into the second question, that of readerly autonomy. I start from the premise that there are many possible ways these images can be read—both from the layperson's point of view and from the vantage point of the sensitized social scientist armed with the tools to deconstruct the meaning contained within them. The complexity of viewpoint is suggested by the discussion in Lutz and Collins (1993) on the "seven gazes" or the "looks and looking relations that swirl in and around" the photographs in *National Geographic*. Lutz and Collins (1993:187) list these as: "the photographer's gaze (the actual look through the viewfinder); the institutional magazine gaze, evident in cropping, picture choice, and captioning; the reader's gaze; the non-Western subject's gaze; the explicit looking done by Westerners who may be framed with locals in the picture; the gaze returned or refracted by the mirrors or cameras that are shown in local hands; and our own academic gaze." But my interest here is with the average layperson and what they see in these images; does their interpretation closely correspond to artist and authorial intent? Do readers, particularly non-expert readers, recognize the masculine technology complex, the feminine nurturing home base, the Eurocentric progress themes? There is certainly evidence that many people read sexual politics into these images, as I will discuss below. The third question (illustrative outcome), is only easy to explore if one assumes a relatively low level of readerly autonomy, and even then it raises many complex issues surrounding science popularization. For example, to what extent does science popularization try to convey the full complexity of the often hotly contested theoretical milieu when conveying "results" to the public? How well can the public be educated as to these points of contention and what level of comprehension will likely be the result? What effect will such comprehension, or its failure, have on public support for funding science research? Here it is only possible to touch on some of these issues. One aspect of outcome that interests me, however, is that human origins illustrations have apparently been consistent enough over the past five decades to have produced a very coherent picture among the wider public. One indication of this is the burgeoning genre of fiction which professes to tell the "human story" behind this history.

For example, in the early pages of a recent novel of this genre, Piers Anthony produces a story line which is obviously based on the *National Geographic* "fleeing the volcano" image described above: "The man walked straight ahead, intent on his mission: to find something to eat.... The woman followed just behind, keeping a wary eye on the child.... She heard something. She turned to her left and paused, listening and looking" (1993:12). It is not so much Anthony's use of this image to construct a fictional narrative that is revealing, but rather the nature of the relationship that exists between his two storybook characters. This relationship is a window into the lay interpretation of the popularization of paleoanthropological findings. In Anthony's narration: "The man grunted peremptorily, and the woman resumed her motion." Later on, after they found food, the woman and child became tired, so the woman "employed a familiar device" and "made a grunt of sexual suggestion," to which the man "reacted as expected." In describing their coupling, Anthony (ibid.:13) writes: "The woman was like a doll in his embrace, allowing him any liberty he chose to take." Her feminine ruse proves successful: "By the time he was done, both the woman and the child were rested." The dust jacket of this book describes it as the "culmination of more than a quarter century of research." Piers Anthony has obviously recognized several patterns in evolution publications during this research and has emulated them in the production of his book. If one examines other books in this genre, he is not alone in his interpretation.

The genre of human origins fiction became popular with the several works of Jean M. Auel, beginning in 1980 with the publication of *The Clan of the Cave Bear*. In this fictional account of the transition period between the Neandertals and the anatomically modern humans in Western Europe, Auel created a female protagonist who is blond (read *white*), tall, and smart—all essential characteristics by which Euroamericans separate themselves from the animals. Auel's book proved to be an extremely popular Stone Age soap opera, with Ayla (the fully modern human) as unwilling victim of the sexual advances of one Neandertal male, and as the loving mother of the resulting half-breed offspring. But Auel's tale is also an exploration of the perpetual nature/nurture debate. On the one hand, the Neandertals in Auel's book possess certain instinctive and inborn talents which Ayla does not share; on the other hand, Ayla consistently proves innately smarter than the Neandertals among which she grows up. In the long run, the inborn traits of the Neandertal prove to be less adaptive under conditions of change than does Ayla's cultural inventiveness.

Although Auel's books have a female protagonist, one of the dominant patterns in this genre of fiction is the naturalization of present day Euro-american folk concepts about gender, and the social and political centrality of the male.[1] While Piers Anthony's book is entitled *Isle of Woman*, for example, it actually spends most of its prose on males. It begins over three million years ago, with the australopithecines described above, and then progresses through all the various stages of human evolutionary history. At each of these stages, the book focuses on the sexual and family relationships of a "pair-bonded" couple. All these stories centre on the male. For example, in the australopithecine case, the female described in the passages above has a sister who is consort to the same male. The behaviour of these females is described entirely in

---

1   Terms such as "Euro-american" and "Western" have become part of our cultural discourse as we have learned to recognize the distancing and inventive patterns in the Western social sciences (see, for example, Said 1978). Lutz and Collins (1993:2) discuss "the important ideological line that Europeans have drawn through the Mediterranean Sea, separating themselves from all others." Western cultures, as the heir to Greco-Roman traditions, have a self-image of progress and enlightenment that has been largely conceptualized by "imagining" the non-Western world as less progressive and less enlightened.

terms of that male's needs, wants and activities. The two females organize their estrus, reproductive and lactating lives so that one of them is always sexually receptive to the male. In this way, they are both able to benefit "from his superior ability to forage and to protect them from both outsiders and other men in the tribe" (ibid.:14). When the story line moves on from the australopithecines, this male-centred focus continues. The pronoun "he" figures predominantly and themes of male technological prowess and the male role in cultural progress are significant story operators. For example, *Homo habilis* is a "he" that lived in the Great Rift Valley of East Africa. "He" used tools and "he" fought with *Australopithecus boisei* whenever they met, resulting in the eventual extinction of the *boisei* form. *Homo erectus* is also a "he" who had a larger brain and who "conquer[ed] the world."

While the male role in evolution is to continuously change, to outcompete other hominids in a survival-of-the-fittest style and to develop culture to subdue nature, the female role remains changeless. The repetitive nature of this female role is aptly summed up when Anthony (ibid.:148) writes: "with the birth of her child, Crystal believed she had truly come of age. She had proven herself capable in every aspect of marriage. What better success could there be in life?" Piers Anthony has interpreted human evolution illustrations, and the paleoanthropological text which they accompany, in many of the ways that concerned Adrienne Zihlman. What is disturbing about these patterns is the extent to which many people, including social scientists working on human evolution, see them as basically factual, if somewhat sensationalized.

Recognizing these patterns and their representation in education illustrations does not necessarily lead to critical analysis of them. After all, perhaps they are a true and accurate reflection of our evolutionary past. If that is the case, then it makes little difference that the fine print in the credits often states that the illustrations are based on an "artist's conception." Nor that the images themselves are presented in a narrative form. The story line in the *National Geographic* "fleeing the volcano" image, for example, satisfies our cultural expectations about the great antiquity of the nuclear family. We can never know for sure if it was a female australopithecine that walked across the volcanic plain three million years ago. We cannot know if she was trailing after a male who was her consort. We cannot know if she was burdened with their joint offspring. We cannot know if this little family was fleeing the volcano that

made the ashes that preserved their footprints. But does any of this ignorance matter? After all, we do know that upright-walking hominids
passed that way because they left their footprints behind to be found
over three million years later. Perhaps the simplest and most logical
assumption is that they were a nuclear family. But in fact these walkers
could as easily have been juveniles as adults, all male and/or female, or
completely separate travellers.

This illustration is not based on scientific conjecture, developed to fit
as many of the facts as possible. It is storytelling. Illustrations in journals
such as *National Geographic* are designed to tell stories, as a picture editor
from the National Geographic organization emphasized by saying: "This
is not travelogue, it is not journalism, it is not an art magazine, it is storytelling" (Lutz and Collins 1993:56). That would not be a problem except
that the power of the story has been enough to subvert science. There is
sound archaeological evidence to suggest that these footprints were
probably made by at least *three* different individuals, and at *different*
points in time. In the *National Geographic* publication on the Laetoli footprints, Mary Leakey acknowledged this and no attempt was made by her
to accommodate the artist's different conception. However, a few years
later in a BBC/Time-Life film, she did speculate that the hominids who
made the footprints in volcanic ash were perhaps a "first family." It is
hard to know when and where these "first family" ideas emerged; did
they predate and perhaps influence the artist's illustration, or did this
illustration later begin to work on Leakey's (unconscious?) interpretation
of the footprints (see chapter 4)?

The question of the influence of art is an important one. It is true that
the comprehension and appreciation of the content of any figurative representation will not be universally shared. Males and females, for example,
may get very different messages from the same image. And yet, it is often
assumed that given the particular cultural and social background of the
people who view them, illustrations will send roughly similar messages to
most viewers. In referring to the Victorian ease of "reading" the face and
body of human figures in Victorian art for information about their moral
character, intelligence, social class and personal habits, Mary Cowling
(1989:9) writes: "The scrutiny to which the painted face and figure were
subjected was a habit borrowed from life itself." This daily habit of reading
faces and figures for information did not die with the Victorians, although
without their firm belief in physiognomy, we perhaps do not feel there is

as much there to discover. But like the physiognomist, we do place some truth value on whatever information we glean. In short, viewers share in common the pattern of reading these illustrations as realistic, and as Gifford-Gonzalez (1993:28) notes: "realism is read as objective truth."

This was brought home to me again and again as I began to systematically document people's reactions to human evolution illustrations. I began by collecting an initial set of illustrations and informally discussing them with colleagues and friends. Later, many of these same colleagues began to come to me with examples that they themselves had collected. I then made slides of a set of twenty-two such illustrations, and discussed them with students in both graduate and undergraduate anthropology gender courses over a two-year period. As a result of issues raised by these discussions, I began to seek out more information on artistic conventions and on the more recent human evolution research. Next, I encouraged three graduate students to carry out a research project around the problem of how a very small sample of undergraduate university students interpreted these conventions.[2]

We designed a blind test procedure which involved one student describing the images to a second student who was placed behind a screen and was thus unable to see the illustrations. The second student was asked to place each illustration into one of four preselected categories, based on the verbal description provided by the first student. These four categories included "the Missing Link," "Man the Hunter," "the First Family" and "the Rise of Civilization," all themes found with regularity in the paleoanthropology literature. If necessary, the second student could ask questions of the first student after the initial description was offered, in order to help them make their choice of category for each illustration. The blind test provided a stimulus for the first student to describe what they saw in the illustrations without any input from the researchers which might direct their attention or lead their interpretations. The questions from the second student were also an interesting indication of how conventions were related to meaning. Fourteen students from a variety of academic backgrounds were involved in the blind tests. In addition to the blind tests, the study involved seven qualitative

---

2   I want to thank Susan Blair, Stephanie O'Sullivan and Vincent Bourgeois for their participation in various stages of this research.

interviews with individual students in order to solicit more detailed responses on a small set of images. These interviews specifically focused on how the students interpreted the narrative content of the illustrations as well as on their opinions as to the realism of the implied story line. We were particularly interested in drawing out student opinions with respect to illustrations of comparable content but with contrasting story lines (an illustration highlighting intra-hominid warfare as a source of early hominid mortality, for example, versus one illustrating predation of hominids by leopards).

Despite the anecdotal nature of most of my information, and the small sample in the more rigorous study, my findings were internally consistent and, in many cases, were suggestive of problems I had not recognized previously. Most students were able to recognize the visual devices by which the female gender was written into a role as sexual partner, nurturing mother and home caregiver, and some were even critical of the images. But a surprising number saw no problem with the gender representation. When they were specifically asked about the gender roles portrayed, students explained them by reference to "natural gender facts" and to "scientific" findings about our evolutionary history which proved the great antiquity of a gender-based division of labour. Challenging the representation of gender roles seemed to verge on denying the validity of modern theories about human evolution and thereby aligning oneself with "the Creationist Camp." Apparently, the gender "facts" in these images are so well submerged in the scientific knowledge being portrayed that people automatically conclude that all the information is equally well grounded in empirical fact. This was in sharp contrast to the racial implications, some of which were also easily accepted by students. But when students had the racist connotations pointed out to them, they often reported feeling offended by them and no one justified racism by reference to authoritative science.

What is science really able to tell about the history of our two genders and their respective roles in the evolution of the human species? Do these illustrations accurately reflect the archeological evidence, or do they better represent the modern politics of gender? For the average reader of popular magazines and books, and even of introductory textbooks, this question is probably never articulated, although there are many who take a critical view of these images for religious or other reasons. But for anyone interested in questions about the production, popularization and dissemination of what has been called "origins research" (Conkey 1991), the sources, validity and ultimate purpose of the imagery in these illustrations is important to investigate. Answering questions about scientific validity led me into several different fields of research, beginning with the state of current knowledge in the field of paleoanthropology, a field I had not followed closely since my graduate school days. I knew that there were new paleoanthropological findings being made every year, but I had not been following how they had been incorporated into the theoretical framework of human evolution. I was aware that origins research had been affected by the feminist upheaval in science, and had become a contentious field of discourse, involving several conflicting theories about the nature of our evolutionary origins. In chapter 2, I briefly cover these conflicting theories of human evolution which have come to be characterized by two powerful images: Man the Hunter versus Woman the Gatherer. I knew that in the struggle for theoretical dominance, the masculine mythology of the hunter was best and longest epitomized by the work of Sherwood Washburn and his intellectual heirs and students, Irven DeVore and Richard Lee. I also knew from my graduate school days that the Woman-the-Gatherer crowd was best represented by the work of Nancy Tanner and Adrienne Zihlman. But I had not appreciated the extent to which this struggle had become a losing battle for the feminists, especially with the recent publications of Richard Leakey and C.O. Lovejoy.

Having brought myself up-to-date on the changing theoretical discourse which is the context for human origins illustrations, I then turned to the techniques by which messages of "race," gender and progress were embedded in the seemingly innocuous medium of the educative illustration. Chapter 3 explores recent critical work by people such as Margaret Miles, Linda Nead, Lynne Pearce and Marina Warner, who have all focused on the female nude in Western art and pornography. Others, including Mary Cowling, Page duBois, and Anne Hollander, have traced the many relationships between historical and cultural influences and artistic expression. Their work allowed me to better understand the Western artistic conventions which are the basic building blocks of science illustrators. In both feminist criticism and art history, however, educational illustration has not received much attention. And so I turned to the relatively new field of "cultural studies," such as the work of Lisa Bloom, Donna

Haraway, Bruce Knauft, Catherine Lutz and Jane Collins, Diane Gifford-Gonzalez, and Stephanie Moser. Each of these has explored mass culture and especially the popularization of science in order to better understand the politics of science and its dissemination.

Mass culture is usually contrasted with popular culture in a distinction that sees the former as generated by powerful interests for consumption by the working classes and the latter as self-generating and thus somehow less manipulative and degenerate (see the discussion in Lutz and Collins 1993:5-6). Educational illustration is part of the larger exercise in mass culture and is explicitly designed to communicate the findings of a scientific elite to a somewhat devalued cultural group–the layperson. An important component of cultural studies has been the critical analysis of the content of and motivations for the dissemination of scientific findings through mass culture. Haraway, Lutz and Collins, and Bloom, for example, all work to deconstruct the dominant racial, gender and post-colonial imagery found in *National Geographic*'s use of visual materials. In the middle section of this book (chapters 4 through 7), I trace the appearance of many of the same themes in human evolution illustrations from a wide variety of educational and quasi-educational publishing outlets, including everything from textbooks to popular magazines.

Investigating how and why females are depicted in the ways they are in such illustrations requires looking into the how and why of patterns of male representation. In chapter 4, I examine gender attributes, roles and relationships as they are represented in various sample illustrations. As far as I can ascertain, the female images in human evolution illustrations are almost always accompanied by male counterparts, although the reverse is certainly not true. The sample of illustrations which I collected does not contain any female-only images. However, in her analysis of eighty-eight Cro-Magnon illustrations, Gifford-Gonzalez (1993) did find eight which portrayed women alone without male counterparts. In contrast, she found fully half the images she surveyed to be male-only. Female and male are obviously very much counter-images. The male form has less meaning without the female and the female form has no meaning without the male. This linked male-female meaning is partially connected to the conflation of female with nature and male with culture, which in turn is part of a larger cultural accretion of meaning which connects "race," gender and progress together in insidious ways. These meanings have led me beyond Zihlman's original questions about human evolution illustrations. In chapter 5, for example, I address the use of cultural and evolutionary "analogous others" in the construction of an idealized model of Western, masculine culture. The march of the hominids along the "road to progress" is also a lineup of modern "races" in condensed form. The physiognomy portrayed in body, cranium and facial type is like a reader for the Victorian application of racial and cultural stereotypes to physical form and to cultural achievements.

In chapter 6, I expand on this selective use of the analogous other to show how it allows women (especially women of colour), non-Western peoples (especially peoples of colour) and non-human primates to be codified as primitive in comparison to the progressive, white, Western male. These contrastive meanings of primitive and advanced have influenced the type of modern-day analogies considered useful in the reconstruction of the behaviour of hominid species long since extinct. Several extant species of apes as well as the peoples of modern foraging societies have been considered good sources of information on the past. But creating a primitive against which our progress can be measured has led to considerable theoretical disputes over the validity of human origins analogies. Some argue that the drive for origins analogy led to serious misrepresentation of the analogous other and indeed to the "invention" of spurious "facts" (the Great Kalahari Debate—Richard Lee versus Edwin Wilmsen; baboon or chimpanzee—Washburn and DeVore versus Zihlman). These arguments over scientific validity have in turn corresponded in complex ways to the changing Euro-american relationships with the so-called Third World. The use of foraging populations and non-human primates as modern-day windows onto our evolutionary past has excited accusations of neocolonial exploitation. Deconstructing human evolution imagery requires a better understanding of these several contested analogies, especially with regard to the diachronic picture of the visual representation of human evolution. As the politics of analogy have raged, various stylistic devices employed in illustrations have waxed and waned. Older-style imagery from a less contentious period becomes immediately recognizable, and the new devices exposed whereby illustrators attempt to avoid "politically incorrect" representations.

But the content analysis of origins illustrations must go deeper yet. Human origins imagery relies not only on cultural stereotypes (of male and female, of "race" and colour and accomplishment) but also on several interwoven inspirations including some very contentious aspects of evolutionary theory. There is the ubiquitous story operator of progress, which appears not only in human evolution, but according to Stephen Jay Gould is also a significant factor in the adaptationist literature of evolutionary theory in general. Survival of the fittest operates to explain all evolutionary questions of persistence, but Gould and his followers argue that evolution more closely resembles a "crap shoot" than it does a process involving the successful adaptation of superior forms. One of the more interesting aspects of the human origins illustrations is the way that such disputes are submerged so that progress and survival of the fittest reign supreme (see chapter 7). Thus, the content of origins illustrations is neither complete fabrication nor constrained by the known facts, but is instead an interesting mix of knowledge privileged as "scientific," theory masked as natural stories, and stereotype masquerading as legitimate hypotheses. This conglomeration makes it all the harder to dismiss their impact, or to critique their logical validity. And illogic is an important attribute of the human evolution story field, which is saturated with flaws in reasoning, flaws which have important interconnections. Examples include functionalism (explaining attributes by reference to their supposed function), presentism (assumed that what exists today must always have existed, and in that form and for that function), essentialism (boiling complex biological and cultural assemblages down to their so-called essential features, which are then explained by reference to their function) and universalism (assuming that specific features have the same characteristics and serve the same functions everywhere they occur and across all time frames). Illustrations preserve and perpetuate these logical flaws.

"Contested knowledge" turns out to be an excellent description of the field of human evolution; conflict characterizes the fields of paleoanthropology, paleontology, comparative anatomy and physical anthropology, primatology and the social anthropology of forager societies. Because of the influence of all of these on the scientific illustrator, these disagreements are all important grist for the mill of deconstruction. And this contentious context is particularly apparent when we do a diachronic analysis. Theories about the development of specific human traits, their order of appearance and the significance of their interaction, have all changed in the past few decades; these changes in turn have affected the illustrations. And yet, it is interesting how certain messages have been consistently maintained, particularly those pertaining to gender, "race" and progress. This constancy is not always overt. For example, a very subtle shift is noticeable in illustrations in recent years, a shift towards increasing "eroticization" of the female image (see chapter 8).

Perhaps this constancy relates to another important contextualizing aspect of human origins illustrations, the way in which they operate as commodities in capitalist systems of exchange. In chapter 9, I address the commercial aspects of illustrations to show how being commodities has a significant effect on their form, distribution and interpretation. This commodity aspect of illustrations requires a significant erasure of their context of production. Science illustrations are produced by artists who are individuals with differing backgrounds and interests; but these differences are submerged in the effort to constitute their work as scientific. These artists in turn are involved in complex relations with scientists, editors, and publishers; each of these have their own commercial and non-commercial motivations which are also submerged. Further, once illustrations are produced, they can be disseminated and consumed under a wide variety of marketing practices. Some illustrations take on a life quite independent of their original creator's intentions. Many types of institutions, with differing kinds of motivations and end goals, play a role in their creation and distribution. Copyright laws allow institutions and individuals who had little to do with the initial production of certain illustrations, to act as gatekeepers over their potential publication outlets. Finally, viewers consume them in widely varying contexts and with quite different interpretive outcomes. As the student responses recounted in this book show, there is no strict correlation between intent, distribution patterns, reader interpretation and ultimate outcome.

To summarize, the critical evaluation of the reconstructive illustrations found in educational publications on human evolution requires an appreciation of complexity. These visual images cannot be treated as simple pictures, nor can they be separated from the (con)text in which they appear. To begin to deconstruct their meaning, one must gain at least passing familiarity with theories, concepts and terms which originate in a wide variety of fields, many of which are now characterized by theoretical conflict. Readers may start out interested in better understanding the pictures they see in old magazines in their local dentist's office, but hopefully they will finish this book with a wider interest in and sensitivity to the political nature of many different fields of science discourse. I have only begun what should be a much larger process of critical evaluation. Much more research needs to be done so that we can think differently about the nature of scientific knowledge, about the history of our species and our cultural institutions, and about the over simplistic and misleading representation in visual form of these many complex ideas.

CHAPTER TWO

Contested Knowledge in the Human Evolution Story Field: Man the Hunter versus Woman the Gatherer

IN THIS CHAPTER I EXAMINE the various theories which attempt to explain our evolutionary history as a species, though I begin not with anthropology, but with literary analysis. Surprising as it may seem, there is an important connection between evolutionary theories and the morphology of folk tales. In his book *The Bones of Contention*, Lewin discusses the conclusions of a Yale graduate student looking into this link (1987:30, see also Landau 1991), and he characterizes them as being as important as any new fossil find. He calls her work "the missing link between literature and paleoanthropology." If human evolution accounts are read with an eye to their morphological structure, it becomes apparent that they have often been couched in the same form as the heroic epics of our cultural history. These epics have the same overall structure, whether we are dealing with Biblical tales such as the Garden of Eden, or Disneyesque versions of old classics such as Aladdin.

Borrowing from Landau, Lewin nicely summarizes the morphology of the Western folk tale, using human evolution accounts as an illustration. This morphology exhibits a basic pattern of several successive stages:

> the *introduction of the humble hero* (an ape, a monkey, or a diminutive prosimian) in an initially stable environment; our hero is then expelled from this safety (because of climatic change) and is forced to embark on a hazardous journey during which he must overcome *a series of tests* (new environmental conditions) and thereby *display his worth* (develop intelligence, bipedalism, etc); thus endowed, our hero develops further advantages (tools ... reason ...), only to be tested again (the rigors of Ice Age Europe); the *ultimate triumph* is the achievement of humanity (Lewin 1987:33, emphasis mine).

17

Why has this narrative organization, which is common to all Western heroic myths, been an enduring feature of origin stories in human evolution?

Do we need to concern ourselves with the narrative correspondence between folk tales and scientific accounts, between story operators and scientific hypothesis? After all, any phenomenon which has a sequential nature is surely best described and analyzed beginning at the beginning and working through to the end. But Landau's thesis is not just that our scientific explanations of human evolution conform in broad outline to narrative approaches, but that the demands of narrative approaches have structured our understanding of human evolution. Human evolution theory has become a "meta-narrative"; it has become theory, couched in the timeless form of a story and then treated as fact.

> Paleoanthropologists have told the same story over and over. This story, first recounted in the days when fossils were few, has constrained the interpretations of new fossil discoveries. It is by constraining interpretations of new fossil finds that narrative has held paleoanthropology captive (Landau 1991:178).

There may be several reasons for this conservatism, including the reluctance of Western researchers to part with interpretations that so closely approximate a central cultural tenet: the inevitability of rewards for innate virtue. Another reason may be that the audience to which these narratives are directed is similarly conservative in terms of what it can relate to, both in content and in the format of the information delivery. Or perhaps, as Haraway (1989) suggests, conservatism is not a symptom but an integral part of the state of evolutionary discourse. Ultimately, whatever the reasons for it, conservatism has blinded us to alternative approaches to the fossil data.

Conservatism and Consensus: The Story Field of Human Evolution

What is the scientific knowledge that is the context for images which attempt to reconstruct something of the physical form and possible lifestyle of various hominid evolutionary stages? In a recent introductory anthropology textbook, we are told that "there is widespread agreement over the broad outline, even though debate continues over details"

(Haviland 1994:134). Two points are important to keep in mind here; first, this "broad outline" has never really changed despite an enormous increase in fossil finds in recent decades; the basic ideas have been around since Darwin's time (Zihlman 1981:77). This conservatism is most apparent in paleoanthropological publications geared to the layperson. Second, the above quote demonstrates how the discipline presents an image of consensus in such publications, despite the highly public disputes on the relative importance of this or that fossil which sometimes rage between leading authorities. This public facade of consensus and conservatism seem strangely at odds with the hyperbole applied to each new fossil find, many of which are claimed to be "revolutionary" and to require the "dramatic rewriting of human history."

In contrast, a far more challenging feminist-inspired controversy has hardly been acknowledged in the literature geared to the layperson, much less described as revolutionary. Yet it was this controversy which struck at key elements of the human evolution story, mainly through the concerted efforts of a few practitioners who attempted to "raise the cost of defending some accounts" over others (Haraway 1988:81). The Man-the-Hunter model told one story of human origins, the Woman-the-Gatherer model offered a different story. It focused on a different "humble hero(ine)," altered the nature of the challenges faced by that hero(ine) and in the process, shook up the "broad outline" of human evolution far more than did some of the highly touted fossils. More importantly, it resulted in significant "rereadings" of the fossil record, which demonstrates just how context-specific those readings are. And finally, the Woman-the-Gatherer model was influenced by and was ultimately influential on the selection of those analogies with which we flesh out our evolutionary history. The feminists relied on different non-human primates (chimpanzees rather than baboons) and focused on the female gatherer rather than the male hunter in extant human foraging societies. This strategy effectively cast doubt on the old Man-the-Hunter stories. But the Women-the-Gatherer stories have been challenged in their turn by yet another narrative of human evolution, which some call the "Love-Joy hypothesis." In this chapter, I recount these various alternative stories told about human evolution, the Man-the-Hunter story, the Woman-the-Gatherer story, and the latest Lovejoy hypothesis in order to provide a diachronic and theoretical context for the many repetitive themes which feature in the illustrations.

Identifying the Contestants: Who Generates
Human Evolution Stories?

For the layperson, the field of evolution seems to involve a bewildering array of specialized fields of study. Paleoanthropology, for example, is a sub-field within anthropology which is specifically concerned with the study of hominid evolution and which in turn has many different fields contributing to it. Primatology, or the study of the primate order, including the human species and our closest relatives both past and present, makes important contributions in comparative anatomy and behaviour, and in taxonomic issues. Physical anthropology studies human biological diversity, ranging across time and space. These three fields have a significant degree of overlap in their research interests, and all are further united in that their central theoretical tenet is Darwinian evolution. For that reason, paleontology, which is the study of ancient life forms through the fossil record, is also relevant because of its influence on evolutionary theory and its ability to provide supporting data. Each of these disciplines has played a role in the development of modern story fields in human evolution. Practitioners drawn from all of these fields have been key players in the contests over what is accepted as human origins knowledge.

One thing that unites the practitioners of paleoanthropology, primatology and physical anthropology is that they all operate on the boundaries of the physical and social sciences and as such, work at the boundary between nature and culture. Many people are drawn to these disciplines, both as specialists and as interested laypersons, precisely because of this boundary status. It translates into tremendous influence in the wider society; much of the research product on human evolution enters very rapidly into political and social debates about human nature, normal versus abnormal behaviour, gender roles and cultural organization. Primatology, for example, has long made authoritative statements on a wide range of topics including appropriate psychiatric treatments, marriage counselling, the natural place of mothers, social disorder and the discussion of the human propensity for territoriality and warfare (Haraway 1983:178). Paleoanthropological models of hominid gender-specific behaviour have been used to explain modern Western patterns of dating, premarital sex and even rape. Paleontology generates theoretical ideas that interact with and impact on social and political beliefs— about the primacy of the individual, for example, and the nature of the struggle for survival. As a consequence of this boundary science position, primatology, physical anthropology, paleoanthropology and paleontology are all rife with what Haraway (1989) calls "contested meanings."

Paleoanthropology, for example, does not produce "facts" so much as it does "interpretations." All so-called *data* in this field must be given some *constructed meaning*, including such things as the significance of the geological stratigraphy of a fossil, its age as established through radiometric or other dating techniques, its characteristics of dentition, hip and skull structure, the evidence of associated flora, fauna and cultural remains found with it, and the wear patterns on teeth or cut marks on bone. Furthermore, constructed meaning, particularly on the boundary between culture and nature, is often value-laden (see Haraway 1983, 1988, 1989) and as such is often politically and socially contentious. So it is that we find the contested concepts of gender, "race," relative cultural merit and other social values becoming significant influences in question generation, research design and theory construction. This contentious aspect of many branches of human scientific knowledge has recently spawned a postmodern field of study which examines, among other things, how such contests shape the knowledge that receives widespread acceptance (see Caplan 1988, Conkey 1991, di Leonardo 1991, Haraway 1989, Sperling 1991). What are the ultimate stakes that promote such contests in the first place, and how do the resulting debates induce strange intellectual alignments for political ends?

While the contentious process of constructing meaning in paleoanthropology has been highly visible to practitioners, the public has not been made aware of the nature of the disputes nor of the stakes in the human origins contest. Behind the scenes there has been a war going on in human evolution research, waged over the provocative issues of "forces for change," "origins" and "gender"—all of which have been core operators in the stories scientists have constructed to explain our history as a biological species. Although there are various "camps" involved in the ongoing skirmishes, the war ultimately boils down to whether or not the significant actor in human history was Man the Hunter,[1] or was

---

1 Elaine Morgan (1972:4) has aptly dubbed this model the "Tarzan theory." Haraway (1988, 1989) also refers us to the Tarzan saga and explores the meaningful content of its narrative structure.

instead Woman the Gatherer. Recent quasi-educational publications and even introductory textbooks in anthropology have tended to obscure the heat generated by these two opposing viewpoints, and to smooth over the controversy as one of minor "details." But anyone evaluating those reconstructive images which were produced while the battles were raging must become aware of the fundamental discrepancies between the various protagonists because illustrators have not been innocent bystanders to the skirmishes.

When paleoanthropological illustrations are examined in chronological order, that is, according to the date they were published, it is apparent that there is significant interaction between the theoretical debates of the period and the product of the illustrator's work. This might be explained by the earnest attempts of illustrators to objectively portray the various arguments developed by each side. But a closer examination which combines knowledge of the Western art world with its meaningful conventions and the controversy within paleoanthropology, reveals that illustrators have been among the front-line troops in the battle for establishing the distinction between scientific knowledge and what some have called the "politically correct" but unfortunately "unscientific" feminist theory (see Haraway 1989).

The intended audience of quasi-educational and educational illustrations comprises, for the most part, non-experts; that is, students in undergraduate anthropology courses, or the general public who read the popular press or visit museums. These are the people for whom some fleshing out of the dry facts is often considered necessary, and among whom there is rarely a good command of the supporting data or evolutionary arguments upon which such theories are based. How is human evolution explained to such an audience in the textual material which accompanies the illustrations they see? Primarily, these laypersons are now and have long been presented with a narrative which fits very well into their cultural expectations.

Man the Hunter

In his Preface to *The Territorial Imperative*, Robert Ardrey (1966:v) writes of the tremendous excitement he felt in 1955 when Raymond Dart introduced him to a room filled with fossilized bones. He speaks of the intellectual stimulation of "discovering" that man's earliest ancestors had been hunters, who for "unknown ages had been killing other species for a living before we started killing each other for fun." During the 1960s, together with a group of other popularizers (Lorenz 1966; Morris 1968; Tiger 1969), Ardrey aggressively promoted this image of the human evolutionary past in an atmosphere of public debate over the legitimacy of the Vietnam War. Whatever else the wider public came to know about human evolution, it received the message that *man*kind was naturally aggressive and fiercely territorial. This image of our so-called, biologically determined characteristics was perfectly in tune with the experiences of people embroiled in three major wars in as many decades (World War Two, the Korean War and the Vietnam War), however much it may have been out of step with student radicalism of the 1960s. In the years since that heady period of intense political debate, this image of Man the Hunter has proven surprisingly resilient. Morgan (1972:2) writes: "The legend of the jungle heritage and the evolution of man as a hunting carnivore has taken root in man's [*sic*] mind as firmly as Genesis ever did." Indeed, the structure of the Biblical story of Genesis and that of the Man-the-Hunter model have significant similarities, with our first evolutionary precursors standing in for Adam and Eve in the Garden of Eden. On the other hand, Elaine Morgan (1972:4) dubbed this model the "Tarzan theory," a theme which Haraway (1988, 1989) explores by reference to the meaningful content of its narrative structure. Whether Man the Hunter resonates to the Biblical Adam and Eve or to the heroic Tarzan, the fact that this highly public and popular version of the human origins story was filled with errors and grossly oversimplified several theories which anthropologists were postulating at the time, was in no way a limitation to its popularizers (Tanner 1981:25-26). In fact, the reverse was probably true. The popular press with its emphasis on hunting stories that resonated to Adam's patriarchal authority, had for many decades a profound effect upon the scientific theorizing. The resulting theoretical model takes the following approach to human history.

During the geological epoch known as the Miocene, a period of time beginning around 23 million years ago and lasting approximately 18 million years, the primate order went through a process of marked species diversification with many species radiating outwards from Africa, spreading into Europe and Asia. In the process, primates relied on several significant characteristics of their order: stereoscopic, three-dimensional vision, nails instead of claws and hands that grasp to facilitate swift movement through trees, shoulder and limb structures adapted to swinging and climbing, larger brains than many animals of their size and relatively unspecialized teeth. However, as the climatic fluctuations associated with the late Miocene unfolded, these animals were faced with an ecological challenge involving significant cooling and drying trends resulting in marked environmental change. The extinction of many forms followed, as did the radical morphological change of others. The Man-the-Hunter model postulates that in order to survive these global upheavals, at least one primate species adapted by leaving the safety of the trees and heading out onto the savanna.

At the time of the widest dissemination of the Man-the-Hunter model, the term savanna resonated with danger and mystery, as can be estimated by some of the rhetoric used to describe it. Pfeiffer (1978:33), for example, refers to it as "dry plains, as wide as oceans" and in addition writes: "In a sense nature was more natural then, the wilderness was wilder than it has ever been since. It might have been an Eden of a sort." Whether or not it was an Eden, the primates who moved out onto the savanna were not adapted to a ground-dwelling life. In order to survive there, a new set of behaviours and morphological characteristics were needed. These changes culminated millions of years later in the human species. The process of change was punctuated by morphological forms which were either directly ancestral to the human line or were side-branches in the same (hominid) family tree. Thus early *Australopithecus* transformed into *Homo habilis*, which turned into *Homo erectus*, which turned into archaic forms of fully modern mankind such as the Neandertals, which finally turned into modern-day *Homo sapiens sapiens*.

Ardrey, Morris and others promoted the hunting lifestyle as the impetus for most of these changes. In the scientific community, a similar narrative emerged which was reflected in the academic publications of major proponents of the Man-the-Hunter model, including Washburn, DeVore, Hall and Lee (see chapter 6). In their view, primitive mankind had first to learn to hold themselves erect to see over the grasses for prolonged periods, both in order to spot their new sources of food and to avoid ground-dwelling predators which they had never had to confront before. Second, they had to be able to move quickly across the grasslands in pursuit of game animals which supplied the bulk of their new diet. A host of new behavioural complexes had to emerge, including running, dodging, turning quickly, and the coordination and balance required to aim and throw accurately and to stalk slowly. Over time, these behavioural changes led to the development of a bipedal gait. Other physiological changes developed in a feedback relationship with bipedalism and new food-getting behaviours, including enlarged brain size, more dexterous hands, the capacity for speech and a prolonged infant dependency. While the grasslands presented many opportunities for surviving the Miocene environmental upheavals, they were also an extremely dangerous place for a small primate to be, especially one that was a relatively weak creature compared to those animals already adapted to life on the savanna. In some ways these hominids became even weaker, as when they lost their large canine teeth. But this anomaly, along with others, is explained in the Man-the-Hunter model by reference to encephalization, which is associated with greater intelligence and the primitive beginnings of culture. As the brain enlarged and became more inventive, cultural solutions to survival problems eliminated the need for biological ones.

The model simply assumes that males took the lead in both physiological and cultural developments. Sexual dimorphism is read as hard evidence that males became larger and more aggressive, most likely in order to defend the group. Analogous primate groups such as the baboon are used to argue that social cooperation among hominid males allowed them to share the twin burdens of group protection and of the hunt. A social hierarchy, where each animal knew its place and how to act in situations of danger, served as the foundation for this social cooperation. The extended period of time that males were required to spend together on the hunt led to male bonding which also enhanced cooperation (Lionel Tiger quoted in Pfeiffer 1978:126). To protect themselves from predators and also to eat, tools were developed primarily in the form of crude stone weapons. Tool manufacture was related to the development of changes in the structure of the hands. Making and using tools may also have reinforced or actually led to bipedality (Washburn cited in Howell 1965:50). Tool use required that the brain become more adept at planning and foresight, requiring larger brains again, as well as language for thought and communication. As intelligence continued to increase, the hominids were able to retain more knowledge about their terrain, the habits of animals, the patterns of plant growth and maturity, and to pass these on to their offspring. Bipedality, encephalization, speech, tool use and the rise of culture all developed together in a complicated feedback relationship, each reinforcing the other and all allowing *man*kind to emerge as the most adaptive and thus the dominant species on earth.

And where was the female in this picture of evolutionary success? Females are relatively invisible in the Man-the-Hunter model, largely because of cultural assumptions about the respective traits and attributes of each gender. For example, females could not play a significant role in evolutionary events for reasons having to do with their biological nature. The new importance of hunting created several problems for the gender. Burdened with a weak and dependent offspring as all primates are, and being morphologically smaller and weaker than the male, the female could not participate in the hunt and thus could not feed either herself or the young. Males had to provision these weaker members of the group. But other aspects of female physiology also caused problems. Estrus females set off mating frenzies in which males fought with each other over access to the receptive female. Given that male cooperation on the hunt was necessary to survival, this old pattern of male competition for mating opportunities became counter-productive (Chard 1975:87; Pfeiffer 1978:128). Thus, pair bonding emerged as an adaptive behavioural complex which at once solved both problems. Since one male and one female mated for life; the monogamous human family emerged; females exchanged sexual fidelity for material support, and male bonding was no longer threatened. Several morphological changes facilitated these lifelong partnerships. In the most important of these, females became permanently sexually receptive through the loss of estrus.

The male-male cooperative social bonds were not the only type of social bonds threatened by mating frenzies associated with female estrus. Mating also placed maladaptive stresses on another important behavioural complex—the mother-infant relationship. This relationship also underwent significant change under the pressure of bipedalism and encephalization. As female physiology changed to adapt to upright walking and as infants were born with larger heads as a result of encephalization, the birth process became more traumatic for females and had to occur at an earlier stage of infant development. This led to more helpless infants and a longer dependency period after birth. Concealing ovulation helped these dependent young in two ways. It protected infants who were still clinging to their mothers from injuries related to mating battles, and also enabled females to be continuously sexually receptive which more closely bonded the provisioning male to her and thus to her child (see

Diamond 1993 for an updated version of this argument). Physiological changes increased female attractiveness to males, including larger breast size, fleshy earlobes and buttocks, and everted lips (Morris cited in Morgan 1972:11). These changes were necessary to "counterbalance the new appeal of male-male associations" (Pfeiffer 1978:128).

From the time of its first appearance, some aspects of this Me-Tarzan, You-Jane model were more highly dramatized than others by its popularizers, and this led to significant criticism. Reviewers of Ardrey's books for example, pointed out that the proto-hominids would have needed the entire evolutionary grab bag of adaptive changes fully developed before they would have had any chance of competing on the savanna against other carnivores (see Tanner 1981:26). Other criticisms focused on the androcentric features of the Ardrey-Lorenz-Morris-Tiger publications, and on their assumption that the male of the species was far more important to the development and consequences of our evolutionary history than the female. In biological terms, of course, this does not make much sense. One of the most interesting of these critiques also appeared in the popular press, where it poked fun at the Ardrey-and-Gang popularization and postulated an alternative hypothesis of the "descent of woman" in an aquatic environment (Morgan 1972). Whatever the weaknesses of the Man-the-Hunter model, it was this lack of a role for the female half of the species that ultimately sparked development of a significant theoretical alternative, one that developed at a time when the accumulating evidence had begun to suggest significant problems with the dominant story line.

Destabilizing a Story Field: New Fossils and New Interpretations of the Old Evidence

The hunter narrative was first developed when the fossil record was relatively limited, as was other kinds of data which play a supporting role in the interpretation of those fossils. What is often downplayed in the educational publications is that fossil evidence is *still* relatively fragmentary and further, subject to a number of possible alternative *interpretations.* Teeth are one of the most durable of body parts and they tend to preserve best in the fossil record. The further one goes back in time, therefore, the more the fossil record comprises portions of jaw or individual teeth. These can tell a paleoanthropologist more than a layperson might suspect, but teeth are still relatively limited sources of information. Remains from the neck down are far less common, and have excited proportionately more interest whenever they have been found, especially since bipedal locomotion is thought to be the first significant feature to distinguish early hominids from their Miocene ancestors.

On the basis of this limited data, textbooks and popular accounts usually present the reader with a bewildering succession of species categories arranged in a chronological series suggesting the progressive development of humankind. In other words, these texts "make a call" on individual fossils and then discuss them in the order of a presumed phylogeny, and of a presumed one-track, physiological and cultural process of change ultimately resulting in the human species. While experts argue over the placement of individual fossils into this chronological scheme, there is little challenge of the overall ladder-of-progress model. I think it no accident that this chronological, progress-oriented approach closely duplicates the logic underlying a Renaissance model of the universe known as the Great Chain of Being (see chapter 7). It could be argued that fossil data is best presented in some logical and *natural* fashion in order to make sense of the mass of information presented in human evolution stories. But the host of assumptions that go into this ladder-of-progress model are never explicitly explored and possible alternative interpretations that could place various fossils in different categories are often downplayed. Interpretation largely focuses on several key areas of the anatomy: the cranium (particularly its overall size and shape as well as the location of the foramen magnum or opening that allows the spinal chord to enter the skull), the maxilla and mandible (particularly the size, shape and pattern of both jaws and teeth), the shoulder (including shape and angles of scapula and clavicle), the lumbar curve, the pelvis (size and shape of ilium, sacrum and pelvic opening), the hip, knee and ankle joints as well as the length and size of femur, tibia and fibula, and the shape and proportion of hands and feet. All of these physiological manifestations are represented as if they relate very straightforward stories about the life of a biological organism and more importantly about its place in our family tree.

But in fact, whether a paleoanthropologist is examining teeth, cranium or post-cranial fragments, the discipline has been extremely conservative with respect to how these fossils are to be interpreted. Since the earliest days of excitement about the "missing link," questions about a particular fossil usually centre around its relationship to modern humanity, rendering paleoanthropological analysis very "*Homo sapiens*-centric." Fossils that exhibit more "archaic" forms of teeth, jaw, hip, knee, hand or foot, are either placed further back along the human family tree, or further away in the phylogenic relationship to humans. A host of assumptions flow from such categorization. Non-ancestors are not thought to have much intelligence, nor to have used tools or other cultural attributes, nor to have been very good at long-term survival. While other kinds of questions are sometimes addressed, such as the adaptive behaviour patterns suggested by morphological characteristics, these are usually only asked when they have some significance to human evolution. For example, the evidence for variation in size and shape among several australopithecine fossils from the same time period is said to represent either sexual dimorphism or species variation. But the way this question is addressed relates to two *Homo sapiens*-centric issues, the origins of human sex roles and the ancestral status of the more robust forms (i.e., are they direct ancestors or evolutionary dead ends?). Public interest will be generated only when a scientist can authoritatively position a fossil in the hominid family tree as ancestral to the human branch.

This *Homo sapiens*-centric tendency in the interpretation of fossils remains unabated, but in recent years the new fossil finds have had the effect of narrowing public interest, from a wider focus on all so-called transition periods to a narrower interest in the "early transition" from the Miocene ape to the australopithecine. The amount of research funding, academic disputes and publication success that the research surrounding the australopithecines has recently received is one indication of this new first origins interest. And it is at this early transition phase that problems first began to multiply for the Man-the-Hunter model. There are several fossils which have been key to this development, particularly by pushing the chronology of human history further back in time and thereby significantly complicating the narrative plot (see Johanson and Shreeve 1989:22). In 1924, when M. de Bruyn found the Taung Child fossil skull in South Africa, the Man-the-Hunter model was already securely entrenched. When the Taung Child was dated at between one and two million years of age, this significantly extended the temporal range of the hominids but did not seriously threaten the model. Together with "Zinj," another fossil found at Olduvai Gorge in East Africa in 1959 by Mary Leakey, the Taung Child established the australopithecines as *the* significant actors in the drama of human origins. Although these fossils and others like them had relatively small brains, their cranial capacity was marginally larger than other members of the primate family and they were definitely bipedal. While Tobias (1974:39) was later to argue that the Taung Child skull forced the realization that brain enlargement was neither the first nor even among the earliest of the developments leading to humanity, the fact that the australopithecines lacked tools and that bipedalism seemed the only definite transition characteristic associated with them was not enough to seriously challenge the traditional analysis or to destabilize the Man-the-Hunter model.

Then in the early 1970s, Bernard Ngeneo, a member of the Leakey research team, uncovered many fragments of a skull which was given the designation ER 1470 and dated to around 1.9 million years ago. When it was reconstructed, the skull had a relatively complete cranium, plus fragments of the facial bones. Although this skull was older than Zinj, Richard Leakey thought it represented something significantly new in evolutionary terms, given its larger cranial size. He classified it as *Homo habilis*, the first representative of the *Homo* line, thus suggesting that the more robust Zinj fossil was a hominid side-branch culminating in an evolutionary dead end. While there are arguments about the status of ER 1470 (it has been variously classified as a late australopithecine, as a transitional form, or as a full-fledged *Homo habilis*), it does suggest that the direct ancestors of humans probably coexisted with other more "primitive" hominids for a relatively long period of time. This finding was clearly inconsistent with a unilineal view of evolution where gradual and cumulative changes over time transformed an inferior ancestral stock into successively more superior forms until the arrival of the human species. Surely our ancestors would have been better adapted than any other extant hominid? Their status as founding fathers of the human line proves their staying power and thus their evolutionary superiority. But then, what were they doing coexisting over such long time periods with clearly inferior forms which were doomed to extinction? There were more australopithecines out there than were needed to play the role of our ancestors.

In 1974, Donald Johanson's research team created more problems by discovering something unprecedented in fossil history. A number of fragments of a fossil found in Hadar, Ethiopia, and dated to over three million years ago, were found to represent one female individual with a significant proportion of the post-cranial bones preserved. Dubbed "Lucy," the extreme age of this fossil represented the best look yet at the early transition period offered by the archaeological record. Her stature as postulated from leg bone proportions, was a diminutive three feet tall. Much of her pelvis was preserved, as were portions of both arms, the rib cage, some leg bones, the mandible and a few cranial fragments. In addition, the bones from approximately twenty other individuals (dubbed the "First Family") were also found at the same site. Although it has been suggested that Johanson and his collaborators have monopolized these fossils and have not published complete descriptions of the finds (Haraway 1989:343-44), his interpretation that they represent a very early stage of the australopithecines has been widely accepted.

In an analysis that surprised many, Johanson interpreted the Lucy fossil as a functional biped, thus pushing back the earliest dates for the transition to upright walking. With her apelike dentition and very small cranial capacity, Lucy also confirmed what many paleoanthropologists had suspected for some time, that bipedality developed significantly ahead of other codes for morphological modernity, including encephalization, tool use and changes to the structure of the hand. Lucy also challenged other sorts of origins assumptions. While the gracile or relatively small australopithecines had long assumed "ancestral status" relative to humans, the Lucy find stimulated heated debate as to the status of the robust varieties which were found to exist at roughly the same time and in roughly the same places. Were they a separate species or possibly the larger male counterparts of Lucy's species? This gender dimorphism argument has allowed some to downplay the importance of the fact that both the gracile and robust forms of the australopithecines appear to have coexisted for a much longer time frame than was ever expected, and to thereby maintain intact the unilineal view of human evolution.

Another fossil find, this one at Laetoli close to the Olduvai Gorge, pushed the origins of bipedality even farther back in time. In 1978, Mary Leakey found the remains of footprints, made in deep volcanic ash, fossilized and preserved for approximately 3.5 to 3.7 million years. These footprints suggest an accomplished bipedal gait with a stride much like modern humans (Tuttle 1985). In order to explain them, the origins of bipedality have been dated to as far back as four million years before the present. This gives the human branch of the family tree significant antiquity, but it also causes problems because bipedalism now appears to have developed more than two million years before other significant morphological changes leading to the human species. It was at this point that many began to seriously reconsider aspects of the Man-the-Hunter model (see Pilbeam 1980). This was followed in the early and mid-1980s by a series of fossil finds which further confused the picture.

In 1985, the so-called Black Skull was found by Alan Walker near Lake Turkana. It dates to approximately 2.5 million years ago but displays a very puzzling mixture of features. It strengthens the possibility that the several gracile and robust species of the australopithecine genus may have coexisted for close to a million years, since it pushes back the time frame for one of the most robust species, the *Australopithecus boisei*, by at least three hundred thousand years. Further, the anatomical features of this robust species appear to have been stable for more than a million years, and surprisingly, it appears to be the robust australopithecine which shows an early increase in brain size (Kottak 1994:164). This find led many of the most influential paleoanthropologists to adopt the idea that at least some of the robust varieties represent a sex-role specialization resulting in sexual dimorphism among a single species of australopithecines (Leakey and Lewin 1992). The latest excitement over the early transition phase was generated in 1994, when Tim White and his colleagues reported finding an early Pliocene hominid, perhaps the precursor to Lucy and the First Family (White et al. 1994; WoldeGabriel et al. 1994). These *Australopithecus ramidus* date to approximately 4.4 million years ago and appear to have been forest dwellers. But their morphological characteristics (especially the placement of the foramen magnum at the base of the skull) are suggestive of some bipedality.

Meanwhile, all this emphasis on the importance of the australopithecines has downplayed the importance of the next evolutionary transformation, from the australopithecines to the *Homo* family. But explanations of this transition also require reconsideration, particulary the scenario of a slow and gentle transition. In 1984, for example, "*Homo erectus* Boy" (WT15,000) was found in West Turkana by Kimoya Kimeu, a collaborator of the Leakey family. The fossil was dated to around 1.6 million years ago and enough of it was recovered to determine that the age at death was approximately twelve years. *Homo erectus* Boy not only demonstrates significant encephalization, but also a surprising and inexplicable jump in body size; he would have been around five feet five inches tall at death, giving a probable height at maturity of around six feet. This is particularly puzzling given that the hominid fossils that predate *Homo erectus*

Boy demonstrate no such dramatic changes in body size. This suggests a "rapid and sudden transformation" occurring sometime around 1.6 million years ago, but the process does not seem to have happened in a steady and uniform way. In 1986, for example, Tim White found a fossil at Olduvai which dates to 1.8 million years ago or very close in age to *Homo erectus* Boy. This fossil has been interpreted to be a *Homo habilis*, the species assumed to be the direct precursor of *Homo erectus*. However, Tim White's fossil find is just as small in stature as Lucy, but with longer arms, suggesting a species with a locomotor pattern adapted to both terrestrial and arboreal environments over one million years *after* Lucy and just a few hundred thousand years *before Homo erectus* Boy.

Given these recent fossils, there is now little support for a process of gradual development, from smaller to larger size, of morphological reorganization, and of larger brain size, nor for a linear evolutionary narrative, although some researchers remain committed to these ideas. While the transformation to bipedalism has been pushed back to more than four million years ago, the other morphological changes such as encephalization, larger bodies and tool use appear to lag significantly behind, with most developments only appearing rather suddenly more than two million years later around the *Homo erectus* stage. As if this were not enough, what went on between is hardly conducive to supporting the Man-the-Hunter model, as there is obviously a far more complicated evolutionary history for which it cannot account. The fossils do not support a pattern of slow, linear and progressive change based on a feedback relationship between encephalization, bipedality, tool use and a hunting lifestyle. While various efforts have been underway to shore up the shaky edifice, attacks have come from another direction; the androcentrism of Man the Hunter has also been subject to a destabilization process, one which originated in the feminist movement.

Woman the Gatherer

In the early 1970s, when I was an undergraduate, a slim little book made the rounds among my fellow anthropology majors. It was not assigned by any professor and it was never covered in any lecture material, yet we spent more time discussing it than most assigned readings. It was funny and filled with a dry sarcasm and heavy ridicule. We delighted in reciting the most biting passages to each other. Another appeal was that it challenged material that our professors were teaching in a very non-critical way. The object of the ridicule was the Man-the-Hunter hypothesis and the book was Elaine Morgan's *The Descent of Woman* (1972). In it she belittled and berated the hunter model until it seemed the most ridiculous, romanticized kind of fantasy concocted especially to please the Western male ego (she saved her most acerbic comments for the pair-bonding hypothesis). Morgan questioned the notion that the transition to a predator lifestyle would have been necessary and also that it would have necessarily required a bipedal gait. She expressed doubt that the required changes could be accomplished quickly enough to prevent our ancestors from becoming a "leopard's lunch." She openly ridiculed the suggestion that breasts, earlobes and everted lips were developed to attract males and thus cement the pair bond. She demonstrated how easily equally plausible, functionalist accounts could be constructed around an evolutionary "beach bum" hiatus in the African coastal waters during the Miocene drought. However little the academic community subsequently took her "aquatic ape" theory seriously (see Roede et al. 1991), her books had the effect of demonstrating the flaws of simplistic functional explanations as well as the deeply androcentric assumptions at work in Man the Hunter. In my mind, the model never seemed quite reasonable again. Of course the reception to this heresy among the scientists was vitriolic. Mary Leakey called it "the outcome of an overfertile imagination" (cited in Richards 1991:115-16).

At about the same time, however, the momentum was building behind other more academically grounded critiques. At the American Anthropological Association meetings in 1970, Sally Linton (now Slocum) presented a paper in which she critiqued the androcentric bias of the Man-the-Hunter model and exposed it for a construct based on Western male-centred interests and self-images. She argued that it was important to rewrite the human origins narrative to include females. She suggested one way to do this might be to incorporate the evidence from modern-day hunting and gathering societies where it was found that females contributed the largest proportion of the diet by weight (see Lee 1969). But she emphasized that the greatest challenge would be to ask questions differently and to ask different questions; this was a challenge taken up by Adrienne Zihlman and her colleague Nancy Tanner (see Haraway 1989:334-35). Zihlman is a physical anthropologist at the University of California at Santa Cruz, who has worked on the early transition phase in hominid evolution with a particular focus on bipedality. Nancy Tanner was a social anthropologist. Together they began to develop an alternative origins story by asking how *female* activities, reproductive investments, and patterns of behaviour could have influenced human evolution (see especially Tanner and Zihlman 1976, Zihlman 1978, and Tanner 1981).

Zihlman and Tanner recognized that while the early transition period is one of significant changes in behavioural and locomotor patterns, answering questions about the source and direction of these changes is made more difficult by the lack of fossil material for the critical period between ten and five million years ago. Given the Lucy and Laetoli finds, the most significant change during this period was bipedalism, but how to explain it? Tanner and Zihlman developed some ideas about this which Tanner discusses most fully in her book, *On Becoming Human (1981)*. While the modern primates have all specialized in either quadrupedal postures on top of branches as with the monkeys, or in brachiation which is "a below-branch hanging, swinging and climbing pattern" as with the apes, the Miocene primate fossils demonstrate a rather generalized locomotor adaptation. What the new theory needed was an evolutionary incentive, one that nudged a few Miocene primates in the direction of bipedality without being an overwhelming threat to their survival. Zihlman and Tanner speculated that as a result of occupying areas such as edge ecotones, where selective pressures were different, some primitive hominoids (Miocene apes) did develop a more specialized locomotion, resulting in the first hominids. That is, these primarily arboreal quadrupeds somehow developed the ability to brachiate and to stand erect on their hind legs, if only for short periods. What was the incentive?

Tanner and Zihlman did not reject the entire hunter model in that they still linked the early transition phase to dramatic climatic change and to resulting new selective environmental pressures. However, they differed with the hunter model on the issue of what the new environment would have looked like. Rather than emphasizing a grasslands habitat for the transitional period, they argued that the Miocene drought would have produced a mosaic pattern of grasslands interspersed with clumps of bushes and trees and with forest corridors along lakesides, streams and river beds (Tanner 1981:178). In this less disruptive environmental transition, the early australopithecines would have been forced to spend more time on the ground, but with a secure retreat to the trees when needed. Food sources from both the trees and the grasslands would have expanded the foraging repertoire rather than requiring a complete retooling of the hominoid food-getting capabilities. Tanner and Zihlman saw new foods and resulting dentition changes as pivotal to the early transition period. As seeds and nuts replaced soft fruits and leaves in the diet and placed different mastication demands on teeth and jaw muscles, there was a reduction in canine size. Primitive weapons (sticks and stones) and patterns of bluff and aggression display may have then been necessary to replace this defensive dentition. It is important here to note that behavioural changes are said to lead to morphological ones, a common approach for both the Man-the-Hunter and the Woman-the-Gatherer models (see for example Tanner 1981:160, 186; Haraway 1989:332).

In another point of similarity with the hunter model, Tanner and Zihlman's model focused on gender differences in food-getting activities, just as the older hunting hypothesis did. However, they privileged the role of the female instead of the male. The reason for this had to do with the distinction they made between individualistic foraging and socio-centric gathering. In most species, including the majority of primates, individual animals forage on their own for on-the-spot consumption of foods. Gathering, in contrast, involves the collection and carrying of quantities of food for later sharing and consumption by more than one individual, as is common with the human species (Tanner 1981:140). Tanner and Zihlman focused on the need to explain why foraging hominoids were transformed into gathering hominids. In evolutionary terms, it is important to note that a foraging-gathering transition is not so great a leap as a foraging-hunting transition. Gathering could have focused on the same kinds of foods that foraging did, including insects, eggs and the helpless young of game animals as well as fruit and starch sources. The only tools required for a transition to a gathering lifestyle would be digging sticks, some means of carrying gathered materials and perhaps chopping blades for processing plant foods. Zihlman argued that given the physical constraints of size and primate locomotor patterns, gathering as a transitional food-getting activity made more sense while in contrast, "hunting must have emerged late in human evolutionary history from a technological and social base in gathering" (1981:93).

What might cause the shift from foraging to gathering? Tanner and Zihlman argued that the gathering pursuit was a subsistence technique by which female proto-hominids continued to support their dependent offspring, under the new environmental constraints of the Miocene drought. Females were under larger nutritional demands given that they had to feed both themselves and their offspring (pre and post partum), in comparison to males who fed only themselves. Zihlman and Tanner suggested that this fact created gender-specific foraging patterns for those Miocene apes who found themselves restricted to marginal environments during periods of dessication associated with the Miocene. This is consistent with a differential pattern of male/female foraging patterns among some analogous non-human primates of today. Zihlman speculated that the impetus for the development of bipedalism developed in the latter half of the Miocene, when females were pressed into searching for savanna foods which were found sporadically, located long distances apart (Haraway 1989:332). In turn, the slow emergence of bipedalism placed biomechanical demands on the procreative process (especially parturition given the changes to the pelvic structure) that resulted in off-spring being born at a more immature stage. This resulted in a longer dependency period for those offspring, which in turn was connected to and used by these females to train and encourage their offspring of both sexes to develop skills in the same gathering pursuit (Tanner 1981:145).

In this model, the primary social bonds in proto-hominid society were not pair bonds between monogamous male and female couples, but the nurturing bonds between females and their offspring of both sexes. The primary impetus to tool manufacture is not male-oriented weapons of hunt and defence but gender-irrelevant tools of digging, collecting and transport (Linton 1971; Tanner and Zihlman 1976; Zihlman 1978). The primary sources of meat—when meat was eaten over alternative foods such as nuts, seeds, shoots, roots, berries and insects—were the helpless young of ungulates, taken and killed by both genders. The questions of the loss of estrus and of the origin of monogamous family fades into obscurity (Haraway 1989:283). Female gatherers did not need male hunters to survive.

The primary role of males was not protection, provisioning and paternal investment, ultimately creating dominant, aggressive and evolutionarily central, modern-day men. Instead the male role was one of "integrat[ion] along with the females into their mother's kin group and contribut[ion] to the survival of long-dependent young (kin selection)" (Zihlman 1978:4). This created "relatively sociable," caring, sharing and cooperating males who were the preferred sexual partners of females. This approach is diametrically opposed to the pair-bonding and nuclear-family hypothesis of the Man-the-Hunter model. Pair bonding postulates that males made the selection of mating partners and that there was a lack of competition between males for available females; competition existed instead between females for males. But this has never corresponded very well with prevailing biological theory on sexual selection. Biologists argue that control over mate selection is normally in the hands of the parent who makes the greatest investment in offspring and among the primates, females make a larger procreative investment than do males. Tanner and Zihlman argued that it made sense that hominid females were the ones selecting their mates (Tanner and Zihlman 1976:589, Tanner 1981:164). And if females made the selection of mates, male preference for "more attractive" females could not have been a driving force in human evolution, although the opposite may have been true. And since bipedality and changing morphology made secondary sexual characteristics less effective as sexual receptivity clues, it is more logical that females would have had to play the role of sexual aggressors (Tanner 1981:154).

The Woman-the-Gatherer model was a significant factor in dislodging the centrality of hunting and of males in models of human evolution. Today most paleoanthropologists will freely admit that the Man-the-Hunter model was androcentric. However, the gathering woman was never popularized the way that Tiger, Ardrey and Lorenz popularized the aggressive, hunting male. Subsequently, the public never took the gathering-woman image to heart and within a very short period this model was undermined by criticisms which described it as "feminist" and "politically correct" rather than scientifically grounded. For example, Zihlman's emphasis on the early transition period and on female contributions to evolutionary change has led her critics to accuse her of ignoring *male* contributions in human evolution. To which her supporters have responded by pointing out that there is nothing in the gathering model to preclude the adoption of hunting as a significant component of *later* stages of human evolution (Haraway 1989:336). But as any cursory scan of recent introductory textbooks can demonstrate, male centrality in the early stages of human evolution has proved an extremely resilient theme.

The Love-Joy Hypothesis

In recent years, the male role in evolution has once again been privileged and assumptions about sexual dimorphism have been the key to dragging the male back to centre stage. For people such as Donald Johanson

(Johanson and Edey 1981), C.O. Lovejoy (1981), T.D. White (Johanson and White 1979) and others, the Lucy find and the associated "First Family" fossils prove that all *Australopithecus* specimens may have come from a single species with a significant pattern of sexual dimorphism. This single species hypothesis not only allows proponents to resist challenges against the linear model of human evolution, but also to assume that such sexual dimorphism may have developed as a result of sex role specialization, with larger males playing the role of provisioner, protector and mate selector. Lucy and her "First Family" have been the fuel Lovejoy needed to restart the evolutionary engines of "pair bonds, home base, sexual division of labor and male initiative in hominization" (Haraway 1989:343). His hypothesis is that proto-hominid females were faced with ergonomic constraints which would not allow them to increase their investment in offspring survival above what they were already doing. However, increased numbers of offspring seem the logical way whereby proto-hominids survived the Miocene challenge to become hominids. Drawing on some recent sociobiology theories about the importance of differential gender energy constraints, Lovejoy argues that the male Miocene ape had reserves of energy because of their low biological investment in reproduction. The leap to humanity was only made possible when that free male energy was directed to provisioning sedentary females and young in order to guarantee a higher survival rate. Lovejoy puts all the gathering activities which the gathering model ascribed to females, into the hands of males, a position which Linda Fedigan (1986:37) calls "a sudden enthusiasm for gathering." She notes that in this "enthusiasm," Lovejoy fails to cite any of the women who developed the gathering model in the first place. She also notes that the frequent citation of Lovejoy's article in introductory textbooks indicates that it has become the "current orthodoxy about human evolution."

This orthodoxy has not gone unchallenged (Tuttle 1988:406), but its sharpest detractors continue to be proponents of the Women-the-Gatherer model (Fedigan 1986, Hager 1991, Haraway 1989, Leibowitz 1993, Zihlman 1985). They argue first that there is some doubt about the methods which are used to sex fossils among the australopithecines in order to make arguments about sexual dimorphism; these methods are based on assumptions about pelvic differences which may not be warranted in the early transition stage (Hager 1991). Also, there is no evidence that human evolution was based on selection for higher

reproduction. Modern-day analogies drawn from extant foraging populations such as the !Kung Bushmen, suggest reproduction rates consistent with those found among modern apes (Fedigan 1986). Another
important problem with Lovejoy's hypothesis is that there has been
significant research to suggest that the relationship between sexual
dimorphism and specialized sex roles is not nearly so simple nor the
causes so unidirectional as this model suggests (Leibowitz 1993). In
Zihlman's research on modern primates, sexual dimorphism is not pre-
dictive of sexual divisions of labour, monogamous pair bonding, or
male provisioning of females. She uses the pygmy chimpanzee as a
model of potential behaviour patterns during the early transition
period and her research, taken together with Jane Goodall's and others
on the common chimpanzee, does not support a passive, sedentary
role for the female. But perhaps the most damning problem of all with
the Lovejoy hypothesis is that there may not be good fossil support for
it; Zihlman, for example, prefers to keep open the question of sexual
dimorphism until more (and better described) australopithecine fossils
are available.

The irony is that various aspects of both the hunting and of the
gathering models are adopted in a rather scattergun manner in some of
the most recent textbooks. For example, some textbook authors super-
impose gathering onto hunting to create a mixed economy with "sharing between gathering women and hunting or scavenging men as the
key human invention" (Fedigan 1986:35). Unfortunately, as Fedigan
points out, and as a cursory survey of recent introductory textbooks
will show, this mixed economy usually reduces down to retaining the
importance of meat in an otherwise fragmented and logically inconsistent model. Perhaps Zihlman's image of a "kinder, gentler" male sex
which responded to the demands of the socially central female during
the early transition period, is not something that modern Western
males can relate to. Certainly the image of a primarily vegetarian
ancestor has never been popular among Westerners, given the high
cultural value they place on meat. Whether for these reasons or for
others, there have been very few lasting changes to the story line by
which we propose to explain our evolutionary past, despite the fossil
destabilizations and the feminist critiques of those stories. A brief
examination of recent editions of several widely used introductory textbooks demonstrates this.

Textbook Human Evolution

The new 1994 editions of introductory anthropology textbooks, whether integrated (i.e., those which include physical anthropology and archaeology components) or solely introductory physical anthropology, show three significant trends. First, there is more emphasis on the fossils and less on possible explanations. Second, there is a noticeable paucity of reconstructive illustrative material. In Haviland's 1994 edition of his introductory anthropology textbook, for example, we do not see a single attempt at reconstructive illustration, with the possible exception of two drawings of modern humans (1994:205, 207). Conrad Kottak (1994) restricts himself to a few cartoons, while Poirier, Stini and Wreden (1994:384) offer only one image: the head and shoulders of a reconstructed *Homo erectus* male. Third, there is a noticeable lack of reference to the Woman-the-Gatherer authors, even when much of their work is co-opted. Some textbooks make a point of critiquing androcentrism and praising the contributions of people such as Zihlman, stating that they were crucial to the recognition that the two sexes evolved together. Sometimes these women are cited in bibliographies and their work is briefly discussed in the body of the text, usually after a longer section on Lovejoy's thesis, as in Poirier, Stini and Wreden (1994:368-73). Haviland (1994:159) even has an "information box" on Adrienne Zihlman; despite this highlighted box on her contributions, however, Zihlman's literature is not cited in the chapter where the box appears, nor in the recommended reading list at the end of the chapter, nor in the general bibliography of the text. Tanner is ignored, deserving neither "box" nor citations. In Kottak (1994), Tanner's ethnographic research is cited but not her paleoanthropology references; Zihlman is not cited at all. When one looks deeper, the Woman-the-Gatherer model is selectively covered and usually found embedded in a discussion which actually returns to the old androcentrism. The selective co-opting of parts of the gathering model taken together with lack of proper citation, leaves the reader not only with little source material with which to construct a fuller picture of alternative models, but also with a set of somewhat disconnected ideas which are difficult to view as functionally integrated.

Several examples will serve to demonstrate this pattern. Recent texts emphasize that the problem of the early transition period has become the problem of bipedalism and then go on to briefly discuss several possible explanations for its development. But this discussion is

couched in such a way as to reinforce male centrality through the introduction of new occupations for them during the critical transition
period. In the feminist-inspired gathering model, bipedality is linked
with the food-seeking behaviour of highly mobile females. According to
recent textbooks, however, males spent more time on the ground, and
ate more of the new food sources found there, while females spent more
time in the trees (see Stern and Susman 1983 for the original argument,
and Haviland 1994:138 for the textbook version). While this might suggest the rise of interdependency between males and females, in the context of a continual emphasis on meat as a driver in human evolutionary
processes, the textbook reader is left with no doubt as to the more
important contribution of the males. The textbooks which I examined
all drew the conclusion that bipedality was linked to a *scavenging*
lifestyle, thereby making male gathering activities meat-based once
again. Highly mobile males provision more stationary females, and in
this context, the Lovejoy hypothesis is raised as the adaptive advantage
of the new male behaviour. Scavenging, the textbooks suggest, required
"covering large areas slowly" and an "improved ability to locate items
at a distance" (Poirier, Stini and Wreden 1994:305). Or alternatively,
bipedalism made "long distance migration" behind herds of ungulates a
possibility, thus enhancing scavenging opportunities (ibid.:307; see also
Kottak 1994:161). In these sorts of arguments, the textbooks rely on a
very old pattern of seeking to explain the rise of certain essential traits
by reference to some adaptive advantage these traits will ultimately confer. This adaptationism is a problem which I address in more detail in
chapter 7. Here I want to stress the fact that modern textbooks once
again privilege male lifestyle changes, and meat-based dietary changes
to explain the rise of bipedalism.

The revised androcentrism of these early transition explanations
makes it possible for textbooks to move sequentially from bipedalism to
subsequent changes in manual dexterity, the thumb and hand structure,
and brain size, as if the old hunting model had never been challenged
(Haviland 1994:147-48; Kottak 1994:175; Poirier, Stini and Wreden
1994:310). The absence of tools from the earliest archaeological record,
for example, is addressed by the argument that the scavenging australopithecines used tools in the form of natural found objects such as sticks
or stones, but did not manufacture them for specific purposes.
However, it is also suggested that female australopithecines (safe and

stationary in the trees) may have used tools to get food (the way that modern chimpanzees will dip sticks into termite mounds) but that the more exposed scavenging males probably needed to use them for weapons (Haviland 1994:138, 144; Kottak 1994:167). Once the earliest representatives of the genus *Homo* appear on the scene, the rise of deliberate masculine technology can again be made an essential (if somewhat belated) feature of human development. Australopithecines (male and female) *used* tools, *Homo habilis* (male) *made* tools. And this argument is reinforced in the new pattern of illustrations which overwhelmingly emphasize stone tool technology.

In a detailed study of fourteen books, including three physical anthropology, five cultural anthropology, and six integrated or holistic anthropology textbooks, one graduate student found that thirteen of the fourteen textbooks include extensive illustrations of stone tools or tool kits, thus linking progress to male-based technological advancements and its supposed application to a meat-driven economy. This link between males and stone tools is reinforced by the fact that in the frequent illustrations of flintknappers, they are always male. This also holds true for pictures of other sorts of scientists. Of the fifty-two illustrations of scientists in general found in these textbooks, fifty are male. The lonely exception is Mary Leakey, who is illustrated twice. Gero (1991) has challenged the perception that lithics were made and used by males and that females were not participants in the development of stone tool technology, but her arguments have been ignored in introductory textbooks–as have the feminist critiques about androcentrism in textbook representations of the science process.

The linked set of meat-and-(masculine)-tools is the most pervasive story operator in paleoanthropology. In a suggestive subtitle, Haviland links: "Tools, Meat and Brains." Poirier, Stini and Wreden (1994:314) speak of the signal importance of the "acquisition of meat protein." Meat remains central to the explanations offered for significant evolutionary developments, and male specialized behaviour is central to acquiring meat. It is argued that manual dexterity, close cooperation and verbal communication would have been more important in male survival tasks (Poirier, Stini and Wreden 1994:316) and thus male behaviour is the driving force for the rise of culture. This model relies heavily on unsubstantiated links between a meat-based diet and increased intelligence and cultural development.

In the past it was quite common to compare our evolutionary history with other "great hunters" of the savanna: lions, leopards, cheetahs, spotted hyenas and wild dogs (Campbell 1982). Other analogies were made to the "99 percent of human history" that we subsisted as "hunters and gatherers" (ibid.). But as Zihlman (1981:82-83) and others have noted, the primate patterns of social interaction are a far cry from those of carnivores, and such comparisons are "superficial, misleading, and essentially an extension of the 'hunting hypothesis'." Recent textbooks still resonate with story operators of meat, tools and male-centred evolution; it would appear that we have not really learned to ask different questions, nor to ask questions differently.

Summary: Mirrors Rather than Windows

This survey of competing stories of human evolution is suggestive of a long-standing pattern of failing to problematize gender traits and roles. Another and more basic problem is that we have failed to problematize human traits and behavioural patterns. If we compare the anatomically modern human species to its closest living relatives, and to fossils of its proposed precursors, the significant physiological and behavioural changes which must be accounted for in human evolution are numerous and very diverse. Historically, however, the tendency has been towards selecting a few of these to receive disproportionate amounts of attention. Indeed, this overly narrow focus has not changed since Huxley's 1863 emphasis on dentition, brain and locomotor structures (cited in Tanner 1981:29). For example, although the Man-the-Hunter model focused on territoriality and masculine aggression, the main emphasis was on terrestriality, bipedalism, encephalization and civilization, and these continue as preoccupations for paleoanthropology today (see Lewin 1987). But the essential physiological and behavioural attributes of the human species can be defined in a number of different ways. Morgan (1972, 1982), for example, argued that many of the physiological changes that characterize the female of the species more than the male have been systematically ignored or have been "deproblematize" by tying them to pair bonding, perhaps because they are seen as peculiar to the female and thus not of general concern. Sally Linton (1971:39) attempted in a similar way to shift the focus of attention, by asking questions about the significance of extended gestation periods, a more difficult birth process, neoteny and long periods of infant dependency. But in general, both she and Zihlman have largely followed the tradition of asking questions about bipedalism, encephalization and culture.

This "essentialist" approach of paleoanthropology has led to "origins research," specifically focusing on the origins of particular traits, which in turn has led to a particularly warped view of the evolutionary past (see Conkey 1991). The first problem, as I have already pointed out, is that all prehistory is treated from a *Homo sapiens*-centric point of view. Second, there is a determined presentist bias to much of the research which seeks to find the seal of antiquity on behavioural practices and physiological conditions of today. Third, and these are issues I address further in chapter 7, we have never seriously questioned our privileging of a few causal factors in the rise of these traits, nor the functional explanatory mode that goes with them. The role of the savanna, of meat-eating, of technology and thus of male contributions to survival have remained central to dominant story lines of the sources of hominid evolutionary changes, however those changes are defined.

The problem is deeper than a simple male resistance to evolutionary images that do not flatter present-day perceptions of gender attributes and gender roles, especially at the level of popularized accounts. It relates, I believe, to a very basic issue in evolutionary sciences, where, as one colleague reminded me, everything we know about the past, we know by analogy (see chapter 6).

> There has long been a dynamic tension in the interpretation of past events between the scientific goal of creating a "window" through which we can observe the past, and the powerful compulsion to create a "mirror" in which we simply reflect images of ourselves (both our realities and our aspirations) onto the past (David Black, pers. comm.).

Many anthropologists realize that the public is attracted to academic disciplines that can relate to their own experiences and problems, that in short, produce a mirror on their lives. If anthropology cannot attract public attention to the discipline, than support—both literal and figurative—for our (often costly) research will dry up. Public support is a problem with which people such as the Leakeys have struggled and their success at garnering it sometimes left them vulnerable to accusations of pandering to funding sources (Lewin 1987). Archaeologists and paleoanthropologists are given two contradictory messages: hypotheses must be supported by the data, *but* we must also talk about people in order for our research to generate interest.

As theoreticians, archaeologists and paleoanthropologists work from remarkably scanty data. Granted, there are now thousands of fossil items which relate to human evolution, and these are supplemented by comparative anatomy and primate research and by extensive studies of human foraging populations. Nevertheless, compared to the amounts of data the average social anthropologist can collect on any given topic, archaeologists and paleoanthropologists are data poor. The pressure to "cloth that data," to stretch and make it go farther and thus to make it of interest to a wider audience is constant.

> It is when we make the transition from the "record" to the "people" that we are at our most vulnerable and our most dangerous—that is where we are most likely to consciously or unconsciously make the transition from creating a window to creating a mirror. Illustrations are a significant aspect of making that transition—they are literally acts of putting flesh back on the bones, and putting tools back into the hands, of our ancestors. Modern Western gender stereotypes are clearly less useful analogies in this context (David Black, pers. comm.).

Anthropologists and natural scientists in general are members of a particular cultural milieu. They tend to put moral messages into nature, and this tendency has effectively blinkered the natural sciences in their understanding of evolutionary processes (see Gould 1989 and chapter 7 in this book). But there is even more to it than this. Scientific discourse has grown out of a narrative tradition which is much more pervasive than most scientists would accept. The public demands, and the scientists themselves demand, what their culture has led them to expect in the way of story operators and story fields. These cultural narrative expectations are also reflected in the conventions used in the realm of illustrations, as I will show in the chapters that follow.

CHAPTER THREE

Reconstructive Human Evolution Illustrations: Utilizing Western Art Conventions in a Contested Story Field

THE FIELD OF PALEOANTHROPOLOGY is full of narrative tales about the rise of present human traits, the origins of male gender attributes, the timelessness of female gender attributes, the antiquity of the nuclear family, the primacy of the individual in the race to evolve, and the struggle to out-compete other forms. These narrative themes have long been accompanied by illustrations which convey the same ideas in a much more powerful visual medium. This medium is more powerful for a number of reasons, not the least of which is its accessibility. In the quasi-educational material such as *National Geographic* and even in the educational world of college textbooks, the visual component of the printed media is often absorbed when the text is not. These visual devices or illustrations can convey a wealth of material to the casual glance and this material will often be uncritically accepted, which is not always true for the text. How is it that the illustration can convey so much in so little time—and what sorts of information are commonly conveyed?

The term illustration refers to a wide variety of visual media materials (print, drawing, chart, photograph or picture) which are inserted in printed text to elucidate or adorn it. Educative illustrations are more specifically aimed at informing the reader. Illustration in human evolution is a very broad visual field, including but not limited to: images of the fossils as in paintings, photographs or line drawings of bones or teeth; narrative pictures which attempt to clothe those fossils in flesh and behaviour and to fill in the environmental background; charts, figures or "family trees" of the hominid evolutionary sequence; images of artifacts accompanying fossil finds, of the areas where fossils are found or of the crews which found them. All of the above types of illustration have meanings to deconstruct.

For example, Donna Haraway (1989:190) refers to the patronizing, neocolonial patterns of Western scientific practice when she discusses a picture of Richard Leakey and his black research assistant and notes that only Leakey is identified by name. She explores the meaning of the high-tech, holographic image of the Taung Child fossil skull which was published on the cover of a 1985 volume of *National Geographic.* She notes how the empty eye sockets resonate with the appeal of little children's "large, beckoning eyes" while at the same time, the holography speaks to the authority of (masculine) science (ibid.:188). She speaks of the fossil bones of an early australopithecine dubbed Lucy, which are most often seen "laid out like jewels on red velvet" in a way that clearly "awe-thorizes" scientific accounts about human evolution (ibid.:2). These are good observations and indicate how much "deconstruction" is necessary.

While I am interested in similar kinds of analyses, I have by and large limited myself here to analyzing portrayals of ancient forms of humanity. Gifford-Gonzalez (1993:27) distinguishes between *anatomical reconstructions* or "the painstakingly built-up anatomical renderings of soft tissues in three dimensions, inferred from details of evidence of the bones" and *dioramic representations* or "compositions of reconstructed bodies in social groups and hypothetical scenes from daily life." My primary concern is with illustrations that attempt to reconstruct the physiology and form, behavioural patterns, environment and relationships with other organisms, of members of the hominid evolutionary family and which do so for the educational or quasi-educational markets. In that sense, then, I am focusing on dioramic representations. What interests me about such illustrations is that they have an iconographic aspect; that is, they attempt to tell a significant story in a way that utilizes pictorial, symbolic and imaginary content in the visual field. These illustrations are iconographic in another way as well, in that the subject matter they portray is of thematic significance in the wider cultural and scientific context. The illustrations are narrative, but the story format is obscure and relies to a significant extent on unconscious contextualization from this wider cultural field. The reasons for presenting the material "as in a story" are not immediately clear nor are they very often questioned or examined closely. Perhaps this is as true of their production as of their dissemination, but that is something only further research could tell us.

Suffice it to say that the narrative format is suggestive of a "plot," that is, of a pattern or a scheme to the event, situation or incident in the story that each picture tells. For example, in the "fleeing the volcano" illustration by Jay H. Matternes, we see a small "family" on a journey across a volcanic plain (M. Leakey 1979). The male leads and the female trails behind with the infant on her hip. The female has paused to glance anxiously off to the side; the male forges on ahead. Her stance, taken together with the weapon that he carries in his hand, suggests that the journey could be dangerous but that he is capable of protecting his little family. When these types of illustrations are examined together as a group it becomes evident that they share a common plot. The arduous journey is a common feature of many of them; the harsh struggle for survival is another. Such illustrations form a cohesive "narrative practice" or "storytelling" (see Haraway 1988), and the stories they take part in narrating are in turn part of a wider "field" of explanatory accounts. As such they are part and parcel of a larger meta-narrative—a single dominant view of events which is written so often and in so many places that it is often treated as fact rather than as theory or as a *point of view*. Human social and biological evolution has been a great journey, one that has taken us as a species from an animal-like dependence on nature to a human level of independence through culture; and as individuals this journey has taken us from susceptibility to security. Elements of the visual field which participate in this meta-narrative take on a "trope"-like characteristic, much like "figures" of speech, and are recognizable in much the same way as standard conventions of speech. They are conventions presented in a visual format, which is the first and most important clue to their deconstruction.

Deconstructing Visual Imagery: Art History, Feminist Art Critique and Western Artistic Conventions

Illustrators are trained artists, and as such, their repertoire of meaningful conventions is drawn from a tradition of Western art production. While the field of art history has long traced cultural influences, sources of inspiration, patterns of production and the dissemination of technique, it has only been relatively recently that this analysis has taken a truly critical stance. The development of the feminist perspective was an important influence. Two strands of feminist critical activity have emerged to deal primarily with "images of women." The first strand relies on a process of interrogation/deconstruction which is designed to expose ideological complexities and contradictions in the images, while the second strand focuses on the feminist reader/viewer and her relation to such texts (Pearce 1991:3). In this book I emphasize the first approach and use the feminist literature to suggest ways of reading more deeply with respect to gender when viewing reconstructive human evolution images. It is not enough for us to simply become familiar with the artistic conventions, because using such knowledge to "decode" these images will only result in our receiving a predetermined message (ibid.:34). What is required is a critical review of the techniques which produce such images, a review which problematizes the conventions of gender and which in turn allows us to question that predetermined message and to challenge wider cultural idea sets which make that message relevant to us.

To begin, reconstructive human evolution illustrations rely heavily on Western art conventions of the naked human body. This is because of a set of cultural values and expectations that link the primitive and the savage with nakedness. In reconstructing images of our earliest precursors then, illustrators craft the hominid form as naked and primordial. This situation presents both a problem and an opportunity since "naked" is inextricably linked with "nude" in Western art tradition, and the nude comes with a freight of cultural baggage which cannot be ignored. Linda Nead (1990:326) writes:

> The signification of the female nude cannot be separated from the historical discourses of culture, that is, the representation of the nude by critics and art historians ... representations of the female nude created by male artists testify not only to patriarchal understandings of female sexuality and femininity, but they also endorse certain definitions of male sexuality and masculinity.

While the nude is an important component in the Western artistic tradition, both nudity and its opposite state of fully clothed figures, are capable of many different degrees and associated meanings, depending on context and period. If we examine some of these degrees of nudity and associated meanings, the representation of gender in the visual arts becomes less obscure, less absorbed without thought or reflection.

The Naked and the Nude: The Western Practice of Bodily Revision

One of the most important features of the Western representation of the human body is its lack of conformity to reality. This plasticity is the key to the nudes' load-bearing capacity in the representation of culturally determined messages: "the body is not the shape that art had led us to believe" (Clark 1956:7). Artists, in the pursuit of the "ideal form" treat reality as only a "corrupted replica" (ibid.:12). The reasons for and the patterns of body revision as practised in Western art are a lesson in the history of Western politics, religion, gender relations and changes in clothing fashion. The dialectical relationship between images of the body and the body's cultural context becomes visible when the nude of different epochs and cultures are compared.

One of the oldest and most persistent influences on the Western representation of the human form in the visual arts is the classical representation of the Greco-Roman period. This is especially true of the many conventions of the male figure, as when it is coded as authoritative, dominant, aggressive or athletic. The aesthetic athleticism popularized during the classical period is still widely reproduced as the ideal male physiology. Broad shoulders, a chest and flat belly ribbed with muscle, a waist positioned well above the lean hips, muscular thighs and buttocks and a subtle redrawing of the proportions of the leg to give extra length between knee and ankle are all conventions of the classical male form (see Figure 1). These attributes are usually combined with a remote gaze and a somewhat rigid neck and head. Because of their connection to Greek literature and philosophy, these attributes denote not only masculine beauty, but also the additional embedded meanings of heroism, divinity and superiority.

Greco-Roman artistic traditions idolized the nude male body and did not demand of it the same degree of modesty that they did for the female form. In contrast, the female nude developed rather late in Greek art, and even then modesty was often preserved by conventions of stance and body language (Hollander 1978:6). An example that draws on the classical tradition but which actually dates to the fifteenth century is seen in Figure 2, taken from the Adam and Eve panel on the baptismal font in the Siena Cathedral. Here Adam stands in the classical erect pose, while Eve twists her body away from the viewer and awkwardly crosses her legs. This posture simultaneously hides her physical sexual characteristics and draws attention to them; she undulates across the panel like the serpent she is designed to suggest. Her fluidity of form echoes the classical period, with its preference for a close drapery over the female form. Western art historians once thought that this drapery was designed to advertise the feminine wiles beneath the fabric, but it is now clear that it required a significant "bodily revision" in that the average female body had to be altered to properly display the cloth; shoulders were broadened, the chest widened and the breasts lifted, rounded and thrust apart (Hollander 1978:3). Without this manipulation of body parts, those folds of cloth which have come to define Greco-Roman classical art would bunch in a highly unflattering way. The contortions which relate to this bodily revision and to the conventions of posture and stance, require that the female form be treated "as if made from some viscous material" (Clark 1956:21).

The classical representation of the male nude body, while not constrained by the same notions of modesty nor by requirements of drapery, also deviates from reality in order to represent in idealized and standardized form the link in Greek philosophy between the human body and nature, between symmetry and moral worth. The proportions of limb to torso and of upper to lower limbs, the definition of muscle mass and the emphatically erect posture all produce an image of athletic competence and physical symmetry at odds with the general run of humanity. In both male and female images, therefore, the earliest and most persistent of Western cultural influences made the distinction between naked and nude which in turn required redrafting the actual appearance of the human body. Generations of real humans have struggled in vain to mould their physical forms to these demanding and idealized standards.

The classical tradition, as a vibrant source for many body-linked allegories, has been found across all subsequent periods of the Western visual arts. For the classical Greek artist, nudity represented a natural state, or *nuditas virtualis* (Warner 1985:303, 304, 315). This state symbolized virtue, justice, and innocence, in both its primordial and aboriginal forms (ibid.:305, 315). In the face of subsequent European political and religious developments, this tradition was transformed so that nakedness could represent not only freedom from society's constraints (ibid.:313), but the very opposite of culture as in "beyond the pale"—no longer enclosed by boundaries either social or physical. Thus it came to take on a double meaning, one side positive and the other negative with significant opportunity for artistic manipulation. It is not surprising that the rich possibilities of this contrast then ramified throughout the Western history of the female nude, who was able to "play nature to man's culture" (ibid.:325) no matter what the relative value given to either of these concepts at various points in history.

Various body parts were elaborated as devices to signify the difference between the virtuous nude and the savage naked. For example, the "absence of pubic hair meant Art and Beauty and its presence meant Gross Sex" (Hollander 1978:140). When female bodies were crafted as objects of male pleasure the pubic hair was never depicted (Caws 1985:268). When female pubic hair was represented it was as a symbol of female-controlled sexual power and passion; as such, it could contribute to the construction of the female form as a major allegory of sin, lust and corruption, all things to be avoided by a properly moral man. Another convention utilized in the classical tradition was the dishevelled diaphanous tunic, slipped down off one shoulder to bare a breast. This signalled the "natural woman" who could not be a fully cultural entity but was instead maternal or passionate, instinctive or ardent. As with artists of later periods, the Greeks represented such unacculturated females as being under masculine control primarily through two devices: first, women did not occupy the centre (of theology, of social structure, of politics, of artistic expression) and second, images affirmed masculine cultural control over feminine nature (Warner 1985:292; see also duBois 1988). Female nudity was portrayed in a way affirming to male control.

The Body and Invisible Clothing

The plasticity of the human body in art has meant that any "image of the nude body that is absolutely free of any counter-image of clothing is virtually impossible" (Hollander 1978:85). This has led Hollander to characterize the Western nude as "wearing the ghosts of absent clothes." There are numerous advantages to this representational approach, which relies on: "a slight widening or sloping of the shoulders, an elongation or shortening of the waist, a thinning or fattening here and there" (ibid.:88). It is through the use of such "nip and tuck" artwork that the distinction between naked and nude is elaborated. The bodily revision details are based on how a body looks encased in clothing, and these details are employed to make the nude look more realistic to its particular audience, and "therefore sexier and more nude, even while safely avoiding exaggerated sexual characteristics and remaining thus theoretically chaste" (ibid.:88). Standard representational devices of each epoch create a nude body as not just nude but "denuded," and thereby able to take on the excess baggage of "erotic freight," making it a highly successful conveyer of complex messages.

For Hollander, Western representation of the human form since the 1300s has required balancing several components, including details from the classical formulas, adaptations to human immediacy and the need to represent "sexy, modish undress" (ibid.:89). The influence of fashion on the nude form is uniquely European, as is the obsession with fashion. Hollander defines fashion as: "constant perceptible fluctuations of visual design, created out of the combined forms of tailored dress and body" and argues that most non-Western civilizations, both past and present, have not experienced fashion as we know it (ibid.:90). Westerners have a long history of "perpetual changes of form" which in turn depend on an "aesthetic lust" for colour, fabric, drape, shape and line of cloth over body. Hollander's point here is more readily understood by examining Figure 3. This Gothic female figure was produced in the early fifteenth century by the artist Jan Van Eyck to represent the Biblical Eve (Clark 1956:319). During this period, painters and sculptors produced the female body in a weirdly elongated fashion, with tiny high breasts, overly thin limbs, shortened ribcage and extended, swollen-looking bellies. This was not because they did not understand the female form, nor because of a lack of the technical skill to create a realistic image, nor because women of their time actually looked this way. In fact, they crafted these nude women to suit the prevailing perception of body form as it appeared in the clothing of the day. If we turn to clothing fashions of the time, we see waist lines were designed to fit just under the breasts, which were lifted high on the chest. Stomachs were padded to make the wearer appear affluent enough to overeat. Sleeves were long, narrow and tightly fitted, as were hose and footwear. In this fashion environment, high small breasts did not signal nubile youth and an enlarged belly did not represent pregnancy (Hollander 1978:109). Other conventions, as when one hand rested lightly on the bulbous belly, were used to indicate that a woman was expecting. In Figure 3, Eve is represented not as a naked, underfed, pregnant woman, as a modern reader might interpret, but in a body designed to look right for its stylistic epoch. The plasticity of the female form creates sensuous curves that undulate across the image, from a head which leans forward demurely, to shoulders thrust back to lift the chest and breasts, to a back and belly curved outwards again, to buttocks curved in the opposite direction, and on down to create a final curve out of a slightly bent knee stance. During the Gothic period, this undulation was facilitated by an emphasis on the belly as the erotic focus of the female nude, but this waned by the late seventeenth century and was replaced by an emphasis on breasts and buttocks (ibid.:98). But it is important to keep in mind here that both the female *and* the male nude followed fashion in artistic representation throughout European history. For example, male images in the Gothic period were also weirdly elongated, with stooped shoulders and very narrow chest and hips. In fact, the classically favoured proportions of the human body tended to appear and disappear during various periods in European art, depending on other fashion-based tendencies to pad or strip the "upholstered parts" (ibid.:100).

These opportunities for play on conventions of proportion, of padding and of invisible clothing, have proven very useful in reconstructive human evolution illustration, in order to meet the demands of representing more primitive or more advanced forms of the human body, for suggesting natural gender attributes and roles, and for establishing images of authority and power as well as weakness and dependency, as is discussed in the following chapters. Other factors have also contributed to the illustrator's artful representation of the past.

Gender and Religious Meaning in the West

Christian art was one cultural arena that perpetuated both the form and content of the classical artistic tradition. Particularly in the third and fourth centuries, the Christian community relied heavily on Greco-Roman art and classical mythology for its inspiration (Volback 1964:12). Recurrent themes, many of them male-centred, such as the Good Shepherd, the Lamb of God, the Philosopher Teacher, as well as the Gathering of the Grapes, all find their precursors in the popular bucolic art of the Hellenistic communities of Alexandria and Rome. For the Christians, however, the instructional aim of both female and male representation was focused on moral truths rather than on aesthetic enjoyment (ibid.:13). In this instructional milieu, the Christians adopted the classical motif of naked male bodies to represent heroic physical strength, clean-living athletic virtues and endurance against persecution. Other representations of the Christian male (with Christ as their template) portrayed "philosopher teachers," endowed with knowledge and a rather more effete physiology. Later, Christian males (particularly Christ himself) were represented as "triumphant rulers," endowed with authority and physical majesty (ibid.:22). But these multiple, positive roles for males have rather limited female correspondents.

If we trace the Christian history of the representation of the female form, it came to be dominated by two meanings locked in perpetual contrast, each tied to the female reproductive role and each represented in a Biblical figure, one drawn from the Old Testament and one drawn from the New (Miles 1989). The first of these is the "Virgin Mary codification," which focuses almost exclusively on woman as submissive wife and nurturing, long-suffering mother. By the fourth century, the Virgin Mary was a favourite figure in the instructional iconography of the catacombs. She is portrayed there as obedient (to God's will and to Joseph's authority), nourishing and maternal, devoted and empathic, grieving and submissive. In these representations she has served as the dominant template for positive womanhood throughout the history of the Church. A second image, the Eve codification, was used by Christian men to "encapsulate" the negative aspects of womanhood (ibid.:120). Over the course of its history, the Christian church modified the classical representation of female nakedness in order to better symbolize this second negative set of meanings, all associated with sexuality and the "fall from grace."

Unlike the rather static Mary image, representations of Eve developed slowly over time. At the time of the institutionalization of the Church and its elevation as the state religion of the Roman Empire, the female nude did not have a necessary association with seduction and sin. Eve, as found on sarcophagi of the fourth century, does not undulate any more than does Adam beside her (Volbach 1964:22 and Plate 43). But an undulating Eve, as a template for evil sexuality and for female seductive power was represented in large numbers by the fifteenth century by which time women had come to "embody sex itself" (Hollander 1978:87).

The means by which Eve was crafted as the temptress relates back to conventions of nakedness in Western art. Over several centuries, the pressure cooker of Christian theology, as well as church politics and the geopolitics and economy of European society, developed a set of standardized Western social readings of nakedness which have since persisted relatively unchanged (Miles 1989:81). A few of these interpretations are positive, as in the association with a committed resistance to secular or "fallen" society; in this context, the nude body denotes purity and resistance to the seductive attractions of an amoral secular lifestyle. However, most meanings attached to nakedness have been transformed by the Christian church in order to embody the lost and damned; nakedness is the mark of powerlessness, passivity and is associated with slavery, captives, prostitutes, the insane and the dead (ibid.:81), a list which should be extended to include the primitive and/or savage. Nakedness is also used to punish, torture and humiliate. Nudity, on the other hand, is associated with sexuality—which, even under conditions approved by the Church, developed a host of meanings with negative connotations. By the sixteenth century, and given the twin codes of Mary and Eve, both nakedness and nudity in the female form represented sex, lust, sin and death to the Christian community (Miles 1989: xiv), while positive femininity was narrowly coded as well-clothed, maternal and compliant.

If we return to Figure 2, taken from the font in Siena Cathedral and attributed to Antonio Federighi, we can see an early example of the contrastive Christian representation of the male and female forms which developed by the fifteenth century and proliferated after that time. Here the classical form of Adam, muscular and well-proportioned, supports the serpent-like, undulating body of Eve. This image is the earliest known example of such a "symbolic contrast of male and female bodies" and Clark (1956:386) speculates that the sculptor may have been inspired by Far Eastern gender representations. But the Western artist did not have to go so far afield to find standard conventions linked to gender with which to portray complex messages. Eve as the seductress underwrites every image where the female torso leans even slightly backwards so as to "invite the gaze," an invitation specific to the male viewer (Caws 1985:274). The placement of the female figures in the frame and the play of light on their naked bodies creates an object which can at once both attract and repel, threaten and delight (Miles 1989:124). The Madonna, on the other hand, is coded differently, with drooping head, bent neck, slumped shoulders and maternal gaze all of which invoke pity, empathy and concern (Caws 1985:274; Pearce 1991:39). The history of Western visual representation of the female gender is largely a play on the tension between these two polar extremes and on the additional contrast that the male gender provides.

Western standards of representation of gender attributes and of
notions of femininity and masculinity hearken back to religious imagery.
In early religious paintings, the eyes of female images are "unfocused in
the middle distance" while male images tend to engage the viewer's eye,
in order to "invite the viewer to acknowledge kinship and empathy with
him" (Miles 1989:99). This device of engaging the viewer's eye is also
useful for "inviting the viewer to participate in the pictured scene" and
thus to feel part of the action portrayed (Miles 1985b:202). The body language in Figure 2 plays on similar conventions of stance, "Adam strides,
upright and purposeful" while Eve "undulates"; Adam's nakedness is less
"exposed and vulnerable" than Eve's, which is "self-conscious" (Miles
1989:99). Such visual images form an iconographic genre long recognized
as "the books of the illiterate" and thus an important source of religious
instruction. Their meaning lies in "common opinions and interpretations"
(ibid.:118) which are reinforced in each generation through the visual
medium. People learn the meanings embedded in standard conventions
and absorb the messages embedded in the meaning; a gold plate outlines
a head and thus represents a halo, which in turn signals divinity (Pearce
1991:33). Authorities in the Christian church have long defended the use
of such iconography, and the source of the power in these images is suggested by the form that defence takes (Miles 1985a). The images are said
to be useful in instructing the ignorant because they act to "move the
mind more than descriptions." Their efficacy is tied to their immediacy as
a sensory experience, for deeds before the eyes "appear to be actually
carrying on," while in verbal accounts the deed is done and over with, is
only "hearsay" and subsequently "affects the mind less when recalled to
memory" (Miles 1989:66). Thus, in Christian art, common opinions and
interpretations of gender attributes come together with standard conventions of other sorts in a powerful, mutually supportive context, endorsed
by one of our major cultural institutions.

In the politics of gender, these images have significant impact. Not
only do they have an instructional aim in the field of religious ideology,
but they are also useful whenever gender roles come under debate in the
political or social realm. For one thing, religious images reinforce
notions of gender attributes and become potent symbols in the contentious issue of public roles for the two genders. In the sixteenth to
eighteenth centuries in Europe, a protracted struggle to curtail women's
rights developed in both the public sphere of church and government

and in the private sphere of family, property and inheritance (see Miles 1989; Goody 1983, 1990). Increased restrictions were placed on female roles in the public sector and on their rights in the private realm, a political struggle that coincided with a new pattern of fetishism in artistic representation. Female nakedness increasingly appeared as evil and associated with forbidden and arcane pursuits such as witchcraft. The visual arts became more sensual, with overt sexual gestures, as when Adam cups Eve's left breast up as an offering to the viewer in *The Fall* by Hans Baldung, c. 1511. Several pictures of this same type were produced, sometimes with Death replacing Adam. Eve's look is very similar in all of these, slope shouldered, eyes averted, absolutely passive in stance (Miles 1989:127). Eve is subdued and thus partakes of Mary's codification; the evil powers of her attractions are made repellent (and thus powerless) by the implication of their ultimate consequences should man fall prey to them. The image is crafted as powerless and by suggestion so is the gender. It is interesting that in the post-Woman-the-Gatherer environment of paleoanthropology, this same visual device of the cupped breast is found in several recent reconstructive illustrations. Two examples are found among the Jay H. Matternes illustrations; the first is a post-Lucy rendering of a troop of *Australopithecus afarensis*, published in *National Geographic* (Weaver 1985:594) and the second is the endpaper illustration of *Homo habilis* in *Lucy's Child* by Johanson and Shreeve (1989). I return to this point in chapter 8.

By the beginning of the seventeenth century, several "established iconographic devices" and their associated meanings were widely understood in Western culture, based as they were on experience-specific referents. And these experiences in turn resulted in a refinement of the devices. The imagery of Christ, for example, was recrafted to appeal to a wider audience in medieval society. He was no longer cast as the knowledgeable teacher-philosopher of a persecuted people, as in the days when Christianity was just another minority sect. Nor was he cast as the triumphant monarch as in the heady days when a routinized Catholic church became the state religion of the expanding Holy Roman Empire. Instead, the medieval Christ took on a form representing long-suffering humility and the powerlessness associated with the crucifixion. His clothes became the humble stuff of working people and his feet were bare to denote the vulnerability that he shared with them (Miles 1989:143).

The female image also responded to new political and cultural realities. During the Reformation, being "inside" or "outside" of a particular religious fold began to take on increasing significance. Clothing, particularly on women, represented a "fully socialized being" and thus a "saved" soul. Female nakedness, on the other hand, was so well "mastered in representation" that the reaction of the viewer was assured: "female nakedness as an object of male desire" (ibid.:144). As the stimulus for sin, therefore, women had the perpetual potential for slipping outside of the charmed circle of salvation. This period of Christian art particularly relied on the subtheme of grotesque imagery. In the unfolding tradition of the grotesque, women came to represent the most enduring "grotesque other" by which reasoned, moral and advanced [male] society was defined in opposition (Miles 1989:150-51). During the late seventeenth century, female grotesque images were particularly widespread in the context of the hysteria surrounding witchcraft and in the belief in the visible stigmata of witches.

These images relied on three main "acts" in the "life of the grotesque body," including sexual intercourse, parturition and the contortions of death. Processes of birth and menstruation, it has been argued, threatened male images of perfect, self-contained individuality (Miles 1989:153) making women particularly apt subjects for grotesque images. Three pictorial devices were used to construct grotesqueness, including caricature, inversion and hybridization (ibid.:155-161). These devices were differentially applied to male and female forms. Caricature plays on certain characteristics and overemphasizes them in contrast to others; one example is to use discrepancies in size, either in body parts or of the whole body itself as in monstrous giants. Caricature and gender can play off each other in complex ways. Monstrous body size when applied to women (who, by Western standards, ought to be small and fine-boned) conveys a completely different message than when applied to males, where it commands respect and admiration. Female caricature often involved gross size for the breasts, vagina and uterus which were thus crafted as obscene or ugly body parts in comparison with the rest of the body, in order to deflate the dangerous powers and attractions of female sexuality.

Inversion involves producing a disturbing composite by selecting components which are expected and pleasing in their own context and replacing them with their reverse. Examples include crafting a feminine face with masculine brow ridges or a hairy torso with feminine breasts (see Figure 7). Hybridization is related to inversion; it is the mixing of random or disparate parts with no functional integrity—as in "laughing, senile, pregnant, hags" (Miles 1989:161). As with inversion, the conflict between parts generates a tension in the viewer. The process of hybridization is also apparent in disintegration, as when pornography selects specific sections of the anatomy to emphasize, sending a message that women are parts to be evaluated separately—thighs, breasts, legs, buttocks (ibid.:161). The overwhelming weight of this tradition of visual representation of the female in the Christian West is such that the female body is almost impossible to reinvent in modern visual representation.

Non-Christian Influences

While the Church and religion-inspired or -endorsed imagery dominated during many periods of Western history, there were other important influences on the visual arts. Many social, cultural and economic influences contributed to the messages conveyed and the form they took. In the more liberal atmosphere of the eighteenth century, for example, rococo art portrayed females as "beautiful, young, always ready and available, but simple and undemanding" (Sydie 1992:70-71). This prompts Sydie to label this the "art of striptease," where the female nudes were designed to excite by "coyness," by the "pretence of modesty" and by being "narcissistically withdrawn into their wholly feminine world of flowers and doves and pretty children" (ibid.). As the century progressed, however, these images underwent a change as a struggle emerged over the control and regulation of female reproductive capacity. At this point, "the promotion of the domestic woman" began to overtake earlier representations (ibid.:72-74). The themes under this influence were all variations of restriction: clean-living rather than decadent, simplistic and wholesome rather than lusty, and the fecund nursing mother in place of the narcissistic tease.

In the next century, this "cult of sensibility" underwent further subtle changes under the influences of the Victorian era on the representation of women. Lynda Nead (1988) traces the development of the discourse of art during the nineteenth century and follows Foucault (1978) in arguing that the Victorian era was not one of sexual repression, as is often generally supposed, but of an enormous proliferation of discourses on sexuality. In this work, sexuality is defined as organized around the definition of a norm of sexual behaviour and by inference, of deviance and the unacceptable. For both Foucault and Nead, the discourse of art plays an important role in the elaboration of each epoch's sexuality. This discourse takes the form of a particular language with its own rules and conventions as well as the institutions in which that language is found, produced and circulated. The art world thus plays an important part in the production and reproduction of sexual politics with overtones of power and domination, not only between genders but also between classes. The production of clearly demarcated gender roles was one of the central features of a process of class definition during Victorian times. Foucault argues that the deployment of sexuality during the Victorian era was first directed against the dominant class as "self-affirmation" and later spread downwards into the other classes. Nead elaborates on Foucault's ideas by emphasizing that there was a difference between male and female sexualities during the Victorian period such that the active male contrasted with the passive female. This dichotomy crossed class barriers and became encoded throughout society in the "double standard." Female sexuality was dichotomized into virgin/whore; both of these were images that were to act on males as a means to control or stimulate male sexual aggression. This female dualization conformed to class lines; for example, the sexual respectability of the elite class was associated with dependency, delicacy and fragility while women of the lower classes were represented as lacking sexual respectability. A contradiction developed in which elite women were represented with a natural moral superiority but a physical inferiority, while working class women had moral inferiority but a physical superiority (see also Michie 1987:30).

The art world became a battleground of proliferating images and heavily coded messages of sexuality, divided on the basis of gender, class, "race" and "natural intellect." One Victorian artistic "trope" was hair, which was used to both cover and reveal, dress and undress the female body and which was thus able to code the contrasting sets of female sexuality (ibid.:100). For example, elite women were represented with smooth and controlled hairstyles, while working women (dangerous and polluting despite their health) were portrayed with voluminous and uncontrolled hair. The woman's white curve of the neck became a "heavily-coded sign of femininity," as did the pliant and dependent stance of elite females, often shown leaning on males in a predominant "oak and ivy" metaphoric manner (ibid.:13). Female shoulders were represented at a forty-five-degree angle of slope illustrating feminine submissiveness, despite the fact that at other times and during other fashion periods, this slope just as easily designated male arrogance (Hollander 1978:130-31). The representation of different stages in the life cycle also took on new significance. The male figure was shown at various developmental stages, including youth, maturity and old age. The female, on the other hand, was always shown of an age to be simultaneously mother, wife, daughter, all roles which rely on males. Further, they were always represented to suggest the cultural virtues of these roles (Nead 1988:14). All of these symbolic devices idealized the middle-class image of femininity and in the process, "disenfranchized" competing feminine stereotypes.

But it was also during the Victorian era that changes in clothing fashion spawned new representations of the feminine which crossed class borders. The use of underwear in the form of panties became acceptable for respectable women at this time while previously it had been taboo to wear anything between a woman's legs (Hollander 1978:133-34). As panties became a widely used garment, a "sexiness" became attached to them with an associated masculine "dirty interest" which generated the "French postcard" as a new popular art genre. In this form of female representation, interest shifted below the waist and the buttocks were thrust out and the back excessively curved in just at the waist (see the female on the right in Figure 15), a pose that has since been "stamped" on the female nude in Western representation not only in pornography but in the field of "high art" as well. This redirection of masculine interest in the female anatomy crossed class boundaries and both upper-class and lower-class women were portrayed in the resulting postcard art.

The more respectable artistic expression of the period promoted non-sexual gender roles of both males and females in a number of ways that naturalized and codified gender differences. The domestic roles of both genders, for example, were suggested in portrayals of the domestic scene where the nuclear family organization was glorified along very specific lines. The natural leadership role in families (especially respectable families) was thought to be patriarchal and this was encoded in the triangular ordering of people in family pictures, with the male standing at the top or apex of the triangle while the woman was seated on a level with the children (Nead 1988:38). Motherhood has been an enduring theme in the representation of Western and non-Western women alike. But during the Victorian era, this highly specific historical construction whereby the primary raison d'être of women was the moral and physical well-being of children "was made to seem natural and universal" (Nead 1988:27), often through images that played on the emotional tribulations of motherhood. In these sorts of family images, art was able to play much the same instructional role that it had in other periods.

During the Victorian period the subject of educational interest was as likely to be history or social pathology as it was religion or family values. For example, the Victorians enjoyed a genre known as the "incident picture" and Powell Frith's "action packed" narrative illustrations such as Derby Day were very popular (Cowling 1989). Critics acknowledged that this genre of painting was designed to be "read like a novel" and that viewers had to "throw" themselves into the plot and learn the characters. The Victorians "read" the physical form of the individuals represented as if nature had clearly printed there all sorts of information on moral, intellectual and psychological strengths, weaknesses and expected behaviour. Artists were trained in physiognomy, with its pseudo-scientific basis in natural history, evolution, taxonomy and physical anthropology, and were expected to conform to representational stereotypes about the characteristics of certain categories of people. This popular belief in the scientific basis of physiognomy was focused particularly on the head and proportions of the cranium and face. The angles and planes of face, forehead and cranium were often compared to other animal forms. Sample faces and their supposed resemblance to animal forms were thought to tell the physiognomist something about the wider national and cultural character and racial traits of human populations from which they were drawn. Paintings such as Firth's work were thus able to confirm every social prejudice and to support a pattern of national and cultural xenophobia. Physical and racial differences were securely tied to different capacities of intelligence and cultural achievements; the African Negro was shown to resemble an ape and the Irish male was mapped against a yapping terrier dog. Pickpockets and murderers each had their moral debasement written into their physical features, with low brows and thick necks, while the elite, the effete and the intellectual each were known by a "high brow" and other "superior" facial proportions. These "physiognomical beliefs" were so influential and widespread that even today we continue to more or less unconsciously accept them, "particularly those of a racial connotation" (Cowling 1989:39).

Another example of the Victorian use of educational art is found in allegorical painting with a historical content, a form that dates back to early Christian art (Volbach 1964:13). During the Victorian period, its popularity led to the development of new characteristics. Military themes were pervasive, as were cultural heroes and historical events of significance to particular cultural groups. The format was often a "rifted-down-the-middle, frieze-space" which frequently contained a matching off of the sexes. What is interesting about this matching off is the lack of explicit gender conflict in the subject matter portrayed which might justify it (Armstrong 1985:225, 228). By the end of the nineteenth century, this format became the staple of artists such as Degas, who made subtle plays on it in order to send ever more complex messages about gender. In the Degas work called *The Interior,* for example, a male and a female figure occupy the same frame with very little about their relationship made explicit by the artist. However, the male figure is upright and is thus coded as dominant; he "gestures and acts through his gaze" (ibid.:229). The female form which is crouching down and thus coded as submissive, is the object upon which the male active gaze acts. The message of females as "objects" of male interest is not so much endorsed as explored. Other Degas images use the simple device of turning the female figure's back on the viewer to create the opposite of the invitation convention. The message is of an unknowable and an unreadable entity, a rejection of the (male) viewer's gaze. As Surrealist art forms developed, such conventions with their associated meanings were retained, but used in different, highly disjointed ways and thus able to carry additional freights of meaning (Caws 1985).

One feature of this recent elaboration of gender conventions is that artists have been able to direct their output towards a more selective audience. In the past, art often played a levelling role in that all members of the community were expected to have the same exposure to it (as in places of worship) and to learn the same things from it (as in moral messages). In societies practising one dominant, state religion, locating art in the devotional settings that everyone used ensured this universal exposure. A visual image, repeatedly depicted in such settings, can be assumed not only to be endorsed by social authorities, but also to have popular attraction for people of its culture because it relates to strong anxieties, interests, longings (Miles 1985b). In this context, nudity plays a multidimensional role. It has a universal element in that it always carries a sexual message and can thus "intensify the narrative, doctrinal or devotional message" mostly "by evoking subliminal erotic associations" (ibid.:203). And yet, even in such "public" art, nudity can convey a range of messages which can be selectively appropriated by individuals depending on their stage in the life cycle or other influences (ibid.:196). Uncritical or unreflective viewers can choose to pay attention to those messages which relate to their own life experiences–the rest of the messages can be selectively ignored. Wider influences will also affect viewer attention. Such things as life expectancy, notions of privacy, availability of food, marriage customs, child-rearing practices, gender conditioning, laws and punishment can all influence the popularity of an image. Thus, at least two levels of meaning can be appropriated by an audience–the person-specific and the culture-specific. Modern art forms have taken these two levels of meaning and have used them to produce much more complex images, making multiple readings possible.

By the twentieth century, the visual imagery of male versus female widened to include photography, film and other visual media, but continued to retain certain accepted patterns of representation. For example, women remain "portrayed in terms of their bodies" more than do men and are judged by more exacting physical standards in this portrayal (Unger and Crawford 1992:103). There is a tendency to "face-ism" or the representation of males from the shoulders up, while females are more often portrayed from the neck down. Males are portrayed in disproportionate numbers compared to females, and are coded as more important. There is a limited number of behavioural roles associated with females as compared to males and this fact is linked to the "natural" differences in the traits of the two genders. Female occupations are limited by a set of cultural expectations about female attributes, as with an evident "unwillingness to grant females authority" (ibid.:113, 117). Representations of individuals of either sex tend to rely heavily on such Western notions of gender-specific traits and "naturalizes" those traits by the act of repetition.

Recrafting gender images without reference to any of these embedded meanings is made more difficult by the resistance against acknowledging that any problem exists. There are three standard defences used against critiques of the representation of the human nude in the visual arts, and these defences make it difficult to demand a reinvention of the nude. The same sorts of defences show up in the field of anthropology. The first argument is that women are not present or are present in fewer numbers than males for good reason, and so there is no need to reinvent their representation. Some archaeologists, for example, have argued that the female role in evolution is difficult to know because their behaviours did not preserve as well as those of tool-making man. Until we develop the technology to wrest knowledge about women out of the archaeological record, drawing them into the picture can only be done on the basis of pure invention (see Conkey 1991 for a rebuttal). The second argument is that the depiction of women is based on natural fact; this is what makes it inevitable, representational and inscribed in women's biology. There is no universal conspiracy by males to represent women in negative ways and as female representation is based on nature there is nothing that can be done about it without doing violence to the facts. The third argument is that representations of women are uninteresting since they tell us nothing about history or society, or in this case, human evolution. And so we are left with images so loaded with cultural meaning that they have become unwieldy and difficult to thrust aside; any attempt to do so becomes "much ado about nothing."

Artists as Illustrators

All of the above stereotypical tendencies can be discovered in the field of educational illustration and specifically in paleoanthropological reconstructive illustration. This is not surprising since human evolution illustrators are both illustrator and artist; they simultaneously engage the history of their field and earn a living with every artistic act.

Scientific illustration has played a significant role since the early days of the rapid expansion of the scientific enterprise in the mid-1800s. In the fields of paleobotany and geology, collaborative efforts between scholars and artists extend back into the 1700s, but the radical impact of including a visual component with scientific arguments was forcibly brought home to the burgeoning scientific community after the publication of *The Primitive World and Its Different Periods of Formation* in 1847. In this publication, the topographic artist Josef Kuwasseg collaborated with the Austrian paleobotanist Franz Unger to develop a series of windows on the "deep past" through "an ecologically plausible view of the *community* of organisms that had lived" during each geological epoch (Rudwick 1989:237, emphasis in original). These landscape images had an artistic pedigree which extended back into the Era of the Voyages of Discovery.

World maps which were drawn to illustrate new discoveries often included a landscape representation of native vegetation and animal life, much of it highly fanciful. These images in their turn were often influenced by the woodcuts of earlier eras, where horrible imaginary humanoids and animals of the unexplored reaches of the world were crafted in frightening detail (see examples from Olive Dickason 1984). Kuwasseg drew on these illustrative traditions when he crowned his series of landscape representations with an image of the rise of humanity by showing a family group "in primal nakedness" standing and looking out over "a sub-tropical Eden" (ibid.:239). This genre of chronological landscape images could not fail to interest proponents of the infant science of paleoanthropology, and the modern form of science and art collaboration was quickly developed.

By the turn of the century, illustrators and the images they produced were often better known than the scientific knowledge on which they relied. In 1909, Kupka's brutish illustration drawn from the Neandertal remains of La Chapelle reinforced Marcellin Boule's interpretation of the species as an evolutionary backwater and generated immense excitement when it was published in the popular press (Moser 1994). A few years later, Arthur Keith's contrary interpretation was buttressed with a contrasting image of a much more progressive Neandertal produced by the reconstructive artist Forestier (ibid.). A specialized field began to emerge, with training and a background in art being combined with the study of many other disciplines, including botany, anatomy and physical anthropology (see Rensberger 1981, Watson 1956). Professional scientific illustrators worked closely with archaeologists, geologists, paleobotanists and paleoanthropologists to provide vibrant images to accompany the theoretical arguments being developed about the "deep past."

In the period surrounding the First World War, many formal institutions concerned with presenting findings on evolution and human origins to the public began to utilize the illustrative talents of such specialists. Charles R. Knight (b. 1874) worked in association with M.F. Osborn (1936:208, 358), who published several popularized accounts of human evolution. Osborn was president of the American Museum of Natural History and Knight became linked with that institution as well. Maurice Wilson (b. 1914) was a British illustrator who had a similar working relationship with the Natural History Museum in London (see Andrews and Stringer 1989). Rudolph Zallinger (b. 1919) began working with the Peabody Museum of Natural History at Yale University as artist in residence in 1942 (see Ostrom and Delevoryas 1977). Even where illustrators were not linked to a single institution, their impact on the public was often considerable. The work of the famous Czech illustrator Zdeněk Burian (b. 1905) became well-known both as a result of his association with widely read publications, including several by Josep Augusta, and because of sheer output. According to his grandson, he illustrated over 600 books, produced thousands of illustrations and collaborated with several important scholars including Jan Filip, Jiří Mally, Z.V. Spinar, J. Wolf and Karel Zebera (Jiří Hochman, pers. com.). His voluminous reconstructions of the Neandertal became the dominant rendering which influenced artists for many successive decades (for examples, see Augusta and Burian 1960: plates 8-22 and Figures 8 and 10 in this book).

As the level of public education increased in the postwar period, interest in human evolution widened and the publishing world responded with more efforts to popularize the subject. Increasing numbers of artists were attracted to scientific illustration and their work became widely distributed as it appeared and reappeared in both textbooks and popular publications such as *National Geographic* and others of the new genre of science magazines. Examples of artists who participated in this expansion include Zdeněk Burian, Jay H. Matternes, Stanley Meltzoff and Rudy Zallinger. The Time-Life book on human evolution edited by Howell (1965) is a good example of this postwar type of publication and it provides an excellent opportunity to study several different illustrators in one place.[1]

However, before going on to examine the form and consequences of this expansion of the work of illustrators in the reconstruction of the deep past there is an important codicil which must first be considered. Several factors affect the output of scientific illustrators: they develop as a product of their social and stylistic time-frame, work for different venues, produce

---

1 The Time-Life book on the Neandertals, which came out in 1973, offers an interesting contrast with this 1965 publication. It relies far less on reconstructive illustrations and instead utilizes a system which superimposes images of the Neandertal onto a landscape photograph (Constable 1973:36-37). The implications for "realism" are obvious; however, one image goes so far as to place the European, cold-adapted Neandertal on an African savanna, in pursuit of a herd of zebra!

their own distinctive styles and collaborate with different people of distinct theoretical orientations. Any diachronic analysis of paleoanthropological illustrations must be careful to fairly consider these differences in comparing and contrasting them. The question of the influence of scientific theories will be addressed in detail in later chapters of this book. Here I will merely touch on the other influences.

Artistic style is an inescapable component of illustrations and it is clear that since the turn of the century illustrative styles have changed somewhat independent of the intellectual debates of which they are a component. Neandertal illustrations produced by Kupka, Forestier and to a lesser extent, the early work of Burian (see Figure 8), all look surprisingly out-of-date today, especially when compared to newer illustrations, such as those done by Richard Schlecht for a 1996 *National Geographic* article on the Neandertal (Gore 1996). This relates not only to the changing theoretical significance of Neandertals as potential human ancestors but also to a differing stylistic emphasis which uses different codes for primitive anatomical appearance. Style affects content aside from anatomy as well. The wider prewar illustration field, including the work of Charles Knight, Maurice Wilson and Zdeněk Burian, tends to have a more romantic and sentimentalized quality which sets it apart from the stripped-down realism of later illustrators. Flipping through the pages of Augusta and Burian's 1960 book, for example, we see images full of drama, danger, suspense and sometimes downright morbidity. A *Picanthropus* is attacked by a sabre-toothed tiger; Neandertals armed only with clubs and fire tackle cave bears in the close quarters of the winter den; they are also shown wounded by wild boars and enjoying cannibalistic feasts; meanwhile, hunters of the Late Paleolithic are tossed into the air by hairy rhinos, attack a bison in a shallow pond, and are mauled by giant bears. In comparison, more recent illustrations rarely tell such dramatic stories about the past.

Influences relating to work environment are also important sources of stylistic differences. Stanley Meltzoff, for example, worked in the medium of large dioramic paintings and subsequently tended to craft his work for a larger canvas. In filling that larger canvas, Meltzoff relied on an impressionistic style which did not lend itself well to scientific authority or to that of accurate and detailed scientific reconstruction. Meltzoff's images which appeared in Howell's publication demonstrate the difference between impressionistic and authoritative voices in the illustrator's work, especially when compared with illustrators such as Jay Matternes. Meltzoff participates in "an artistic conception" of events, while Matternes works towards making a scientific statement. Meltzoff is unashamedly a romanticist in his material, both in form and in content. While both Meltzoff's and Matternes's illustrations rely on a narrative format, Meltzoff makes his storytelling more explicitly *story* than *telling.* Nevertheless, his museum pieces have often been photographed, cropped and marketed by the museum image library, ultimately to appear in more authoritative textbooks or magazines.

To a lesser extent this is also true of Zdeněk Burian (see Howell 1965:155-57). Burian is now deceased, but a few decades ago his work was very widely published in textbooks, popularized accounts of human evolution and in mass publications such as *National Geographic.* Although he was less impressionistic than Meltzoff, Burian also loved a good story and a fine example of this can be seen in Figure 13, where "one of the world's first artists" is portrayed in front of a buxom trio of women who represent his living models. These women are dark of skin and of Polynesian attractiveness with particularly luxurious tresses; their faces show mischief, humour and respect in equal measure while that of the male artist has a classical haughtiness and self-absorption. Burian was obviously fascinated by the thoughts going on behind the faces he created and his storyboards were rarely a simple stiff concoction.

Many illustrators do not restrict their work to hominid reconstructions and different work environments sometimes act to cross-fertilize an illustrator's various work projects, if only by lending the artist an air of scientific authority. Stanley Meltzoff had a long involvement with the journal *Scientific American,* and produced covers for them on topics as varied as insect navigation, bird flight, and ion exchange resins in electronics (Watson 1956:26). Maurice Wilson and Charles R. Knight both worked in the fields of natural history, paleontology and biological illustration. Knight's (1942) work for the *National Geographic* magazine on the "parade of life through the ages" is a direct descendent of the "landscape illustration" pioneered in the 1847 Unger publication. In his "Parade of Life," Knight likewise begins his chronology with the life forms of the Silurian seas, but his images are full of struggle, of the test for "fitness" and of predator and prey relationships. And he extends these themes to include such "primitive forms" of humanity as the Folsom point hunters of North America shown attacking a bison (Plate

XXI), the Neandertal of Germany shown repelling an "invader" (Plate XXII), the Cro-Magnon artists of France shown representing the hunt in their cave paintings (Plate XXIII) and peoples of the early Bronze Age shown attacking an elk (Plate XXIV). These various story lines, of individual struggle and of survival of the fittest, have proven to have equal utility in and are easily extendible to both the geological "deep past" and our own human origins.

Cross-fertilization works in other ways, as well. The British illustrator Wilson, for example, was admired as a refined craftsman who was particularly adept at portraying the natural beauty of extant animals in their environmental (read landscape) context, and for making these portraits widely available to the public. He worked in various mediums, including publications of all types, museum dioramas and the Brooke Bond Tea picture cards. In his human origins reconstructions, particularly those done for Le Gros Clarke's anthropological handbooks, he participated in the romanticism common to Meltzoff and Burian (see Figure 12) but in addition, relied heavily on the heroic Greco-Roman classical style which emphasized simplicity in visual field and the beauty of the human body. His frame and the narrative field it portrays is subsequently less dark, sombre or "cluttered" than those of Knight, Meltzoff or Burian. But however much these men's *styles* may have differed, when it came to the illustration of prehistoric human life their ultimate goal appears to have been the same: simple messages, forcefully conveyed, and always focused on significant operators of the story of human evolution—hunting, the sexual division of labour, and the family unit. And this is a trend which has carried on into the present day.

The best-known illustrator today is Jay Matternes whose work appears in many different kinds of venues in the publishing world, as well as in museum displays (see the examples of his work for the American Museum of Natural History reprinted in Tattersall 1993). His illustrations are so regularly seen in popular venues such as *National Geographic* and *Time* magazine (see Lemonick 1994) that students could easily identify examples of his work. Haraway (1989:196) calls Matternes "the anatomically expert scientific illustrator" while F. Clark Howell has commented that "Matternes is unique. I don't know whether to call him an artistic scientist or a scientific artist" (cited in Rensberger 1981:41). The Matternes images are certainly aggressively realist (or at least detailist) in style and this realism is accomplished through intensive study of primate anatomy.

Rensberger (1981) emphasizes the "scientific accuracy" of Matternes's work; a photo of Matternes shows him dissecting the corpse of an orang-utan that died in a zoo, and the text describes his method: "he inspects teeth, pushes a needle to the bone to gauge the thickness of flesh, measures between the eyes, and, after dissecting away the skin, begins a study of facial muscles." Rensberger sums up Matternes's expertise by stating that: "If you see it in a Matternes painting, you can be pretty sure it's true or, at least, that it represents a scientific consensus" (ibid.:45). But Matternes's illustrations are also found in Howell (1965:66-69) and this scientific emphasis on anatomical detail is less clear in early work by the illustrator. In comparison with Meltzoff, for example, Matternes produces faces that are rather sterile surfaces, almost cartoon like, and there seems little attempt to suggest that any complex thoughts are going on behind their surface features. His scientific detailism seems to have developed as a personal style later in his career. Nevertheless, in both his early and later work his favourite format is consistent with those of other illustrators. Matternes relies on a narrative representation verging on the "incident picture" of Victorian fame. Like Wilson, he utilizes a highly classical approach to the human body *and* very simple storytelling. His work, as a result, is a particularly efficacious combination of realism and narrative, having a significantly authoritative voice and at the same time spinning highly imaginative yarns.

An interesting feature of paleoanthropological illustration then, is that it is broadly divided between the more artistically grounded "artist's conceptions," which have been losing ground in terms of popularity in recent years, and the anatomically realistic reconstructive illustrations which now dominate. Nevertheless, both of these quite divergent styles turn on the same story operators; both artist and illustrator participate in the same narrative field. And as I will show in the following chapters, the artistic training and use of Western artistic tropes that they share in common allows them to play an integral role in the propagation of particular idea sets. One of the most problematic themes in Western art is the representation of gender; it is no surprise then that this theme is treated in human evolution illustrative material in ways consistent with the larger art world, a theme I turn to in the next chapter. Scientific illustration endorses, indeed promotes, traditional gender roles based on traditional assumptions about gender attributes, despite the fact that such uses of art have been extensively critiqued by feminist art historians. Unfortunately, the illustrative art world has not received the same attention from the feminists as has the more highbrow art world. And this lack extends to the other conventions in the world of scientific illustration, including xenophobic trends such as racial stereotypes, themes of Western progress and of the "natural superiority" and thus dominance of our species, our history and our culture. I turn to these additional themes in chapters 5, 6 and 7.

CHAPTER FOUR

Gender: The Ubiquitous Story Operator

AN IMPORTANT FOCUS IN this analysis of paleoanthropological illustrative material is gender, which as a concept is often treated in the mass media as straightforward and non-problematic. But anthropologists have long recognized that it is not so easy to develop a working definition of gender which is sensitive to cross-cultural variation. I follow Kessler and McKenna (1978) in defining gender as culturally specific constructs central to the definition of social categories of personhood. Such categorization usually involves designating physiological, psychological, social and cultural aspects considered essential to maleness or femaleness. This categorization happens in the West as it happens elsewhere, although not in exactly the same ways. It is important therefore to distinguish three aspects of gender which taken together allow for significant cultural flexibility in creating social categories of personhood (see Spector and Whelan 1989:69).

The first of these is gender attributes, which are the physiological, psychological, behavioural and emotional attributes considered diagnostic of a particular gender construct in any one social milieu. The attribution of traits to categories of gender may define two, three or more "types" of gender depending on the culture involved, as in the controversial "extra genders" of the berdache of North American native tribes or Hijras of India (Callender and Kochems 1983, Nanda 1993, Whitehead 1981). Gender attributes contribute to, but are not solely determinant of the construction of two other components of gender: gender roles and gender identity. Gender roles are the socially constructed and commonly accepted patterns of behaviour which are more or less ascribed to a particular gender category in any one culture. As such, they form the constellation of behavioural "options" for members of that society, depending on the person's placement into a gender category. While there is no doubt that a certain amount of "play" exists in the boundaries of these behavioural categories and assigned statuses—so that assigned status can lead to behavioural choices while behavioural choices can modify assigned status—it is also true that some societies are more restrictive in these options than are others.

In this regard, the third aspect of gender, which is gender identity, always involves, to a greater or lesser extent, the accommodation individuals make to their cultural milieu. Gender identity is central to, while not being the same thing as, self-identity. We each have a gender identity which helps to guide us in our self-perception of who we are and how we should be obtaining satisfaction in life. Our personal ability to meet cultural, social and self-expectations will have an impact on how we view ourselves as individuals. A basic assumption in much gender research, including gender aspects of paleoanthropology, is that natural gender attributes restrict behavioural options and thus limit gender roles and control gender identities. I will show how this assumption underwrites most of the illustrations developed in the human origins field. But other assumptions are theoretically possible. The human species is capable of considerable "play" with its ideological constructs; individual and cultural inventiveness in creating and defining new behavioural options and thus social categories of personhood must be considered when investigating the deep past.

Changing the way we perceive and work with the concept of gender cannot proceed without a discussion of the impact of feminism. Although feminism has been a highly vocal and politicized influence on many Western disciplines over the past several decades, the relationship between feminism and anthropology is longer and more complex. Anthropology has been involved in the production of gender discourse for as long as it has existed. Early cross-cultural studies of kinship and especially of matrilineal societies proved a significant jolt to complacent Western European notions about male primacy which scholars such as Maine, Morgan and McLennan tried to explain away with evolutionary models (Fox 1967:16-21). Later, Margaret Mead's 1928 research on Samoan teenagers was widely read in American society, challenging people to reconsider various common notions about age and gender. Donna Haraway (1989:351-52) comments that:

> The ideologies and symbols associated with woman as mother, with woman constituted as object of another's desire and pleasure, and with the female body as the stakes in the contest of honour among men

have all been problematized by other cultural discourses on gender and sex. Only some of these challenging moves have been feminist, however defined.

Such material proliferated in the Western consciousness and interacted in complex ways with developing feminist ideas; these in turn influenced the further theoretical development of anthropology. The upshot is that anthropology and feminism have long interacted, but the relationship is not always smooth. One complicating aspect of the relationship has been anthropology's position as simultaneously a product of Western discourse *and* as purveyor into the West of non-Western discourses of culture and society.

Anthropology was shaped on the anvil of the Western obsession with dualism and its many subdisciplines focus on the artificial but deeply rooted boundary between "nature" and "culture." In addition, it has tried to work within the Western trend to dualism with respect to gender such that the human species is divided on the basis of "natural" distinctions into two mutually exclusive categories: male and female. But this dualistic view of gender is not always compatible with the nature/culture contrast. For example, the plentiful anthropological evidence (both biological and cultural) of diversity in human sexuality has resisted being neatened away under the category of deviance and it has proven difficult to assume that male and female are universal "natural" boxes and that people everywhere classify the members of their society only into one of these two options. The result is that anthropological studies have as often challenged these "fully constructed" boxes as they have worked within them; many now take the approach that they require careful *cultural* deconstruction or interpretation (Errington 1990:8-9). Others, particularly in the fields of paleoanthropology, archaeology and physical anthropology, seem comfortable working within the dualist distinction between male and female (see Haraway 1983, 1988). As a result every position in the Western gender debate can find anthropological grist for its mill.

In the resulting dialogue between anthropology and feminism, some gender-relevant meanings have come to be shared to a significant extent by the two while others remain contentious. For example, many anthropologists and feminists can agree that gender is a "cultural system of meaning pertaining to the differences and similarities between men and women as they are lived and interpreted in particular contexts" (Errington 1990:8).

But Haraway (1989:290) notes that feminist theory and practice around gender "seek[s] to explain and change historical systems of sexual difference whereby 'men' and 'women' are socially constituted and positioned in relations of hierarchy and antagonism." Some feminists have politicized and in the process universalized these gender relations, assuming a priori a universal pattern of political and social male dominance, much to the discomfort of many anthropologists who remain focused on the broad implications of heterogeneity in human cultural patterns. Within anthropology, the feminist influence on research has been contested by those for and against feminist political agendas. Some anthropologists have wanted to treat female subordination as an empirical problem to be investigated— while others have chafed this, seeing it as collaboration with the universal patriarchal powerhouse. There have been occasional flare-ups, with accusations and counter-accusations (see Harriet Lyons 1981 and Fran Hosken 1982, as one example). As a result, non-feminist gender research in anthropology has often proceeded along a different track than that of critical feminist thought.

As such Western cultural discourses about gender have proliferated, dissension has increased, much of it in a highly public venue. Haraway (1989) notes, for example, that there are always attempts to "resuscitate" the "traditional view" of women and that these have operated primarily through "reproductive politics" as in contests over abortion clinics and birth control. This has shaped the way that all scientists have gone about doing their work such that the resulting gender debates have been continuously fueled with fresh ammunition from psychology, primatology, anthropology, law, literature and sociology. Of particular interest is research that professes to delve into the "origins" of reproductive behaviour, of gendered behaviour and of human behaviour. This has placed precisely those branches of anthropology most comfortable with the traditional view of gender, and of the nature/culture divide, directly in the public eye.

The Western obsession with the relationship between "natural" attributes and "logical" gender roles has meant that the issue of whether gender is inscribed in nature or is mostly a cultural artifact is one of the more popular and regularly funded research questions. Over the years, the pendulum has swung back and forth, first nature having theoretical ascendency and then nurture. Kessler and McKenna's (1978) approach obviously leans toward the cultural end. Others have argued for a stronger role for biological influences, particularly in gender attributes and gender roles. Sociobiology, for example, has tended to treat gender as an issue primarily decided at birth with ascribed characteristics written in the genes and thus onto the individual. What nature dictates culture can only slightly modify. Even when nature and nurture are conceived of as end points on a single continuum, rather than as two mutually exclusive sources for gender specificities, the question remains as to whether nature or nurture is the primary influence, and what are the limitations on human behavioural plasticity? What is flexible and what is not?

Within anthropology there tends to be a division of labour in the exploration of the relative influence of nature and nurture on questions of gender. In those fields where evolution remains the dominant theoretical paradigm, as in archaeology, physical anthropology, primatology and paleoanthropology (all fields in which males have historically outnumbered females), the influence of biology is considered paramount, and gender attributes are thought to control social gender roles. In these disciplines, explanations of change, whether biological, cultural or social are couched in evolutionary models. That is, such transformations are explained by reference to gradual change over time involving increasing complexity and diversity and systematic progress from earlier (more primitive) to later (more modern) forms. Furthermore, the explanations offered are primarily structural-functional, that is, they seek to explain the existence of a trait or attribute by reference to its function in supporting the continued viability of a larger system, whether biological or social. The result has been that these disciplines have largely worked within an overly narrow definition of gender.

Gender attributes and roles are generalized and universalized. Male as a category is the same whether in the past or the present, whether in North America or Africa. Female as a category differs very little even across species boundaries. Explanations of the attributes and behaviours associated with these gender categories are not only structural-functional, but are generally materialistic, falling into four broad approaches: male strength hypotheses, male bonding hypotheses, male aggression hypotheses and women's childbearing hypotheses (Brettell and Sargent 1993:2-3). Since another assumption is that gender is a significant influence on differential access to local resources and to power and prestige, each of these approaches postulates that males have more access than females and that there are evolutionary reasons for this. Those reasons have to do with an assumed survival function which works to maintain the structural group.

In structural-functional models of this type, the biologist's *population* gets replaced with *social group* and adaptationist theory finds a survival function at the group level for every imagined gender trait, particularly those of the male (Haraway 1989:213).

For example, the many variations of the male strength hypothesis all argue that males dominate by virtue of their greater muscular strength, which not only enables them to make greater contributions to the group's survival, but also gives them greater prestige and power. One example is the "plow theory" of agricultural intensification (Boserup 1970, see also Ember 1983) which argues that while females are able to make significant contributions of labour in horticultural societies, once plow-based agriculture is introduced, male physical strength is necessary for production and thus males become dominant in agriculture and in society. This hypothesis, and other variants of it, are bound up in the Western ideology of social hierarchy that has long ignored a history of serfdom and slavery in which larger contributions of labour do not equal greater power and prestige. In evolutionary terms, this model views male superiority in strength as an adaptive response to past environmental threats that struck at the group. However, the mechanism that links group needs to male phenotypical change, and the one that links brute strength to reproductive success for the entire group, are both very crude in this model and continue to be so under the more recent sociobiological approach.

The male bonding hypothesis explains male dominance in similar fashion by reference to an inherent psychological advantage which allows males to better and more easily form cooperative bonds among themselves for purposes of defence or the hunt, again with resulting advantages to group survival. In this model, females are viewed as "atomistic" and unable to cooperate as they are concerned only for their own offspring. Haraway (1989:200) notes that an "implicitly gendered" and explicitly functional social cooperation was rooted in the physical anthropology of the 1960s and 1970s. The early baboon studies of Washburn and DeVore (1961) are an example of and an influence on this perspective. The male aggression model, on the other hand, argues that certain hormonal and psychological differences between the sexes have resulted in the male sex being more aggressive and thus better suited to defence, the hunt and sexual mate selection. This "testosterone model" is based on assumptions about the gender-specificity of certain "sex" hormones which have been proven erroneous; nevertheless, it has a surprising resilience.

The women's childbearing hypothesis argues that women are absent from the public sphere, and indeed from most spheres of life, because nature has demanded a greater investment of them in reproduction which, while vital to offspring survival, limits the time and energy they can expend on other pursuits. A recent variation on this approach is the "biosocial" perspective on female reproduction strategies (see Lancaster 1989).

Such research, with its implicit assumptions about natural gender attributes and roles, contrasts sharply with the paradigmatic heterogeneity common in social-cultural studies. Social anthropology has moved away from evolutionary models, particularly in the past three decades, and has rejected the universalities and grand theories which subsume the vast diversity of human cultural arrangements into equations of material advantage and adaptive success. This is not to say that evolutionary models are absent; they are merely less influential and the universalizing tendency, while it can be present as a sub-theme, is not written a priori into the theories. Therefore, socio-cultural anthropologists and sometimes archaeologists can feel somewhat uncomfortable with the treatment of gender in archaeology and in paleoanthropology (see Spector and Whelan 1989:67). But the problem of gender politics in archaeology and paleoanthropology is a deep-rooted one which is inevitably worked out in supporting data sets that tend to reinforce fixed ideas.

Idée Fixe: Gender in Paleoanthropological Illustrations

Reinforcing fixed ideas proves to be a significant theme in the representation of gender in educational and quasi-educational human evolution reconstruction artwork.[1] A survey of these illustrations demonstrates that the gender components of their thematic content follows long-standing androcentric patterns and continues to do so despite recent feminist challenges to the "male active" theories of human evolutionary history. These long-standing patterns are summed up in the title for this book, the terminology of which is taken from two sources. "Undulating women" is borrowed from Margaret Miles (1989:99), who employs it to describe a dominant trope in the Western visual representation of female attributes

---

1 An earlier version of this chapter was published in 1994 under the title "Undulating Women and Erect Men" in the journal *Visual Anthropology*.

(see chapter 3). In the European visual tradition, this fluidity in the female form is often contrasted with an upright and aesthetically athletic male figure. The male terminology in the title is a play on the paleoanthropology category *Homo erectus*. This terminology nicely encapsulates the stereotypical and contrastive imagery of the two genders which dominates in the Western art world and is the basic building material for messages about the timeless nature of gender in origins illustrations.

The interrogation/deconstruction of such imagery is designed to expose ideological complexities and contradictions through a wider "familiarity with conventions" (Pearce 1991). As a student of anthropology, the visual arts conventions employed in origins illustrations eluded me and given their "incipient narrative context," I absorbed a pre-designed message without critical reflection until Morgan's (1989) collection of readings on teaching gender in anthropology sensitized me to the issue. As I explored the hidden messages contained in the images, I grew more and more disturbed since, in my experience, most students viewed educative illustrations in a relatively uncritical way. Over a three-year period, I showed slides of many different reconstructive human evolution illustrations to my gender classes. After hearing about some of the standard conventions of representation in Western art, the students were surprised by what they found embedded within these images. As my research on this topic continued and expanded, I became more and more aware of the need to focus greater attention on the place of the illustrator in designing messages absorbed by students and the wider public.

Art historians have commented on the educational function of visual representation, particularly in the case of the narrative or anecdotal format where the representation "tells a story" to the viewer (Armstrong 1985:225). As discussed in chapter 3, Miles (1989:118) calls religious visual images "the books of the illiterate" which church authorities defend because of their ability to move the imagination of the viewer in timeless ways. Images of Eve, for example, have for centuries warned of the destructive power of female sexuality, while images of Mary have provided an equally timeless template for positive femininity (Miles 1985b:196; 1989:120). And all this is achieved without the necessity of moral harangues which might antagonize more than convince. But it is exactly this "timeless" aspect of visual representation which creates problems for educational purposes. Caws (1985:268) notes that the narrative power of such imagery "erodes doubt." Can such thoughtless absorption of predetermined messages have a place in education?

In this chapter, I examine a set of images which attempt to portray the physical form and something of the lifestyle of a succession of proto-hominids and hominid species, in order to show the ways in which gender roles are irrevocably tied to "natural" attributes through long-standing visual conventions. The representative sample of illustrations which I discuss below has been selected from educational and quasi-educational sources such as magazines (*National Geographic, Time, Newsweek*), popular works on paleoanthropology and introductory anthropology textbooks. In a later chapter, I will return to the gender issue with a specific focus on more recent illustrations to show how these gender roles have remained basically unchallenged while the female attributes have been subtly eroticized (see chapter 8).

The Iconographic "Ladder of Human Evolution" and the Invisible Gender

The "iconography" of the ladder of human evolution (Gould 1989:33) almost always appears whenever a popular magazine publishes an article on human evolution. Since I could not obtain the copyright necessary to reprint existing examples of this ladder iconography (see chapter 9), I commissioned an artist to produce an example especially for this book (see Figure 5). The sources for several other examples are discussed below. All such ladder illustrations that I have seen conform to the basic pattern shown in Figure 5, of a series of male nude or almost nude figures, representing various evolutionary stages and lined up in single file from left to right of the frame. It is possible, however, to have considerable variation within this basic pattern. In Howell's (1965) book, a very impressive illustration by the artist Rudy Zallinger includes *fifteen* figures representing "the road to *Homo sapiens,*" from the Miocene ape *Pliopithecus* to fully modern humans. The emphasis has been placed on demonstrating in full anatomical detail, the many stages on "man's long march from apelike ancestors to *sapiens.*" Another example from Bernard Campbell's (1982) textbook *Humankind Emerging* shows an very attenuated version with only six figures, from *Australopithecus afarensis* to modern humans. Here anatomical detail is less important than the overall idea of developmental continuity throughout our human family tree (i.e., bipedality,

large-brain, tool use). A third example, produced by the artist Jay H.
Matternes and published in *National Geographic* (Weaver 1985:574-77),
shows nine figures ranging from the australopithecines to modern man.
The figures are running across the page, giving the viewer a sense of
unstoppable momentum. These images all beautifully convey the very
old idea of the "march of progress," a theme I discuss further in chapter 7. Nevertheless, they also reveal much about our taken-for-granted
gender assumptions.

In comparing a number of examples of such imagery, several common features stand out. For example, artists generally lean very heavily
on the Greco-Roman classical tradition and particularly on aesthetic athleticism in order to develop the male figures. These males are well-muscled and healthy representatives of physical perfection, whatever their
evolutionary stage. Other devices suggest evolutionary change to the
male physique. Beginning at the point at which *Australopithecus* is portrayed, and intensified at the representation of the *Homo* line, we usually
see heads held more erect and rather rigidly on top of the shoulders as
opposed to hanging ahead of them. The shoulders are laid back (as
opposed to hunched forward) and increasingly well-muscled. The back
grows ever more flat, the stomach ever more lean, and the thighs and buttocks ever more muscular and powerful looking as the hominid family
evolves. Despite the striding action of the figures, their posture is rigidly
upright; usually the stepping action of the right leg modestly hides the
male genitals. The facial expression is "remote" and since they face to the
right, the figures do not engage the viewer's eye, but appear to have their
attention on some highly desirable end goal just off the page.

There are no overweight, injured, elderly or sick males in these
iconographic ladders of progress. The message is that males are athletic,
competent, healthy, pure, upright and progressive. Although the *National
Geographic* (Weaver 1985) example shows the male figures in rather
more of a hurry (to evolve?) than the other two examples (the action in
the gait speeds up considerably at the level of *Homo habilis*), even there
the effort is clearly not beyond masculine capabilities. They will succeed
in their desire to get ahead, and their images leave us in no doubt as to
their ability to do just that. This convention of an erect, ambitious, forward-looking and aesthetically athletic male directly "endorse[s] certain
definitions of male sexuality and muscularity" (Nead 1990:326). It is one
seen repeatedly in paleoanthropological illustrations.

And what of female images to provide a foil for these males? In fact, in the iconography of human evolutionary progress which these ladders represent, the female of the species is rarely if ever represented; she is notable in her erasure. Even when such iconography is borrowed by the advertising world, as it very often is, the male remains the dominant, indeed the only choice for the "line up" of evolutionary stages (see the examples in Gould 1989:29-35). Gould reprints one example from the cartoon world which contrasts two evolutionary line-ups, a female versus a male, but the female form (an elderly looking woman dressed as a peasant) remains unchanged in the series of representations which cross the frame of the illustration. These women stay down on their hands and knees, scrubbing across all time (the woman that never evolved), while the male goes from chimpanzee to *Homo sapiens sapiens.* The author of this cartoon has represented two aspects of the role of the female in human prehistory, their relative invisibility and the timeless nature of the portrayal of their essential attributes. Representations of males are found with far more frequency than those of females and when females are found in the imagery or in the accompanying text, their attributions are static, unchanging across millennia and across species boundaries. This is true even of the more interesting, "narrative or anecdotal" representations which provide additional scope for the use of artistic conventions and for the contrasting representation of gender. In these images, gender attributes are suggested in such a way that the gender roles portrayed seem natural and with roots in deepest antiquity. In what follows, I discuss such anecdotal images in the presumed phylogenic order of the various hominid species.

The Australopithecines: The Deep History of Gender Attributes and Roles

Since the discovery many decades ago of the Taung skull, certain species among the australopithecines have been classified as the oldest representatives of the hominid family and have thus become a topic of considerable public interest. But of equal interest is the fact that the australopithecine family contains species which are *not* presumed to be ancestral. As a category, therefore, the australopithecine group has been able to resonate to Biblical stories of Adam and Eve and of Cain and Abel, as well as to modern stories which pit nurture against nature, success against failure. And these stories in turn have undoubtedly influenced the theories developed to explain the survival of the ancestral australopithecines and the extinction of the other types. As a result of the centrality of the australopithecines to origin narratives and of the popularity of these Biblical and nature/nurture story operators, the australopithecines have figured in an enormous number of reconstructive illustrations. Indeed, one of the better known illustrators, Jay H. Matternes, has almost made a career out of drawing them.

Examining how Matternes has approached the australopithecines over time proves to be instructive of several processes at work in the art of illustration. The first process has to do with the *Homo*-centric character of reconstructive illustrations. Whenever the form being represented is presumed to be ancestral to the human species, subtle anatomical conventions of modernity come into play, a number of which have even more subtle gender overtones. These conventions can be reversed to emphasize primitiveness for those forms considered non-ancestral. This *Homo*-centric focus is very apparent as we examine the Matternes australopithecine illustrations across time; they go through a definite transformation from the early 1960s to the mid-1980s. This transformation relates to the changing status of the australopithecine as an ancestral form, a status which has come under increasing debate in the discipline as the fossil record has become more complex and confusing. The visual representation of the australopithecine has obviously been an important component of the resulting disputes (see chapter 5 for a further analysis of this transformation).

The second process that is obvious from Matternes's work, however, has to do with continuity. Despite the above transformation over time, these australopithecine illustrations also demonstrate how some Matternes thematic content has never changed. They show what amounts to an obsession with both the "origins" of and thus the "naturalness" of sex role specialization, the nuclear family and male dominance. For example, Howell's (1965) book on "Early Man" contains a number of early examples of Matternes's australopithecine illustrations in which these themes are dominant. In later Matternes work done for *National Geographic*, we see these same origins themes maintained alongside a significant modernization of the australopithecine physiology. In examining several selected examples of these illustrations, I discuss the relationships between the theoretical and fossil evidence, the bodily revision of the australopithecine form, and the central conservatism in the origins and gender messages.

One of the Matternes illustrations published in Howell (1965:69) is a typical example of how Matternes naturalizes gender messages such as the respective roles of male and female in the nuclear family. In this image, he has drawn three australopithecines, who despite their hairy and apelike physiology, are presented in a Victorian-style grouping of the "triangle of family life," with the "father" standing erect and thus forming the apex of the triangle, coding him as authoritarian. The successful hunter has just returned home to his rock shelter, where his more sedentary "wife" and "child" await him. He stands holding up his trophy for admiration, while the female and juvenile are placed lower in the frame to form the other two points of the triangle. The female is busy skinning game; however, as is consistent with most such illustrations which invoke the hunt through the presence of a dead animal, the butchering process is not very far advanced (see also Figures 7, 11). This allows hunting to be sanitized so as not to offend Western sensibilities. The male brings in a second kill in order to make clear the source of the game animal the female is skinning. Matternes thus enforces two messages; the male is not only *the* hunter but is also highly skilled at it. Meanwhile, the juvenile in the background lacks any clear social role, and consequently is more of a caricature-like representation. In one image Matternes gives both gender attributes and roles a timeless character, and in addition, gives the nuclear family with its dependence on a natural gender division of labour, a pedigree of considerable antiquity.

In addition to this narrative content, the illustration is also a classic example of many visual devices which have remained constant throughout the history of reconstructive illustration. Attention is drawn to the male figure in several ways. First, his larger size in the frame signals his relative importance compared to the other figures (see also Figures 6, 8, 9, 11) and at the same time, manages to suggest sexual dimorphism in size and muscular strength. Second, in contrast to the male, the female crouches low in the frame, occupying less visual field and placed "closer to the earth," suggesting the attributes of smaller stature and more timid demeanour. Third, and of great importance, the male figure is the *stimulus* to the action in the scene. The other two figures are responding to him. In the many images I have examined, particularly the older ones, women are rarely the stimulus for the action of the scene and this is even more true of juveniles and infants. Thus females and the young are linked together in their opposition to the male: passive to his active, nature to his culture, symbols of his masculinity and thus coded as limited in their significance.

It is interesting to compare an early, non-Matternes example of the australopithecine representation, such as the work of Zdeněk Burian, with the above Matternes illustration. In Augusta and Burian (1960: Plate 1), Burian has carried the apelike convention of hominid primitiveness to an extreme, representing the australopithecine as having rather chimpanzee-like facial features, apelike bodies and long arms. The narrative field symbolizes origins, but the origins of masculine technology rather than of the nuclear family, through the rather lurid device of having the australopithecine figures pick over the bones of an ape in their search for suitable tools. And with the total erasure of the female form, there is little gender content. Burian's australopithecines appear to have lived the lifestyle of the Victorian exclusive all-male club, in contrast to Matternes's "australopithecine Victorian family triangle."

A second nuclear family is seen in another Matternes illustration appearing in *National Geographic* (see Leakey 1979:448); this was published fourteen years after the Howell (1965) image and is entitled: "Hominids travel northward beneath the volcano's cloud." It shows a male figure with a female figure carrying a child, crossing a volcanic plain together. Although the male and female are equal in size and prominence in the frame, their activities and placement are used to suggest traditional gender roles and attributes; the female trails behind the male who walks ahead. She is burdened with infant (nature) while the male carries a stick (suggestive of a weapon and thus of culture). The female portrays nervousness in her glance off to the side while the male forges straight ahead. In this volcano image, Matternes is ostensibly attempting to recreate how two sets of footprints were preserved in volcanic ash around four million years ago. But the most frequent description obtained from students who viewed this illustration was: "It's a family, a man and a woman and their child." This family theme has been commented on before. Nancy Tanner (1981:175) notes that Jay Matternes chose to illustrate the footprints as a "First Family" despite the fact that Mary Leakey (1979:453) interpreted the two sets of footprints as having been made in the volcanic ash at different points in time.

The question of the means by which these footprints were created is an important one. Later publications comment that the footprints seemed to represent *three* distinct individuals, with two sets of impressions some-what overlapping. Stern and Susman's (1983:309) argument is that these prints represent the locomotion of a transitional biped, one that spent as much time climbing trees as walking, in which case, the Matternes illus-tration would be a misrepresentation of more than one aspect of the sci-entific evidence. Tuttle (1985) disagrees, arguing that the gait represented at Laetoli is exactly like that of modern humans. While the Matternes illustration represents a very premature stage of the analysis of these foot-prints, the fact remains that the image is a misrepresentation, even of the data as it was understood at the time that the drawing was made. However, it may be that Mary Leakey, as the science author responsible for the article in which the Jay Matternes illustration appeared, was her-self ambivalent. In a later BBC/Time-Life film, for example, she sug-gested that the footprints at Laetoli were "perhaps a family party" (quoted in Haraway 1989:196); was Mary Leakey influenced by Matternes's image or was Matternes influenced by Mary Leakey? Another feature of this illustration is the Biblical narrative content. Haraway has commented that she sees Adam and Eve fleeing the Garden of Eden, the volcano operating as "the sign of destruction and banishment"–paleoanthropol-ogy resonating with Biblical themes. She also makes the acerbic point that the infant is not carried in a sling, despite the Woman-the-Gatherer postu-lation that such a device was the "first humanising tool." I think one of the most interesting features of this illustration, however, is the way in which Matternes has linked these several themes: Bible and family life, the origin of family and the origin of the species.

As is true of most reconstructive illustrations, this linkage of the origins of family and of species is ultimately a gender message. In both the "fleeing the volcano" and the "australopithecine family triangle" illustrations, the female is there to provide more information about the male; through her he is coded as provider or protector. In the same way that females provide more information about males, infants and juveniles are present to provide more information about the natural gender roles of males *and* females. This may be why Gifford-Gonzalez (1993:31) found no examples of "child only" imagery in her survey of eighty-eight Cro-Magnon illustrations. Nevertheless, we should not underestimate the role juveniles and infants play in the images where they *do* appear. In the first Matternes image discussed above, the juve-nile codes the male as a progenitor, and more importantly, codes the female as maternal. This pervasive code of motherhood crops up in most Western discourse about women. Lutz and Collins (1993:166-71) trace the motherhood code through the pages of the *National Geographic* magazine to show how these romanticize the idealized mother-child bond and at the same time universalize and trivialize the female category. In the vast majority of the illustrations I have examined, this pattern holds true and it is one that viewers intuitively use to position themselves vis-à-vis the narrative plot of the illustration.

Students' responses to the Matternes "fleeing the volcano" illustration are very interesting when contrasted with the comments on Figure 7. Figure 7 is a Maurice Wilson illustration which was produced in 1950. It shows three adult *Homo erectus* at the mouth of a cave engaged in tasks such as stone tool manufacture, collecting firewood(?) and preparing to skin game. Many students expressed ambiguity with regards to the gender of the figures, even though clear physiological evidence of "femaleness" is present (i.e., breasts) on the figure on the left. With no infants or young present in the illustration, students proved to be less likely to identify this figure as female. It may be that student confusion over the gender identification of these Wilson figures also related to the fact that the figures form a loose "family triangle," but in this case the female represents the tallest point. On more than one occasion, students would go so far as to place their finger on the image and say: "This guy here ..." or "This man here is feeding the fire." Clearly, the most important indicator of female status is the maternal gender role represented through the presence of juveniles or infants.

Such stereotypical gender roles are reinforced by their association with suggested natural gender attributes. In another Matternes example found in both *Human Origins. Louis Leakey and the East African Evidence* by Isaac and McCown (1976:270) and in Jolly and Plog's (1986:202) fourth edition of their introductory textbook, a group of robust australopithecines is represented. The physiological devices used to distinguish male from female are small, high and pointed breasts on the females and more rotund chests and bellies on the males. A large male dominates the central frame and is portrayed in an upright (leaping) position directly engaging the viewer's eye. This eye contact links him to the observer and makes the viewer play the role of the stimulus to the scene's action. In this case, the action is a threatening display by the male, who is the only one to wield a weapon or to challenge the viewer's right to peer into the image. The females, on the other hand, project docility and timidity in stereotypical fashion, through conventions of posture (slump-shouldered) and facial expression (see Pearce 1991:39, and Hinde 1975:123).

Another Matternes illustration found in Howell (1965:66-67) shows a large group of similarly crafted, non-ancestral, apelike australopithecines in a savanna-like environment. The majority of the females are portrayed lower frame, crouching or sitting, and again found in association with off-spring. Their activities consist of nursing or resting. The males, on the other hand, are all shown in an erect, purposeful, upright stance, walking or reaching up into a tree. These images suggest a restricted evolutionary role for females based on the limitation imposed by their reproductive attributes. However, one female stands out. Despite having the usual juvenile in attendance, she is obviously not passively awaiting the rewards of male provisioning but sits digging for roots with a stick. Is Matternes deviating here from the usual pattern of natural male/female attributes and roles? Since this illustration was published in 1965, we can safely assume that the active female is *not* a representative of Woman the Gatherer. Instead she is another example of how Matternes crafts the australopithecines when they are presumed to be non-ancestral.

The caption identifies this active female as part of a foraging band of *vegetarian Paranthropus*, a species believed to have been an evolutionary dead end. The head of one female looks very like that of a chimpanzee and the bodies of males and females alike are shown with a very apelike representation, with hairy pelts, squat heads and extremely robust physiology. As will be discussed further in chapter 5, these more apelike representations are not only used to represent the primitive forms of deeper antiquity, but also to suggest non-ancestral status. The behaviour illustrated becomes a code for evolutionary failure. As is true for all hominid illustrations, whether ancestral or not, the males are more actively engaged in their environment in comparison to the females; but in such non-ancestral cases, the females are less passive than in the ancestral species, thus signalling the failure of their less-advanced males to properly provision them.

This non-ancestral masculine failure in the survival-of-the-fittest test is sometimes more explicitly addressed. One Matternes illustration in Howell (1965:74-75) resonates to early theories about masculine aggression, technological aptitude and defence roles. In this image, two more advanced-looking male hominids with stone weapons confront a group of *Paranthropus* males. The four male *Paranthropus* make ready to retreat with only crude rocks for defence. In the background, several female *Paranthropus* with their young can be seen fleeing the encounter. The text comments that coexistence ended for australopithecines and *Paranthropus* because the former was a hunter and "his hunting ways continued to sharpen his wits," while the latter was vegetarian. Presumably being vegetarian had no sharpening affect on the *Paranthropus* male wits; thus they were easily eliminated by our wittier ancestors in an all-out war for territory and resources. It is interesting that students universally responded positively to this image. They had no difficulty identifying the thematic content of survival-of-the-fittest in intra-species warfare and were able to describe what they saw with ease. Students also had no difficulty identifying the gender of the fleeing figures, partly because these females were running away while the males stayed behind to protect their retreat and partly because they carried children with them.

When Matternes illustrates the australopithecines who do represent our ancestors for the Howell book, the active male imagery is differently elaborated. Here essential male attributes of aggression and athletic prowess are more directly linked to success, to achievement and to masculine roles in provisioning. Males are shown leaping onto a bush buck, spearing a porcupine, cracking open bones or clubbing rodents (Howell 1965:68-69). One Matternes image (ibid.:64-65) foreshadows the scavenger hypothesis, since a group of male australopithecines are shown attempting to drive off hyenas from the remains of an antelope. Meanwhile, the females crouch in the background, often in the safety of a cave or other shelter, with highly dependent infants in attendance.

Probably as a direct response to the 1974 Lucy find and the increasing emphasis this placed on the australopithecines as ancestral forms, Matternes refined and modernized the australopithecine in his post-1974 illustrations. In 1976, a Matternes image was published in Isaac and McCown's *Human Origins* which modernized the physical form of the ancestral australopithecine but maintained the standard representation of gender roles. Most of the group is shown relaxing in the foreground while a few members scavenge meat from an animal carcass in the background. A female sits forward frame sharing meat with her child while behind her several males sit eating unencumbered by offspring. Particularly in contrast to the earlier Matternes examples, there is a noticeable shift in the physiological representation of these early hominids. They are less ape-like and more humanoid. They have no fur, and the overall proportions of arm length, chest and belly size, hip and knee angle, and facial features suggest a refining process. Obviously Matternes is leaning less on the non-human primates for sources of inspiration and more on modern foraging populations such as the !Kung bushmen. Given the ambiguity of the caption on this illustration, "early hominid life" could theoretically refer to *Homo habilis* or to some transitional form between australopithecine and the *Homo* family, and given the way that illustrations circulate in the publishing world, it is difficult to tell just what Matternes was trying to convey with this modernization of the australopithecine form.

The "fleeing the volcano" image published in *National Geographic* (Leakey 1979) solidifies the revised body image of the australopithecines in Matternes's later work (see also his australopithecines in Weaver 1985:594). In comparison with the australopithecines in Howell, these later *National Geographic* versions are lighter boned and less muscular; there is less emphasis on barrel chest and large belly and the head is less apelike, primarily because the cranium is subtly enlarged and the eyes humanized. The Lucy discoveries, and the subsequent positioning of the early australopithecines as directly ancestral to humans, appears to have influenced Matternes to represent even the early forms in more modern physiological terms. One student response to this image was that "they walk upright like humans and their backs and legs and stuff all look like human features." Nevertheless, the gender messages embedded in these recent and physiologically updated images have not shifted at all. Male and female remain coded much as they always had been.

And Matternes is not alone in playing with physiology to allow hominid forms from the deep past to play games of "ascending anachronism" or "descending anachronism" (see Conkey 1991:109). Ascending anachronisms are "pushed back" in time and thus naturalized while descending anachronisms come forward in time to participate in defining our own "cultural prowess" (ibid.). The game is intimately connected to the "facts" on which the science author wishes to focus and the arguments to be made with them. The illustrations provided by John Gurche in Donald Johanson's latest article on his Hadar, Ethiopia, "First Family" finds (*National Geographic* 1996:96) are a good example. Here the *Australopithecus afarensis* are portrayed in ways that hearken back to Matternes's pre-Lucy, robust and non-ancestral images. In this article, however, Johanson is reasserting his single species, sexual dimorphism argument which allows him to maintain a unilineal evolutionary model by incorporating all the widely varying australopithecus fossil finds into a single ancestral category. Thus the Gurche images show males considerably larger than the females in order to match their physiology with the heavier, more robust fossils. These males, however, have body-builder muscles and lithe confidence rather than the gorilla-like lethargy suggested in the earlier Matternes images. The combined gender messages are extremely suggestive, with one female walking beside and making what can only be described as "googoo eyes" at the central male figure of the illustration. These Gurche males are ancestors of which modern men can be proud.

The Post-Australopithecus Patterns of Representation

If we leave the genus *Australopithecus* now, and move on to early illustrations of the genus *Homo*, we see that the conventions used to suggest the essential attributes and natural roles of male and female remain consistent across species boundaries. Stanley Meltzoff contributed a number of illustrations to the discussion of *Homo erectus* in Howell (1965:90-99). As noted earlier, Meltzoff paints in an impressionist style that differs from the Matternes commitment to scientific anatomical reconstruction, taking as it does a more romantic approach to the material. In the first of his series of illustrations on the *Homo erectus*, Meltzoff presents a fireside scene in which a female nurses an infant and adolescents roughhouse on the grass beside her. Meanwhile, two men prepare for a hunt by sharpening a hand axe and setting out weapons. Only the female engages the viewer's eye, but her look in no way invites viewer response—nor does it respond to the viewer. It is a passive gazing outward. In the majority of these Meltzoff *Homo erectus* illustrations for Howell, the females are represented in much smaller numbers than the males and are usually found breast feeding (ibid.:90), holding children, carrying burdens (ibid.:92-93) or passively watching males recreate the hunt (ibid.:98-99). They are absent from the hunt scenes themselves; males control not only social provisioning, but also the cultural activities such as ritualized recreations of the hunt which are linked to that provisioning. Furthermore, males control the landscape, where females rarely venture. This is consistent with Gifford-Gonzalez's (1993:31) findings that less than 25 percent of

Cro-Magnon female images are portrayed on the landscape whereas over 75 percent of the male images are found there. Across the *Australopithecus,* the *Homo erectus* and the *Homo sapiens* stages, females are "tied down" while men wander. Control, particularly control over nature through the rise of culture, is inextricably linked to male gender attributes and roles.

In Figure 6, we see an illustration produced by the Czech illustrator Zdeněk Burian which was published in textbooks such as Pfeiffer's (1978:88) *The Emergence of Man* where it was entitled: *"Homo erectus* foraging in the wilderness of Java." Burian was a realist but he did not go so into detailism as did Matternes, perhaps preferring to focus on the romantic narrative content. In Figure 6, the male figure is again crafted as dominant by virtue of being placed upright, central and forward in the frame. His athleticism, with its faint echo of the classical Greek style, is in contrast to the only female figure in the illustration who is bent over and burdened with offspring. In such older illustrations, it is common to see males significantly outnumber females because the Man-the-Hunter model assigned more "jobs" to males which the artist could then illustrate. The female in this illustration is foraging for food, as are some of the other males in the image, but only she carries a child. The males around her perform purposeful tasks including heavy labour, defence and provisioning. Two males carrying weapons lag behind and look alert; the upfront and central male also appears "on guard." Two other males turn over a boulder, perhaps to find edible grubs underneath while yet another reaches up into a tree. The lone female, symbolized by the child hanging around her neck, seems outnumbered and outperformed by her masculine counterparts. Fewer in number, smaller in size, peripheral in placement and with less tasks to perform, the females are made insignificant to evolutionary history.

Another *Homo erectus* illustration which has already been discussed (Figure 7), appears in several textbooks where its use as representation of past hominid forms is not always consistent. In two of these, (Louise B. Young 1970:212 and Haviland 1979:152), the figures are identified as a group of *Homo erectus,* while in Staski and Marks (1992:469) it is entitled "Artists rendition of Neandertal life" and the caption questions their nudity given that the Neandertal had tools for skinning animals and lived in a cold climate. In Young and in Staski and Marks, the artist's name and date (Maurice Wilson 1950) are clearly visible while in Haviland they are not. The Natural History Museum in London, which holds the copyright on most of Maurice Wilson's work, classifies Figure 7 as *Homo erectus* (Peking Man). The fact that some publishers have used it to represent Neandertal life demonstrates the plasticity of the iconography and the continuity of the gender messages. The format in Figure 7 is typical of that described by Armstrong (1985:225) as the "rifted, divided-down-the-middle, frieze-space" format common to the painting of Western religious and historical subjects and in which the sexes are "matched" in opposition although the narrative content gives us no explanation of this. In this illustration, the figures are placed in an explicitly cultural space with evidence of a dwelling (cave) and the domesticity of a fire. The two males are full of purposeful activity; one crouches at an anvil stone and strikes off stone blades while the other drags in a deer. Meanwhile the lone female, intent as she is on the male's hunting prize, has no clear role except perhaps to stoke the fire.

Wilson has made interesting use of several artistic conventions which denote primitiveness as well as natural gender attributes. The female image is an example of hybridization, where random parts of disparate nature are mixed without functional integrity. A tension is created in the viewer by mixing these disparate parts into one visual image, often to denote grotesqueness. For example, in the upper body, the female's sloped shoulders (docility, submission) conflict with the jutting forward head stance and almost belligerent set of the jaw (aggression). On the other hand, the representation of the eyes and forehead make her upper face appear almost wistful (feminine). The torso also contains disparate images, with feminine breasts, shoulders and upper arms above a classically masculine midriff and belly. Perhaps the jaw, midriff and belly explain why students often identified her as a male. In contrast, the two males in the image are well-muscled and athletic, and all their parts are functionally integrated; they look far less grotesque, with broad shoulders, flat stomachs and muscular thighs. Only their facial features and lack of neck place them in a primitive category. This has allowed them to pass as Neandertal, in cases where the author of the text wanted to emphasize the distance between the Neandertal and anatomically modern humans. In general, gender role content for the *Homo erectus* imagery remains consistent with australopithecine patterns. The only difference is the increased activities and mobility for the males which links them to change and to technological endeavours such as hunting, tool manufacture and use. The females remain static and represented much as they were at the australopithecine stage, nurturing offspring, tending fires, and preparing food. In all these activities, they remain dependent upon the male.

These themes continue when we turn to illustrations of the Neandertals. In both Howell's (1965:131-35) book and the Augusta and Burian (1960) publication, Zdeněk Burian published many such images. Males and females are equally grotesque in Burian's illustrations, in keeping with the robust physiology of the Neandertals which is suggested by their heavier skeletal structure. Burian represents their chests as enormously broad, the shoulders as massive, the figures as hairy, with large hands and feet and practically no neck. In a Burian illustration used in Pfeiffer's (1972:187) textbook, we are shown a Neandertal community portrayed "at the beginning of a rhinoceros hunt" (Figure 8). In this image a male figure centres the visual field and male figures remain numerically dominant. The lone female is placed low in relation to the males as she is seated while they mostly stand. She continues the female association with "timeless" roles of caring for the young and of feeding them, cradling an infant in the nursing position. One male carries a club and gestures towards the rhinos in the distance, while another male, interrupted from his flintknapping, rises from his work. These Neandertals differ little from the previous *Homo erectus* material with respect to gender, being represented in a familiar dichotomized fashion. Females are represented in fewer numbers than are males, generally being outnumbered three to one. They also are involved in fewer activities, usually tending children or following male leaders, heavily laden with burdens. Male hunters are shown driving ibex off of cliffs, or butchering rhinoceros who have fallen into camouflaged pits (Howell 1965:134-35). It is important to note the pervasiveness of these gender conventions. They appear not only in "artists' conceptions" published in the mass media, where the academic world could be said to have less control over the messages conveyed, but also in the other venues by which the public learns about our ancestral past, the museum diorama (see Tattersall 1993:128-29) and its modern-day equivalent, the historic theme park (ibid.:155).

The Neandertal images are notable for one difference. We begin to see a very explicit association of adult males with cultural pursuits such as art and ritual because of the several archaeological finds that suggest that the Neandertal regularly buried their dead with some care. Illustrators such as Burian rapidly responded to sensational findings such as those at Shanidar Cave where Ralph Solecki and his team worked between 1951 and 1960 and where several adult and infant Neandertal burials were found. Pollen evidence suggested that one adult Neandertal had been apparently buried with a large number of wildflowers (Solecki 1971:214), leading Solecki to dub these Neandertals as "the First Flower People" and to hypothesize that they had respect for their dead and some form of burial rituals. In many subsequent publications (see Pfeiffer's 1972:190, *Reader's Digest Quest for the Past* 1984:15) Neandertals were shown at the graveside. Neandertal burial excavations obviously fascinate illustrators and the public alike, but what is more important is that this topic is treated very consistently in such illustrations. In the example shown in Figure 10, Zdeněk Burian has produced a robust and somewhat grotesque Neandertal image consistent with his earlier work used in the Howell (1965) publication. The corpse is positioned as if to sleep, with one hand under its head and knees drawn up. It is wearing primitive clothes and is accompanied by cultural artifacts. The attendants are all male. Burian was also interested in the between-war theories that circulated around other supposed Neandertal ritualized behavior, including those involving cranial cannibalism, cave bear skulls and the horns of wild goats (see Trinkaus and Shipman 1993:257-58). In his 1960 publication with Augusta, he included many illustrations which played on the masculine rise of such "fully-human" cultural attributes. Trinkaus and Shipman (ibid.) comment that these supposed ritual behaviours projected "very human ideals, values, and religious beliefs" back "into the remote past inhabited by Neandertals." Among these beliefs were those concerned with the cultural supremacy of the male.

The Neandertal imagery does not escape from the cult of the nuclear family, either. In a painting by Maurice Wilson, Neandertals are shown in a nuclear family setting (Figure 9). Two juveniles are placed low, squabbling or playing behind the female. She also crouches low to the ground, cleaning a skin. Her body is positioned in a sexually suggestive posture which Gifford-Gonzalez (1993:35) has dubbed the "Drudge-on-a-Hide." Meanwhile the male stands erect, wrapping an animal skin around his shoulders. The group thus conforms to the Victorian family triangle. In these images, low continues to be associated with nature (juveniles, females, dirt) while high is increasingly associated with culture (adults, males, clothing, tool manufacture).

One of the more interesting aspects of these gender-loaded images is that the students in both the blind tests and in the interviews were very inventive in creating story lines which justified the gender roles being portrayed. The link between central male and authority, for example, was often made explicit by student narratives: "There's one man standing, I don't know if he's the boss or what. There's also an old man looking elderly, but he's sitting on a dead log. He doesn't appear to be the man in charge." Students tended to describe central male figures using terms such as "the leader of the band," "a very strong person obviously," "he looks powerful" or "the headman of the tribe" and build their commentary around them. The blind test results were also revealing in that the students who had to categorize the illustrations on the basis of another student's description of them often classified *any* image with a male holding a weapon as "Man the Hunter." This was true of both older and newer images and we included both to provide a contrast for the student who was giving the descriptions. For example, we included both an older Zdeněk Burian Neandertal illustration in which males took centre stage (see Figure 8) and a newer Jay Matternes Neandertal illustration in which the only male holding a tool is a flintknapper while a group of centre-stage females skin a carcass (Weaver 1985:599). In both cases, students classified the images under the "Man-the-Hunter" category.

Illustrations of the *Homo sapiens sapiens* show both continuity with some themes and the introduction of some new and different themes with respect to gender. In Figure 11, we are shown that "Early neolithic populations in Europe were also hunters." This illustration was painted by Charles R. Knight and often appeared in textbooks (see Poirier 1982:405). It is a personal favourite of mine because of the richness of the visual art conventions such as the heroic central male figure with the light falling on him directly from above. This religious convention from the Renaissance period symbolizes divinity or closeness to God. The male figure takes a classical stance, standing with his arms crossed on his chest, presenting his athletic physique to the best advantage. He is bracketed by his fellow hunters, who have helped him to bring down a stag and who now crouch around the prize. The suggestion is of royalty since in many societies the stag was preserved for the king's hunt (see also Figure 12). Once again, male images numerically dominate and are placed central and forward in the frame. One juvenile male is "spear carrier" to his elders, and in good classical form, his youth makes him appear effeminate (see Clark 1956:54). True femininity, however, is marked by Victorian tropes of voluminous hair, unruly to signal "natural sexuality" (Michie 1987:100; Nead 1988; Pearce 1991), as well as by the burden of infant nurturing with the associated bared breasts (Miles 1985a, Warner 1985), and by peripheral placement. The meaning of such "marked" bodies is suggested to us by linguistics, where the term "marked" refers to the way that language alters the meaning of a word by adding to it a linguistic particle that has no meaning on its own; adding *ess* and *ette*, for example, mark the word as feminine while the unmarked forms are masculine (Tannen 1993:18). In the same way in artistic representation, "marked bodies" are added to in ways that change their meaning away from the implicit standard, the white masculine body. Their deviance from this standard can be elaborated in a number of different ways: long unruly hair to mark the feminine body, attached child to mark the motherly body, hairiness and black skin to mark the primitive body.

Males continue their role as the major breadwinner in these images. In a Maurice Wilson painting of Swanscombe Man, for example, several men with spears bring down a stag while an older man supervises from behind a bush (see Figure 12). Although Swanscombe Man is often classified as one of the archaic *Homo sapiens* (along with Neandertals), the hunters' physique in this image is so aesthetically athletic that they could have come directly off a vase or frieze from Classical Greece. Universal male providers, their essential capabilities are mapped onto their physique. Such essential gender attributes crop up as embedded messages throughout the imagery of the Cro-Magnon; women are restricted to child care, hide working and butchery, while males make tools and other artifacts, carry game, hunt, do rituals, make art and dominate the landscape (see Gifford-Gonzalez 1993:32).

Summary

As the discussion in this chapter demonstrates, crossing species and even genus boundaries is no barrier to portraying the universal nature of gender, both male and female. It is obvious from even so brief a discussion of reconstructive illustrations (and the number of examples could have been much wider) that very definite patterns prevail despite the fact that the subject matter encompasses many millennium and a number of extinct species about which we really have very little information.

Females are to nature, naked, childbirth, nurturing, low, dirt, stasis and peripherality what males are to culture, clothing, the hunt, defence, progress, high, clean and centrality. The bodies of both genders are marked by these associations and their representation in illustrations faithfully reproduces these markings fully created at the earliest stages of evolutionary development. Furthermore, these markings are extremely flexible and thus useful props for the major theoretical arguments, around which they swirl and for which they provide the verification funded by their verisimilitude to what we know from our own lives. What is has always been–a very comforting thought.

We can acknowledge the explicitly androcentric focus to the prevalent narratives of human evolution, and we can deconstruct these images sufficiently to identify the significant connections made between nature and female and between male and culture. But these observations are not new (see Ortner 1974). I have found colleagues initially tend to respond to this material in one of two ways. The first response is that the visual representations of gender, much as the "politically correct" might deplore them, are grounded in "natural facts" and are thus inevitable, representational and inscribed in male and female biology (see also Miles 1989:219). Students often took this view when asked in interviews about the realism of such images. Many commented that men were the providers and women raised the offspring and the reasons for this had to do with gender differences in strength and aggression. One student commented: "It's actually how we existed through most of our time on earth, as hunter-gatherers, so why not? Very accurate." A second student said: "Usually women and children, as far as I know, didn't go on a hunt." They felt confident that such "facts" were empirically established and often cited their introductory anthropology course discussions of the "hunter/gatherer economy" which were couched in evolutionary terms, as supportive evidence. Consequently they found the older illustrations with an emphasis on male roles very easy to interpret and largely realistic and representational.

The second response I got from colleagues with respect to such images was that the older, androcentric and old-fashioned models have long been under critical attack and are in the process of being dislodged, as is their illustrative material. Certainly it is true that in the textbook world, such illustrative material has almost disappeared entirely. However, I would argue that the problem is real, remains so and is much more intransigent than either of the above positions suggest. These images continue to be produced in large number, especially in the popular press. A recent television series on human evolution, for example, generated a glossy hardcover publication entitled: *Ape Man: The Story of Human Evolution* (Caird 1994). Dr. Robert Foley was the scientific advisor to this series and produced many of the reconstructive illustrations for the book. These illustrations conform exactly to the patterns of gender representation discussed in this chapter, despite having been produced so recently. The *National Geographic* magazine also continues to publish gender-loaded illustrations. In addition, students continue to access older materials when doing research on human evolution and very little is done in the high school or university environment to provide them with the tools to critically evaluate what they see there.

We need to pay more attention to the specifics of the illustrative content as well as the uses to which illustrations are put in order to interrogate the subliminal messages they convey. The patterns are clear and disturbing. The portrait of the evolutionary history of the two genders corresponds very closely to Unger and Crawford's (1992:103-20) findings with respect to Western visual representations of women in general, including the following: disproportionate representation of numbers of males versus females, cultural specificity of gender traits portrayed, limited behavioural roles and occupations of females versus males, and different physical properties associated with each sex. No modern introductory textbook is going to baldly state that human nature is naturally divided into two mutually exclusive categories, male and female. Nor is it going to go on to argue that the male contribution has always been the more "active" and important one while females have remained essentially the same for over three million years—burdened by their role in reproduction and passive observers of the evolutionary process. But textual material can indirectly lead students to such conclusions, and the repetitive nature of the narrative illustrative material suggests that such ideas are still propagated, consciously or unconsciously.

Where do these ideas come from? David Pilbeam (1980:270) has commented on problems in the paleoanthropological models by stating: "We do not see things as they are. We see things as we are." The messages which are found in reconstructive illustrations have their source in our present day cultural arrangements, moral and value systems, division of labour, social and political disputes and family structures. But they come through various side doors. Paleoanthropology can only clothe the fossils by analogy (Sperling 1991), and the analogies selected have shifted in popularity in recent years (see chapter 6). The ethnography of "primitive" peoples and the work of primatology have traditionally been the two sources from which paleoanthropologists attempt to clothe the fossils. The relative popularity of either of these two fields waxes and wanes with the political climate. From at least one perspective, however, it makes little difference whether the ethnography of so-called "gatherers and hunters" or the stories of primatology serve as templates for human evolution; what is important to note is that both rely on universalizing tendencies.

The narrative line and the assigned roles of male and female are unchanged by various shifts in emphasis from one source of analogy to another. It also does not matter if we refer to older illustrations such as those prepared for the Time-Life series on human evolution (Howell 1965), to anthropology textbooks of ten and twenty years ago or to more recent work for *National Geographic*. It is clear that there has been no substantial reconsideration of gender attributes, roles and relationships in the history of the human species; the illustrations show that stereotypical physiological, psychological, behavioural and emotional attributes are conceptualized as fully formed at the earliest proto-hominid stage. From that point on, the male-active and female-passive pattern persists relatively unchanged.

Gender attributes and roles link females to timeless traits of nurturing, food preparation and dependency on males. Males, on the other hand, have been fitted since time immemorial to be protectors, provisioners, inventors, tool-makers and the artificers of art, ritual and culture. This connection with culture has made their roles and attributes less immutable than the females', although physiologically they remain remarkably athletic and ageless. Each of the two genders is tied by functional theory to "essential" traits and characteristics that are universal and cross boundaries of species and time (see chapter 7). These essential traits have more to do with the present than with any real knowledge of the past. And as I will demonstrate in the next chapter, the construction of "others" against which a select group of males are contrasted provides scope for other messages; messages about "race" and the culture of white, Western society, which is linked in important ways to the gender messages discussed here.

CHAPTER FIVE

Conflation and the Significant Other: Racism and Codes of the Primitive

MESSAGES ABOUT GENDER are not the only information coded into the visual format of human evolution reconstructive illustrations. Gender attributes and roles are inextricably tied together with images of progress such that primate, non-white and primitive are linked together with nature and with female, while advancement is linked with culture and with the white male. In specifying "whiteness" here, I do not refer to a racial category of biological extraction, but as Haraway (1989:401, n 15) notes, to a "designation of political space." This space has been occupied by various peoples at various times. The space also expands or contracts based on political and social issues of "us" versus "them." The Irish used to be considered "black" by the British, although perhaps less "black" than the Punjabi; the Chinese are less coloured than the African Negro, but more than the European; the Jewish Israeli is white by present-day American standards while the Middle Eastern Muslim is definitely a "person of colour," especially since the Gulf War. As marked categories, with political and even evolutionary connotations, racial categorization is a very useful device for sending subtle and not-so-subtle messages about relative status and worth. In the Western construct of social value and worth, the highest-ranked category has long been the white, Anglo-Saxon male. According to feminist readings, this ranking is consistent with a larger social construct such that male is to culture what female is to nature (Ortner 1974). In the Western cognitive universe, this pattern of conflating some concepts into a category called "nature" and of conflating another set of concepts into a category of "culture" is inextricably linked to the ranking of the universe of things such that some are better than others, so that nature, while not entirely negative, is often out of man's control and thus relatively devalued in comparison to culture.

This cultural bias led some Western feminists to assume that such conflations were universal. In trying to explicate the "universal devaluation of women," for example, Ortner (1974:72) writes: "woman is being identified with—or, if you will, seems to be a symbol of—*something that every culture devalues*, something that every culture defines as being of a lower order of existence than itself ... and that is 'nature' in the most generalized sense" (emphasis mine). She defines culture as the product of human consciousness, including systems of thought and technology by which humans attempt to have some control over nature. She argues that in every human society males are associated with culture while females are associated with nature. Woman, as a universal category, cannot transcend her biological self and thus cannot be associated with culture:

> It is simply a fact that proportionately more of women's body space, for a greater percentage of her lifetime, and at some—sometimes great—cost to her personal health, strength, and general stability, is taken up with the natural processes surrounding the reproduction of the species (ibid.:74-75).

This argument has proven enormously stimulating in the feminist/ anthropological analysis of gender (see for example, Strathern 1980, Valeri 1990, Haraway 1988; see also the discussion of "nature as female" in Merchant 1980 and Haraway 1989). But as many feminists have pointed out, historically and cross-culturally, there are also good grounds to argue that culture and nature are not so easily nor rigidly classified (Haraway 1988). Rather, they meet at a complex boundary zone, with permutations capable of conveying very complex messages back and forth across the boundary, depending on time period, subject, object or value system under discussion.

Nevertheless, it is true that to a broad extent "woman" as a category *is* conflated with nature in the Western conception of things (see Miles 1989). And so, while feminists may irritably state that "we won't play nature to your culture anymore" (Barbara Kruger quoted in Warner 1985:325), the systems of thought that generate these associations are firmly intermeshed with most of our accepted paleoanthropological and archaeological theories. This fact is highly visible in origins illustrations, where female is always playing nature to male culture. The pernicious influence of these logical (illogical) constructs may be one reason that Euro-american archaeology has tended to respond to criticisms of androcentrism by trying to "add women and stir" (Conkey 1991). It has sometimes been argued, for example, that the paradigmatic changes necessary to integrate women into the "history of mankind" will come with time, and that these will be a product of new methodologies that will produce the data necessary to draw women into the picture. An oft-cited example is pollen data, which if found in sufficient quantities, could "counteract the overwhelming visibility of the more durable residues left by scavenging (formerly hunting) males" (ibid.:127). But as Conkey (ibid.) argues:

> this is not the point at all: adding pollen studies to document the role of women is a methodological diversion away from the more fundamental and unquestioned assumption–and object–of knowledge–that there is a gender-based division of labour (man-the-hunter/woman-the-gatherer) in early hominid life (some 2 million years ago!), a specific division of labour that is then taken as an *essential* feature of human social life (emphasis in original).

These and other "objects-of-knowledge" are produced artifacts of our systems of thought, not empirically discovered realities.

In the reconstruction illustrations discussed in the last chapter, woman and nature are conflated, and man and culture similarly so. In this chapter I want to address the question of what *other* categories are found on the woman/nature side of this divide. Women are not alone in their "otherness" in opposition to males. And not all males are together in their unity with culture (read progress) and in their opposition to females. In a sense, this chapter echoes many of the themes discussed in the last since the division between *woman* as a category and all the other categories conflated into nature carves apart what is presented to the viewer as a seamless whole. Nevertheless, it is important to highlight these other categories and to give their position within the evolution narrative the same emphasis that gender has received.

The "Significant Other" in Paleoanthropological Thought

Without the foil of an alien other, how could the progress of man be measured? Or to ask the same question in another way, how have white Westerners managed to construct their history as "the story of the family of man" (Haraway 1989:153)? And to paraphrase Haraway to ask yet another question, just what about "race" is visible to whom in the evolution story? Women, children, "coloured" racial categories and the "primitive" are all grist for the mill which links the adult, white, male, Euroamerican with evolutionary progress. All others are coded as contrasting to some degree or other with that exemplary progress. Categories of otherness include class as well as "race" and gender, and these three form part of a common system of meaning (Sacks 1989). Not only did males bring home the first meat, whether scavenged or hunted, but they rapidly learned how to parlay this new commodity into family dominance and ultimately world dominance. This success is not the prerequisite of all males; male as a category is not universal as is female. Before all other ranking, there is first the ranking of males over females. But hierarchy is not satisfied with this achievement, some males are obviously better than others.

As Marcus and Fischer (1986:23) note for ethnography, much of the anthropological exercise is focused on a "significant other," but the reason for that focus is usually not acknowledged: "The underdeveloped, relatively implicit side of ethnographic description focused on a cultural other is the reference it makes to the presumed, mutually familiar world shared by the writer and his readers." Pelto and Pelto (1978:31) have commented that anthropology is seeking contrast and usually the implicit basis of comparison is "modern, middle-class North American society." One might add "white" and "male" as further categories to this list.

Marcus and Fischer (1986:23) note that "ethnographic realism" assumes that the exercise of anthropology aims to "represent the reality of a whole world or form of life" by reference to "parts" which "evoke a social and cultural totality." On the surface, paleoanthropological reconstruction is a similar kind of exercise. But in paleoanthropology, the "parts" are relatively small in number, difficult to decipher, and cannot be said to easily evoke their total social, biological and cultural context. The reconstruction effort is seriously compromised by this fact, but this has never been accepted as an insurmountable difficulty. Analogy and inference have always stepped in when fossil evidence proved insufficient. These attempts to clothe the fossils have always had more to do with endorsing *today* than with uncovering *yesterday*.

The others which have been significant in this process of analogy and inference have largely remained the "primitive" (read forager) peoples of Africa and the African apes, despite protests that this approach descends into the unscientific world of ethnocentrism and anthropomorphism. The Man-the-Hunter model, for example, has been criticized for over-relying on analogies drawn from DeVore's (1962, 1965a, 1965b) questionable work on the baboon which posited the male as central to social organization, and on the ethnographic descriptions of the Kalahari San peoples provided by the early work of Richard Lee (Lee and DeVore 1968). While this research has been criticized for conforming to Sherwood Washburn's androcentric agenda for the human evolution story, the Woman-the-Gatherer model is susceptible to a similar kind of critique. The use of analogy is fundamental to both models. The Woman-the-Gatherer model, for example, utilized the chimpanzee as well as the post-Richard Lee descriptions of the San foragers of the Kalahari Desert (Tanner 1981, 1987). And there is an equally visible pattern of interlocution in much of the research which makes this use of analogy possible. For example, research on the chimpanzees by figures such as Jane Goodall, often responded to (eco-)feminist-driven gender political issues unique to the Euro-american scene (see Haraway 1989:136, 172-78). Goodall's (1967, 1971, 1986) work made the female chimpanzee the most important variable in understanding chimp social organization. And the post-Lee work on the !Kung (see Shostak 1981) was no more "fact" than that which proceeded it; all research upon which origins analogy is based is equally "contested knowledge." Thus while Lee's work on the !Kung has been disputed on the grounds that he has treated the San as if they were ahistorical time capsules representing the evolutionary past of the entire species (see chapter 6), Marcus and Fischer (1986:58) note that Shostak was an interlocutor for Western feminism when she collected the biography of a !Kung woman. This led her to focus on concerns such as the "coercive powers of conventional sex roles." Obviously, changing Euro-american perceptions of what is important and what is not in regards to otherness is a significant lens through which all empirical information must pass. Otherness is characterized by what the Western observer is capable of seeing at a particular point in history.

One alarming consequence of this type of interlocution has been that human societies such as the !Kung San and non-human primates such as the chimpanzee are often discussed interchangeably. Tanner's book, for example, argues that chimpanzees remain "the best available model for suggesting features of the ancestral ape population" (1981:65). Although the chimpanzees have gone through an evolutionary history which is as long as modern *Homo sapiens,* Tanner argues that the chimpanzee is "conservative," and thus a good model of our ancestral population. Further, she argues that the chimp can point to the ways in which behaviour has remained unchanged and to the ways it has changed for both the transitional proto-hominids and for modern humans. At the same time, her book uses many illustrations drawn from the !Kung foragers as well as from other non-foraging African tribal groups (1981:10, 12, 27, 142, 144). She often refers to the numerous similarities between ape and !Kung social structure and behaviour. In discussing social organization and group size, for example, she postulates that

> the early hominids' communication system would not be adequate to the task of coordinating social activities in communities much larger or more complexly organized than chimpanzee communities ... small, very flexible and mobile living groups are utilized by human gatherer-hunters today. Dobe !Kung San camps range in size from only about 4 to 34 individuals.... Perhaps small communities were utilized not only by our ape, transitional and early human ancestors but also by most humans prior to the invention of horticulture and agriculture (1981:87).

In one paragraph, we find early hominid, chimpanzees and the Dobe !Kung San all conflated together. One suspects that their most important similarity is that they are all found in Africa, that *dark* continent.

African analogies for proto-hominids life and behaviour are considered suitable because their position under the Western gaze is one of primitiveness *as compared with ourselves.* When we deal with people such as the !Kung Bushmen in this way it remains essentially ethnocentric and racist, no matter how such assumptions are dressed up with codicils which refer to our shared millions of years of history as "hunter-gatherers." Because the fact is, we no longer share this lifestyle and the implicit comparison of ourselves with the !Kung cannot fail to present them as "survivals," primitive time capsules lacking the progress that the rest of the world enjoys. Thus, their unique history, their colonial past, their relationship with neighbouring peoples are all ignored as significant factors in the !Kung present-day lifestyle, as are other ethnographic descriptions of them that emphasize these aspects (see chapter 6). Their *minds*, as a product of their own unique history and life experiences are invisible, while their *bodies* do the work of evolutionary representation.

It may be unfair to single Tanner out in respect to her use of these analogies, since they are widespread in the discipline. There may even be good scientific reasons for using the !Kung and the chimpanzee to postulate our evolutionary past (Zihlman 1991 lists several). But no matter how carefully we word these analogies, the assumptions drawn from them are not always under our control. And it may be that the use of such analogies is based on cultural stereotypes which if taken out into the light of day would make us feel rather uncomfortable. As Haraway (1989:152) notes, "*white* is the colour code for bodies ascribed the attribute of *mind*," in the former "white settler colonies like the U.S."–in formal intelligence tests, in patterns of professional occupation, in political enfranchisement, people of colour are not associated with the symbolic powers or with any powers of rational thought. In fact, there has been a burgeoning social anthropological debate on the topic of the native mind and rationality which is epitomized in Geertz's (1995) discussion of the Sahlins/Obeyesekere conflict over the death of Captain Cook in the South Pacific. Was the death of Captain Cook on the island of Hawaii a result of native superstition? Could the native mind really have failed to comprehend Cook's human nature and did Hawaiians really confuse Cook with their fertility god Lono, thus leading to Cook's death when he failed to act in a Lono-like manner? Sahlins says that the native mind, as embedded in a totally different cultural system of human action, is different from the Western mind; Obeyesekere objects to any view that might promote the notion that the coloured *body* lacks rational *mind*. When one observes the significance of black bodies as analogies of the prehuman and their importance in retracing the transition across the great boundary from animal to man, the significance of such politicized debates takes on new meaning. How much more deplorable is a discourse in which the coloured body lacks any presence of *mind* at all, where the *body* (especially the politically powerless, black African body) is coded as "the subject of control and the object of appropriation" in exploring human origins.

Lutz and Collins (1994:115-16) found that naked black women were a central image in *National Geographic* magazines and that no white-skinned women were represented as naked, with a few recent exceptions which were "photographed discreetly from behind." But because women-as-beautiful-objects is one of the dominant codes by which females are represented in Western cultural rhetoric, use of the female black body allows the *National Geographic* magazine to combine art and science in such a way that it increases readership and legitimates the magazine's status as a purveyor of truth and beauty, although "in this context, one must first be black and female to do this kind of symbolic labour" (ibid.:116).

Blackness is also coded as *body* in terms of occupational activities in the pages of *National Geographic*. Individuals who were dark or "bronze skinned" in Lutz and Collin's coding scale, were more likely to be represented in strenuous labour while light-skinned individuals were more likely to be shown at leisure (ibid.:161). In evolutionary analogy we see similar kinds of symbolic work for the black body and for the non-human primates; the line of advancement goes from chimpanzee (or ape, or baboon), to coloured (female), to primitive tribal male, to white female to advanced white male. Gould (1989:31) draws attention to this progression in the way that primitives and primates are useful to the false iconography of progress in the advertising world and in the media, by allowing for the substitution of the familiar and devalued modern ape and persons of colour for the unfamiliar proto-hominid. In the popular reading of quasi-educational discourse, we appropriate the body and the inferred racial attributes of the other to stand for a time before us.

We need to challenge these underlying patterns of thinking. The !Kung San remain locked, along with women, juveniles and chimpanzees, into a category of more "natural" things, a category of things whose essential characteristics make them less subject to cultural control and thus a category marked as symbolic of the ascendancy of culture through their implicit contrast to the Euro-american, white male. No matter how warm and fuzzy we conceptualize the relationship between chimp mothers and their offspring to be, and by extension, the family life of matricentric proto-hominids, this was not the force that drove the rise of civilization. Despite the critical stance of the Woman-the-Gatherer model, "warm and fuzzy" and the rise of civilization have seemed antithetical since Hobbes. Foraging may have been the "original affluent" lifestyle (Sahlins 1982), but like Eden, there was little progress until we were expelled from it.

Racial Connotations in Paleoanthropological Illustrations

For examples of the symbolic work of the non-white or female body, we can turn again to the iconographic ladder of progress images discussed in the last chapter. In Figure 5 we can see the implicit assumptions at work with regard to the relationship between racial categories and progress. I have never seen a single example of this convention in which the final figure on the right-hand side of the frame is not Caucasian. Darker skin colour is often used interchangeably with hairiness to suggest primitiveness the further left in the frame you go. As the male figures proceed from left to right they either go from hairy to smooth skinned or from black to lighter skinned, or both. Other biological codes for primitives include "ape-men" faces with low foreheads, prominent brow ridges and prognathous faces. These are rather blatant devices which are anatomically justified, but they can be used in more or less subtle ways. For example, the nose becomes more aquiline (read Caucasian) and the brow ridge becomes less pronounced from the left side of the page to the right. On his figures produced for the Howell (1965:40-45) book, Rudy Zallinger has progressively modernized the hair and beard style from *Homo erectus* to modern humans. The hair on the fully modern male to the right of the frame is shorter, neater and more Western in style than that of those before him, although Cro-Magnon's rather "swept back" locks would also be acceptable by today's standards if not by those of the time of the illustration's production. Jay Matternes produced a somewhat more ambiguous male figure to represent anatomically modern humans in his progress ladder produced for the *National Geographic* magazine (Weaver 1985:574-77). The hair could be Negroid, but the nose and face remain a giveaway. Modern "fully evolved" man is Caucasian; the hominid forms from the deep past are apelike, and in between lies a realm in which racial stereotypes fill many functions.

If we turn to the anecdotal illustrations and to the places that they are published and the ways that students read them, these multiple coded uses to which racial messages are put become obvious. The work of the "anatomically correct scientific illustrator" Matternes provides a set of excellent examples. In his early work, such as that seen in the Howell (1965:69) publication, australopithecines are represented as hairy and apelike. But by 1976, in a "scavenging meat" image published in a textbook which promotes the ancestral significance of the Leakey early hominid finds, the australopithecine form has been significantly modernized (Isaac and McCown 1976:424). In this "scene from early hominid life," one group of five individuals sits eating meat (a culturally loaded action) in the foreground, while a second group in the background hacks away at the carcass of a large animal. As discussed in the last chapter, Matternes has rejected the hairy pelt, the barrel chest and the extremely apelike head with which he had developed earlier australopithecine images. These conventions have been replaced with very human-looking bodies and Negroid skin and features. In this way, the alien otherness of the australopithecine is retained by crossing racial borders rather than by crossing species boundaries (see Miles 1989:150 and Szwed 1975:255). This mechanism allows Matternes to respond to the Lucy fossil, and to suggest the direct ancestral status of the gracile australopithecines using slightly different but equally powerful codes of the primitive. For another comparison of the Matternes manipulation of the contrasting apelike and Negroid conventions of the primitive, see his illustration of *Zinjanthropos boisei* which is also found in Isaac and McCown (1976:270). Here he uses the ape conventions to distance the robust australopithecines (non-ancestral) from the supposedly ancestral gracile forms. Apelike morphology is a convention of primordial beginnings while racial barriers become demonstrative of the ancestral boundary between animal and human, between nature and culture.

This contrast between hairy, apelike primates and dark-skinned primitives is found in many places and remains as popular today as it was in the 1950s. In the original paintings he prepared for the 1993 American Museum of Natural History's new *Hall of Human Biology and Evolution*, Matternes turns back again to the ape convention in illustrating *Paranthropus robustus* (see Tattersall 1993:91). In the foreground, a large male figure is hairy, dark skinned and apelike but with the cultural attribute of a unmodified tool (a pair of antelope horns). Other males are shown in the background, driving off baboons by throwing rocks. Females are shown crouching foreground with digging tools (broken bones) or carrying infants. However, to represent the *Homo erectus* stage, Tattersall (ibid.:106) reprints another image by Matternes, originally published in *National Geographic* in 1982. Here a group of *Homo erectus* are shown in the much more culturally suggestive action of using a prairie blaze to acquire fire. They have no body hair, their skin is bronze rather than black and the hair on their head is Negroid. Their cultural toolkit includes rudimentary clothing as well as the knowledge of fire technology. This mixture of racial features and cultural attributes allows Matternes to craft the *Homo erectus* as more "modern" than the australopithecines but less so than the anatomically modern humans.

Racial stereotypes are marked on the images in reconstructive illustrations, as are the linked interdependencies of "race"-gender-sexuality and black-female-unrepressed (see Lutz and Collins 1993:115) which are equally remarkable for their resiliency. The proto-humans whose remains are found only in the African fossil record are almost without exception represented with darker skin. On the other hand, *Homo erectus*, which is known to have radiated geographically out of Africa and throughout Asia and parts of Europe, is often represented with less dark skin and less apelike features. And with each successive stage of human evolution, the figures are crafted with successively lighter skin and with more Caucasian features. In Figure 7, a 1950s Maurice Wilson reconstruction of the *Homo erectus* finds in Choukoutien Cave in China, the skin tone is considerably lighter and the facial features less apelike than in the australopithecine images of that time (see Burian's australopithecine image in Augusta and Burian 1960: Plate 1 for comparison). The Zdeněk Burian reconstruction of Java Man (*Homo erectus*, see Figure 6) combines the conventions of hairy body with a play of light used to suggest a lighter skin beneath. And this pattern of lighter skin continues with the archaic and fully modern humans found in illustrations such as Figure 9, 10, 11 and 12. In most of the fully modern human reconstructive illustrations that I have seen, the people are coded white, and one rarely sees them represented as Asiatic, Negroid or Native American in appearance although there are a few exceptions. One such example comes from an engraving prepared for the 1889 Exposition Universelle, entitled *Tragedy of the Stone Age*. It shows an Asiatic-looking *Homo sapiens* hunter returning to the home cave to confront a tiger that has just killed his female mate (reprinted in Langness 1993:11). In the *Knowledge through Colour* series on *Fossil Man* by Michael H. Day, the illustrator (A. Oxenham) also uses Asiatic features, this time to portray a *Homo habilis* (1971:cover and 101).

In such illustrative sleight of hand, a connection is established between coloured racial characteristics and uncultured savagery, a "closeness to nature," and with Africa as the source of hominid evolution. Africa is the repository of more primitive hominoids such as the great apes, fewer cultural accomplishments than the West, and an extant "native" condition rather than one that has been effectively overlaid by a white presence. Lutz and Collins (1993:131) comment that: "In the scale of evolutionary progress, which was thought to reach its pinnacle in the English, Africans were found at the bottom of the human scale, while Asians fell midway between the two groups." Illustrative conventions "play" with these deeply ingrained cultural and racial stereotypes, both using and reinforcing them at the same time.

There is little doubt that viewers of these illustrations absorb the implications of such racial connotations, for the most part without critical reflection. Students in the blind test, and even in the interviews where they were more conscious of the motive of the study, frequently lumped hairiness and dark skin together as primitive–that is, of existing in a condition with less command over nature and of being distant from ourselves as representatives of the fully modern human. One student in a blind test, who was asked to describe a Matternes image of the australopithecines (Howell 1965:69) responded with: "The faces are presented in a kind of a primitive way. Their skin colour is dark." Another student, also involved in a blind test, commented on a Zdeněk Burian illustration of a group of Neandertals (ibid.:132-33) by stating: "They have dark skin. They look like Early Man." The often unconscious nature of the student response to these codes is interesting. When a student involved in the blind test was asked to describe Figure 11, a Charles Knight illustration showing a group of Cro-Magnon people clustered around a fallen stag, he commented that: "this group of people doesn't seem to be that long ago." He went on to add: "They keep furs of the animals they killed, which means maybe they trade with Indians. Because these seem to be what we would term white men. They are definitely white-skinned." He then went on to describe their "more advanced" weapons and clothing styles. Figure 13, the Zdeněk Burian illustration of "one of the world's first artists," proved to be very confusing for many students and almost all of them commented on the mixed skin colours in the illustration. One student said: "They just look like a native African population, with women standing behind a male. He's kneeling in the foreground and he's white and they're black, for starters. He's got a little idol." This student came back to this contrast later, repeating: "he's white and they're black" several times, before going on to say: "the man in the front is definitely an elder. The women behind him don't look to be elders." A third student said: "He's so white, he's so blatantly white, really white, that it's the first thing I saw. Like, he's so blatantly white and everyone else is so dark skinned." And finally, yet another student noted: "That [picture] is weird! It's like he's not part of the same race or something."

Figure 13 is one of the few illustrations I know of that codes the anatomically modern human as black, since many of the people portrayed have very dark skin. But I also find that this illustration is one of the more heavily coded examples of the conflation of black, female and primitive in contrast with white, male and culturally advanced. For example, the white male portrayed centre frame is marked with religious authority, with artistic talent and perhaps even with invention; meanwhile the females behind him are distanced from these cultural developments; they only stand and watch; their dark bodies providing a contrast to his whiteness and an inspiration for his talents. His talent *acts upon* their bodies. In this context, the Haraway (1989:154) observation that the union of dark bodies and female gender in Western cultural fields is to be read as "sex, animal, dark, dangerous, fecund, pathological" is instructive. Note how in Figure 13, all the males in the distant background are lighter skinned than the three females in the middle ground of the image. White males (*mind*) employ black females (*body*) to produce objects of artistic/erotic pleasure for other white males (*mind*) to enjoy.

White is definitively coded as "advanced" in evolutionary terms by student respondents. They connect white with *Homo sapiens sapiens* and persons of colour with more primitive hominids. On several occasions students qualified the relatively advanced evolutionary status of the images in an illustration by prefacing the species name with the term "white," as in: "This one is white *Homo sapiens.*" Another approach was to speak of "regular skin" in contrast to "too hairy" or "too dark" to be "regular skin." Without exception, the illustrations containing hairy or dark-skinned images were identified as "more primitive" or "very primitive" in comparison with lighter-skinned images. And what is more telling, although students often critiqued the physical appearance of images that were "too apelike" or "bowlegged" or "out of proportion" (i.e., "the arms are too long here"), skin colour rarely received criticism, nor did the gender attributes and roles portrayed. In sum, the codes of primitive are "hairy," "apelike," "naked," and lumped into that same category, "dark skinned" and "female." These are bodies with little or no mind. In contrast, white bodies are explicitly mind and body, linked together in fully evolved aesthetic masculinity.

In image after image, artists link the rise of cultural knowledge, ritual, symbolic and artistic expression, religion and technology to the (older, white) male. In Figure 14, for example, five anatomically modern males who are wearing furs, head bands and bear-tooth necklaces, are seen in the ritually charged environment of a cave with painted walls. Two men paint scenes of a mammoth hunt on the wall while two others hold up primitive oil lamps for light. A fifth and older male, holding a shamanistic-style tall staff with a bone handle, stands to the left, supervising the work. All of these males have white skin and Caucasian features. In this and in other such images, few or no females are present, and when they are present they play no active role. But these assumptions about the subordinate role of women and associated assumptions about woman-as-object during the earliest stages of the development of art, have come under increasing attack. Russell (1991), for example, argues that there are no grounds for assuming that males were the painters of cave art and that females were the audience or excluded entirely from such ritualized actions (see also Conkey 1983). McDermott (1996) demonstrates that the "plastic" arts of the Upper Paleolithic, such as the famous Venus statuettes, could easily have been produced by females based on autogenous or self-generated information about themselves. Thus, the highly remarked-upon "anatomical omissions and distortions" of the female body which these figurines seem to represent and which had been explained by reference to male-generated symbolic manipulations of the female form, can better be explained by the "relative effects of foreshortening, distance, and occlusion" as women look down on their own bodies (ibid.:227; see also Marshak, Bolger and Dronfield in the same issue of *Current Anthropology*). Nevertheless, interpretations of such art as a masculine product continue to crop up in modern publications; for example, Figure 14 is reprinted in Tattersall (1993:174-75).

This pattern of linking the category *male* to ritual and to all higher cultural accomplishments is often collapsed together with the representation of such early ritual or artistic experts as white, as in Figure 10, which illustrates a Neandertal burial scene. Here the ritual activity centres around a male corpse which is surrounded by three other males. The dead man is being interred along with cultural artifacts such as weapons. Students invariably placed such illustrations into the "Rise of Civilization" category and never commented on the absence of females. They seemed to accept the subtext that males were the only innovators and thus the creators of culture, and even more narrowly, that white European males progressed, while the female, the dark skinned and the hairy of the earth lagged behind in evolutionary developments. White and male is also coded with authority, particularly when accompanied by centrality in frame and an upright stance. In commenting on Figure 11, which shows a group of Neolithic humans clustered around a fallen stag with a central upright male dominating the image, one student said that this central figure is "lighter" and that he "seems to be the wise man, or the big hunter that everyone is listening to." Forward frame and central placement of a single male is thus suggestive to students not only of importance, but also of more complex subtexts of political hierarchy and power.

Students obviously felt most comfortable when both white skin and explicit cultural accomplishments appeared in the same image. Any attempt to mix the codes for modernity and the codes for the primitive seemed to confuse them if there was no explicit narrative plot to explain it. In Figure 16, for example, the artist Angel Martin has attempted to illustrate the evolutionary niche of the human species as one of seed collection. The scene shows a small band of anatomically modern humans standing naked in a field of wild grass, collecting seeds. One student described the scene by opening with: "This one has a female in the very most foreground with an infant on her back and she's white. Everyone in the picture is white skinned. She's picking some wheat." Like all of the other students who saw this image, in the classroom discussions, in the blind tests and in the interviews, this student went on to interpret the illustration as an agricultural one showing farming peoples among their domesticated wheat and horses. None of the students recognized the illustrator's attempt to represent the human species as one which was based on an early and prolonged adaptation to a predominantly grass seed diet. We had anticipated that students would openly laugh at this image and perhaps comment on the "Playboy-esque" bodies of the females. However, not a single student in the blind test nor in the interviews criticized this illustration for its sexual overtones. While students often commented on the relative realism of other body portrayals ("the arms are too long," "that seems too hairy"), these white and sexy bodies were accepted without comment. The students were disturbed by the naked bodies, not because of their explicitly sexual overtones but because of the way naked is usually coded primitive in contrast to white skin as a code for modernity. On several occasions students commented that this nakedness was not logical given the agricultural adaptation. Naked and female as dual codes in a single image were not confusing to them, but naked white males and obvious cultural accomplishments (as in assumed domestication of plants and animals) were jarring.

Summary

This chapter has addressed the potent brew of conflated messages which mark human evolutionary reconstructive illustration. In these pictures, the white, European male mind is the apex of evolutionary progress while female, dark skinned and body are all codes for the primitive. The textual material never baldly makes such statements, but the illustrative material which for decades brought life to the dry textual analysis, both in academic and in the public media, has made these messages easy to convey. Perhaps artistic conventions of the West have made the logical choices for representation of "otherness" rather limited. The conventions of grotesqueness, of hybridization, of caricature, of hairy bestiality, of racial and gender stereotype, of *nuditas virtualis* and of the innocence of ignorance have all been deeply embedded in our cultural psych. But should they be the useful tools which promulgate a set of ideas that archaeology and anthropology have always been loath to challenge? The watchword of human evolution is *progress*. The weak and the ineffectual eventually die out and leave the field to the quick and the strong. Cultural advancement depends on cultural evolution, and despite the discrediting of White and Steward in cultural anthropology (see Hatch 1973), archaeological theory descends in a straight line from the cultural evolutionists. Extinction only takes place for cause; there is no "crap shoot" of evolutionary history in which the "winners" are there merely by the luck of the draw. However long the tenure of australopithecines on earth, however stable the history of Neandertal culture, however persistent some remnant forager populations today, these are simply temporary stops on the one-way track to modern human society. While women have been central to and constrained by the reproduction of the species, and by their affiliation with nature, the males, especially white males, have been the driving force behind change. That change, whereby culture has replaced nature as the means of adapting to our environment, is the defining feature of the human species. Evolutionary progress has created modern, civilized humans and they have a decidedly masculine character as well as Caucasian features.

CHAPTER SIX

Window or Mirror? Primates and Foragers: Analogies of the Pre-Cultural Life

Introduction

When people are first confronted with human origins illustrations, it is very common for them to comment on the "ape-man" appearance of the figures portrayed, especially in older examples. Students involved in our blind test commonly used phrases such as: "monkey-like faces," "looks like gorillas," or "ape-looking." Students also used verbal descriptions of imagery that resonated to racist views of persons of colour. These terms included: "looks more African," "look like a native African population," "more dark skinned than us." Such comments demonstrate that viewers correctly identify the two dominant codes of the primitive, non-human primates and modern African foraging populations, if not the implications of these specific choices. While baboons and chimpanzees served as models for origins illustrations for many years, and continue to have their uses today, I would argue that recently the forager peoples of the Kalahari Desert have become *the* preferred model. Indeed, I would go so far as to argue that anyone who has taken an introductory course in anthropology, especially one where the more widely used ethnographic films about the San or !Kung peoples of the Kalahari Desert have been shown (including *The Hunters* and *N!ai. The Story of a !Kung Woman*), will immediately recognize the influence such visual imagery has had on recent human evolution illustrations. Some may argue that it is only reasonable for illustrators who focus on scientific realism to have real models to work from. But I have often thought that if some members of the !Kung peoples had a more litigious turn of mind there would have been law suits testing the morality of such co-opting of the physical appearance of a modern population to the imaginary world of our human evolutionary past. And if Rosemary Coombe (1996:218) is correct, such a litigious strategy may be the only method open to people who want to challenge the "thingification" of their body and cultural practice through mass media visual entrapment, as it has been successfully employed by North American First Nations people to reject "Indian" trademark labels developed by sports organizations, liquor manufacturers and tobacco corporations. Some very blatant examples of !Kung-esque illustrations are found in the recent Caird (1994) publication *Ape Man,* but this reproduction of the long, lean !Kung body and its various stances at work and in leisure is pervasive throughout the more recent reconstructive illustration field.

The !Kung-esque tendency, and the related tendency to put the primate body to work illustrating the origins of our species, is a result of a combination of factors. Probably the most important of these is the sheer volume of research generated on foragers and on primates by the Sherwood Washburn school of human evolution, which deliberately sought to construct an appropriate world of analogy for origins research. Playing the role of analogical support for the preferred human evolutionary story is predicated first and foremost upon the ready availability of "realistic" images of the lives of primates and so-called primitives. The history of the Sherwood Washburn school of research, then, is important to a better understanding of the ideas behind the illustrations and behind the patterns of change in illustrative material. Another factor to consider is the role that realism plays in buttressing scientific argument (Rudwick 1989, Moser 1992). Since the research results of the Washburn school have formed a body of highly contested knowledge (see chapter 2), an important prerequisite for reading the subtext within human origins illustrations of the postwar period is some understanding of how these contests related to politics within the discipline and the way that realism in illustrations is used to participate in the debates.

Why Analogy?

The exercise of analogy attempts to gain more knowledge about our evolutionary history than the bones, stone tools and faunal assemblages can directly tell us. It is an application of logic which argues that it is reasonable to use observable phenomenon to infer things about relatively unobservable phenomenon if there are grounds to assume relationships or resemblances in form or function between the two. In the case of hominid evolution, the observable phenomena have included a wide variety of extant primate societies, everything from langurs to gorillas, as well as historical and extant human foraging populations. The relatively unobservable phenomena cover a wide time-frame and number of species, from over four million years ago and the earliest proto-hominids, to the relatively near-past of the Neandertal and Cro-Magnon populations of Europe. Analogy in one form or another has been the single most important factor in building pictures of how precursors to the modern human species may have looked and behaved.

The logic behind analogy is that we can infer relationships or resemblances between the known case and the unknown case on the basis of reasonable grounds for coordinating the two. Washburn and DeVore (1961), for example, felt that the reasonable grounds for coordinating the social life of baboons and early hominids was that they were both terrestrial primates, both predominantly vegetarian, and both lived in social groups of between ten and two hundred members. But the real incentive appears to be a serious lack of options; since there are no time machines, we cannot directly observe the characteristics and behaviour of precursors to the human line. And yet, it is exactly the unobservable attributes of those precursors that fascinate Westerners. Paleoanthropologists argue that there is no other way to circumvent the limitations of the discipline and to find out what we are interested in knowing. The practice has been questioned, especially when the analogical evidence seems to make the theories relatively "fossil proof" (Pilbeam 1980:267). But the heavy reliance on analogy has never been seriously challenged and the general assumption appears to be that the method has generated useful knowledge in the past and with refinements can continue to do so in the future. As later discussion in this chapter will show, most Western students of origins research owe their use of analogy to Sherwood Washburn. And yet when Washburn's own publications are examined, there is little evidence of a rigorous rationale and methodology for the approach. In Washburn and DeVore (1961:91), for example, the only acknowledgement made to analogy is as follows: "The purpose of this paper is to present a brief account of the daily life of baboons to serve as a background for the discussion of the social life of early man." However, the real practice is also suggested: "here an attempt has been made to outline only those points that proved to be of greatest interest to the participants of the conference on "The Social Life of Early Man" (ibid.). In their more recent article: "The Reconstruction of Hominid Behavioral Evolution through Strategic Modeling," Tooby and DeVore (1987) support analogy by citing the history of deductive reasoning (Newton's theory of gravitation, Einstein's theory of general relativity, Darwin's theory of natural selection) as a scientific pedigree for the practice (ibid.:183-84). Zihlman (1991) simply states the importance of analogy, refers to Washburn, and then gets on with the job without further comment. But some very basic and interesting questions are being ignored here: what is it that we want to know about our ancient ancestors and why? And how reasonable is it to expect to find it out? The problem is that when questions about the use of analogy have arisen, they have focused instead on the scientific accuracy of the research on which it is based.

Selecting Useful Analogies: Washburn and Crowd

In the 1950s and early 1960s, the physical anthropologist Sherwood Washburn and his students made concerted efforts to render apes (Washburn 1961, 1962; Washburn and Avis 1958; Washburn and Jay 1968; Washburn, Jay and Lancaster 1968; Washburn and Hamburg 1965) and foragers (Lee and DeVore 1968, 1976; Washburn and Lancaster 1968) relevant to human evolution. The success of these efforts may be measured by the successful research agendas of the many members of Washburn's "patriline" and by their prolific publications which have dominated Western human evolution model-building. The most enduring product of these collective efforts was the Man-the-Hunter story, which was endorsed and reinforced at an early stage by the baboon research Washburn did in collaboration with his student, Irven DeVore (Washburn and DeVore 1961). Their view of baboon social life as being male-centred for reasons of defence has proven extremely resilient. Until very recently, introductory anthropology textbooks were more likely to discuss the baboon over any other primate, even though it has long been recognized that baboons are not as closely related taxonomically to humans as are the gorilla or the chimpanzee. The baboon model also continues to crop up in many popular books, media reports and even in school curriculum. In a recent *Time* magazine article on the human propensity for infidelity, for example, an illustration is captioned with the statement: "Among baboons, the higher a male ranks in the social hierarchy, the more sex he has" (Wright

1994:34). The article goes on to argue that infidelity is as natural to human males, especially those who strive for high social status, as it is to the baboon male.

In the years after Washburn's baboon research, he encouraged the practitioners of primatology, physical anthropology, social anthropology and archaeology to expand the analogy-based contributions essential to building and reinforcing the Man-the-Hunter model. The specific target was to draw on as many sources for analogy of the human past as possible. The result was a considerable redirection of the research energies of these subdisciplines. Richard Lee and Irven DeVore (1968), for example, worked under Washburn's guidance to mine the social anthropology of what were then known as "hunter/gatherers" for material of use in reconstructing early hominid lifestyles.[1] Foragers are defined by their food-getting technology which is often said to represent the major behavioural adaptation of "99 percent" of our evolutionary history (Washburn and Lancaster 1968:228); they neither cultivate crops nor keep domesticated animals, relying entirely on wild foodstuffs and game. But Washburn promoted a rather narrow view of the relevant "hunting and gathering" material (ibid.:215-16). "Late adaptations" were not useful, being too tainted by the "great technological progress in [the] late pre-agricultural period" which included among other things, the use of dogs, traps, nets, snares and poisons. This eliminated groups such as the Northwest Coast Indians of North America and the Inuit of the Arctic and placed the preference on "large-game hunting" foragers such as the !Kung. Their lifestyle attributes were thought to include the small scale of basic social units, cooperation between males, divisions of labour between males and females, and exchange patterns of generalized reciprocity. These attributes were said to reflect a unitary culture, rooted in the deep human evolutionary past and offering all the basic prerequisites to the rise of other uniquely human characteristics (ibid.:217). All of the

---

1 In the heady days of the Woman-the-Gatherer model, the term hunter/gatherers became politically incorrect. Lee (1992) uses the terms "hunters and gatherers," "hunter-gatherer" and "gatherer-hunters" interchangeably, while the feminists tend to favour gatherer-hunters in order to emphasize the female role as reliable provisioner of society. In recent years, the term hunter-gatherers has had a resurgence, and people are again using it in publications (see Jolly 1996). Perhaps the least contentious term is "forager" and it is the term I adopt here.

analogy-oriented research had this basic characteristic; it was designed around predetermined interests based on deeply rooted assumptions about what it is to be human.

When considering these patterns of analogical research, one cannot help but be curious about Sherwood Washburn, who played such a central role in its development. He not only had a vision of paleoanthropological reconstruction which was multi-disciplinary and grounded in an empirical comparative approach, he also had the energy and influence to make his vision a meta-narrative in American anthropology (see Haraway 1983, 1988, 1989, Kurtz 1994). How did Washburn manage to be so influential? And how was it that he became the founding father of an "academic patri-line" in primatology and physical anthropology (Haraway 1989)?

Washburn received his Ph.D. in physical anthropology at Harvard in 1940 under Ernest Hooton. Hooton was involved in the postwar UNESCO statement on "universal manhood" which attacked racism using the scientific authority of population genetics and physical anthropology. His influence on Washburn's thesis, which addressed the comparative anatomy problem of skeletal proportions of adult langurs and macaques, may have been less important than his influence on Washburn's subsequent interest in building the intellectual foundations for a "unity of mankind," a unity that was based on a shared evolutionary history. In his article with C.S. Lancaster on "The Evolution of Hunting" (1968:213), for example, Washburn refers to the "unity of mankind" as having its source in "the selection pressures of the hunting and gathering life [being] so similar and the result so successful that populations of *Homo sapiens* are still fundamentally the same everywhere." Washburn's education was based on medical and comparative anatomy and the somewhat racist anthropomorphic physical anthropology of his day, but this focus on the unity of mankind meant that he spent a good deal of his career challenging racist science.

The pragmatics of Washburn's approach to science are also revealing. After graduate school, he went to teach medical anatomy at the Columbia College of Physicians and Surgeons and there he formed a friendship with Paul Fejos, first director of the Wenner-Gren Foundation. This friendship persisted after Washburn left Columbia in 1947; it formed the beginnings of an institutional power base which gave him control over dollars spent on research questions. After moving to the University of Chicago, Washburn developed specific research projects around the application of primatology and physical anthropology to questions of human evolution (see Washburn 1962). By 1958, he was receiving substantial funding for an animal behaviour experimental station as well as for field studies of primates at various sites around the world. He began to attract students to behavioural studies, as opposed to functional anatomy, and his connections meant that these students received solid funding support for their own research. His influence at Wenner-Gren was such that 74 percent of the budget of the foundation between 1965 and 1980 went for primatology and origins research. Many of his students used this support to good advantage, going on to make names in the discipline and in turn attracting their own students.

In 1958, he relocated to the University of California, Berkeley, where he remained until retirement in 1980 and where he is still listed as professor emeritus. The Ph.D. program with which he was associated at Berkeley produced a large and respected alumni of primatologists, paleoanthropologists and physical anthropologists; all of these have shown an interest to one degree or another in the origins applications of their research. And it is in the origins field in particular that Washburn's influence was not just limited to who received funding, but also extended how students thought and did research. Haraway (1983:179) writes that he was able to graft "primate science as a branch of physical anthropology onto roots of modern neo-Darwinian evolutionary theory and structural-functional social anthropology." If Washburn's students didn't always follow exactly in his footsteps, these ideas were the intellectual springboard off of which their own work sprang.

Irven DeVore is a case in point. He was a social anthropology student with a background in British structural-functionalism when Washburn encouraged him to study baboons (Haraway 1988:108 and 1989:219-20). DeVore received his Ph.D. in 1962 and very quickly began crossing subdisciplinary boundaries to publish widely in primatology (1965a, 1965b), in paleoanthropology (with Washburn in 1961), and in social anthropology (with Richard Lee in 1968). A short time after Washburn and DeVore worked together on the baboon research, DeVore collaborated with Richard Lee in establishing the Harvard Bushman (San) Project (1963-74) and in editing the results of a seminal conference ("Man the Hunter" 1968) which entrenched the masculine role in behavioural reconstructions of human origins. When DeVore became interested in sociobiology, his collaboration with Washburn ended, but his career demonstrates the Washburn ideal, which was that students should be well-grounded not only in the fossils, the primates and human anatomy, but also in the ethnographies of modern-day foraging populations.

Washburn and his students believe that there are many windows on our evolutionary past and that any single analogy should not be taken too far. It is foolhardy, for example, to try to pinpoint the one non-human primate species that most closely represents our evolutionary past. Primate evolution (including the hominids) has touched on several different environmental pressures and has been linked to many different adaptive responses (Haraway 1983:188). This palette of primate possibilities is still represented in many diverse extant species. Each one of these species can contribute something to our understanding of anatomy, and of locomotor, food-getting, reproductive and social patterns that we have shared at one point or another in the past with other members of the primate family. Thus, the deep past is as accessible as the more recent past; we only need to know how to cull the modern primate species' stories for narratives applicable to specific stages of development in our own evolutionary story. In addition, given the argument that over 99 percent of human evolutionary existence was spent as foragers, Washburn and his students also feel that modern foragers can play a seminal role in the reconstruction of the most important stage of development, the one that took us out of *nature* and into a *cultural* adaptation. But given the wonderful variability in the field data from physical anthropology, primatology and social anthropology, it is interesting in retrospect that Washburn's legacy, and that of his students, has been dominated from the outset by a few idées fixes. These have so collapsed the corroborative field into one tight human origins argument that no significant challenges have ever been seriously considered. This resistance to alternative explanations requires that questions about the relationship between Washburn's objectives, his use of analogy and the pervasive influence of these two on the origins research product be examined.

Idées Fixes: The Washburn Legacy

Several idées fixes have always dominated Washburn's work, particularly his early work, and these ideas have been both the groundwork and the foundations of human evolution model-building. What were these idées fixes, how are they reflected in the illustrations and why was it so difficult to dislodge the edifice they helped to construct?

First and foremost, Washburn worked towards a behavioural, adaptational and ecological understanding of our past. His ideas addressed a void in prehistory which up until then had been filled with "static chronology," whether of fossils, tools or "protocultures" (Hallowell 1956, 1961). Constructing such chronologies (Oldowan tradition, followed by Acheulean, Levallois, Weimarian and so on) had been the main goal for many decades, with the pursuit of logical typologies, the recognition of intermediate forms and a command of minutiae being the stock in trade of the discipline (see Chard 1975:vii, viii). Before analogy became so popular, typology was felt to be the only way to inject people into the archaeological record. The resulting historical and cultural chronologies were reflected in the illustrative world by the "series of landscapes" genre inherited from the field of geology and paleontology (see chapter 3). Whatever its disadvantages, this approach at least recognized variation and culture history as a central feature of the hominid line. Illustrations of the period tried to draw attention to distinct cultural differences, such as the types of tools and material artifacts crafted and the uses to which they might have been put. Zdeněk Burian's Neandertal illustrations, for example, separate the Teshik-tash variety of burials with its emphasis on ibex horns (Augusta and Burian 1960:Plate 19) from the Le Moustier type with its different types of grave goods (Plate 18). In Charles Knight's (1942) "Parade of Life" article, Cro-Magnon men not only engrave on mammoth ivory and paint pictures on cave walls, but also have distinctive cultural attributes such as ringlet hairstyles, neat beards and moustaches, necklaces and anklets which distinguish them from the lake dwellers shown in the next illustration. The Washburn legacy was to replace this cultural and historical variability with an emphasis on the analogous example as representative of an adaptive type.

One result was that in the scientific viewfinder, human evolution narrowed down to one focus, the origins of the hunting lifestyle; hunting was assumed to be both the most important adaptive behavioural change in the history of human evolution and the causal factor in a unitary cultural lifestyle which did not vary in any significant way across boundaries of space or time. Foley (1988:207) notes that the publication of *Man the Hunter* was pivotal to this reorientation of paleoanthropology away from the historical mode and towards "an approach in which the evolution of humans *was* the evolution of the hunter-gatherer adaptation" (emphasis in the original). Washburn's fixation on the origins significance of baboons and other primates had a number of similar consequences for the discipline of primatology. In discussing the increasing postwar popularity of primatology data in paleoanthropology, Sperling (1991:208) notes that using monkeys and apes as "exemplars" of human evolutionary progress tended to collapse the wonderful diversity of primate lifestyles into a single category, "primate society," just as it had collapsed the diversity of differences from one stage of human evolution to another. Further, a "guarantee of continuity" (Conkey 1991:105) was extended to all primates, so that researchers could speak of "kinship bonds" (see Tanner 1981:91-92), and a gendered "division of labour" (Sperling 1991:208), and even "parenting skills" in non-human primate societies as if they were all interchangeable with human society. This pattern of continuity has become entrenched in primatology and appears to be only weakly resisted by practitioners, however much some of them might be uncomfortable with it.

These trends in social anthropology, prehistory and primatology have together collapsed the number of "evolutionary problems" paleoanthropologists have to solve; behaviour, and most importantly, structural-functional assumptions about adaptive behaviour have become the driving interest. Anatomy, although important, is reduced to a signifier of adaptive (read cultural) behaviour and there is only one cultural process important to human adaptation and evolution (see Washburn and Lancaster 1968). Foley (1988) draws attention to how this new and narrower focus changed the relative importance of several ancestral species, including the Neandertal, which Foley calls the "*bête noire* of previous generations." Under the Washburn reorientation, questions about the Neandertal suddenly became less significant given that their lifestyle as foragers placed them "in the mainstream of human evolution," and "being a hominid, being a human and being a hunter-gatherer were very nearly the same thing." In illustrations, their bestial appearance began to be tempered with the same refining process already discussed with respect to the australopithecines; the trend is clear when Burian's "at the beginning of the rhinoceros hunt" (Figure 8) is compared to Matternes's "Neandertal living group" (Weaver 1985:599).

The second idée fixe of Washburn's work was one that he shared with many Western philosophers and scientists. A central tenet of Western discourse is that all of human history has been one steady upward drive characterized by progress (see Ingold 1986). For Washburn, this progress has been marked in particular by a steady increase in human mastery over nature, over the environment and over the skills and industries that make such mastery possible. In this regard, Washburn is in the company of other influential figures in the broader origins discourse such as Walcott, the great American paleontologist. Given this trust in progressive development, evolutionary models have tended to lean more towards Spencer than they have towards Darwin (see Ingold 1986:47-48, Gould 1989). Acknowledging this fixation on (human) evolutionary progress allows us to make sense of specific passages such as the following:

> If there were great variation in social behaviour from species to species of monkeys or if man's social behaviour were very similar to monkey's, then the chances of reconstruction of the social life of early man would be very poor, but man is unique in his social life, as he is in his locomotion and intelligence ... because of the great behavioural gap between man and his nearest relatives, some reconstruction of behaviour is possible (Washburn and DeVore 1961:103).

This "great behavioural gap" is the divide between nature and culture and because monkeys have not crossed the gap as humans have, we can know something about human evolutionary history and about the time before the progressive rise of consciousness and culture by looking at these non-human primates. They are ciphers of a pre-cultural past, of a time when we had not yet progressed beyond them.

A third idée fixe of Washburn's work (one later contested by many of his students) is that the transformation from nature to culture is primarily a male accomplishment. For Washburn, the seeds of an early and prolonged male leadership role are clearly observable in other extant primate societies:

> Adult male baboons are much larger than the females and have large canine teeth. When danger is near, it is they that protect the troop, and as a result they are actively sought out by the younger and weaker troop members (ibid.:100; see also Washburn, Jay and Lancaster 1968:204).

The essential difference between non-terrestrial and terrestrial animals is the greater danger the latter faces from predators, and an essential similarity between humans and baboons is that their terrestrial lifestyle has forced them both to adapt to this greater danger largely through the development of *social* "coping mechanisms." Washburn and DeVore's work represents baboon social life as hierarchical, with males stratified by dominance-seeking and yet cooperating to protect the females and young. Terminology used to describe this functional and cooperative social life leans on militaristic and androgenic metaphors, as when the social groups are referred to as "troops," and the male bodies as "fighting machines" (see Fedigan and Fedigan 1989:47). The females are not viewed as socially important and although they make valuable contributions to reproductive success, this is very much an automatic biological "reflex" (Washburn and DeVore 1961:98). Their role in the survival of their species is passive, based on instinct and nature. In contrast, hierarchy and dominance as well as aggression and cooperation between the males function together to ensure group survival. The adaptive success of such behavioural survival strategies is demonstrated by baboon population levels, which exceed those of pre-agricultural human societies (ibid.:92-93). These behavioural traits ultimately led to hominid progress and to masculine provisioning.

Washburn and DeVore acknowledge that in baboon society, males do *not* provide economic support for the females and dependent young. Since individual patterns of baboon food procurement do not allow the male physical superiority to lead to domination in the realm of food acquisition, the baboon can simultaneously represent a good analogy for early hominid adaptive stages and as a negative baseline for measuring how far humans have progressed. The role of the male baboon in the physical protection of females and their offspring is said to be the natural start of more explicitly hominid cultural patterns of male provisioning.

Masculine aggression, for example, laid the groundwork for a hunting lifestyle. Once hunting was adopted, other "ordering mechanisms" came into play to regulate social life and to make cooperation and sharing possible despite such aggression. These ordering mechanisms then propelled the proto-hominid *away* from the baboon food-procuring pattern. Male physical superiority is inferred to be something proto-hominids and baboons have in common, so it is logical to assume that this physical superiority would have ensured a central place for the male in the new proto-hominid ordering mechanisms *as it did in baboon social life.* Hunting, taken together with the development of uniquely hominid anatomical features (bipedality, larger brain, prolonged infant dependency), created conditions favourable to the generation of uniquely human cultural features such as incest taboos, exogamous mating, the monogamous patriarchal family, and delayed social maturity among others. But Washburn and DeVore *begin* by assuming that proto-hominid males were central to the social defensive organization, as they were to later hominid developments, and their entire baboon analogy can only support this assumption through an intellectual sleight of hand. The questionable leaps of faith required in the story line can be traced through a close reading of the text of this seminal article.

Washburn and DeVore effect this sleight of hand in several locations in their text, as well as by moving from specifically *nature*-based topics, such as "troop size," "range," "diet" and "population structure," to specifically more *cultural* topics such as "subgroups and play," "mother-child relations" and "economic dependence." The key transformation in the narrative takes place on page 99, *and without explanation!* The text just suddenly and inexplicable jumps from discussing female child-caring practises, to male provisioning. The key passage reads:

> In the evolution of society, the most important rules are those that guarantee economic survival to the dependent young. Human females and their young are efficient gatherers, so the crucial customs are those that guarantee the services of a hunter to a woman and her children.

How is it that we can go without explanation, from "efficient" gathering females and young, to the need for "the services" of a male hunter? Other examples of such sleight of hand can be cited.

For example, Washburn and DeVore found that baboon ranges were inconsistent with what was common for human hunting populations, being much smaller in size. To resolve this contradiction, they turned to the "large living carnivores" as alternative analogies, and argued that our earliest ancestors must have diverged from the baboon behaviour model to pursue game over many miles (ibid.:93-94). Since the connection between the rise of bipedality and high mobility over the landscape is a very old one, a primate with a baboon-style territory would not have fit the high mobility requirement of a bipedal, hunting ape. Washburn and DeVore also viewed the baboon troop as an inbred population structure which was inconsistent with what they expected for early hominids relying on hunting. Hunting, they argued, would have been "incompatible with the kind of society that does not allow any of its members to leave the group" (ibid.:95). The proto-hominid would have tolerated far less inbreeding than do modern baboon troops. Thus, in making baboons relevant to human origins, Washburn and DeVore constructed them more often as contrasting rather than as analogous models–the list of differences in all arenas other than male centrality in social life is striking. Baboons did not practise manipulative play with objects as do humans (ibid.:96), baboon mother-child relations were more dependent on biology than on culture (ibid.:97) and baboons did not have the human family pattern which allowed for the long period of infant helplessness, the lack of competition between males for a female's reproductive capacity and the male role as provider (ibid.:97-98). Even in the matter of a home base for operations, Washburn and DeVore concluded that the human species demonstrates significant advances over baboon adaptive behaviour (ibid.:101). But the culture/nature divide allows Washburn and DeVore to save the rather unsupportive data on the baboon for the construction of a *pre-cultural* proto-hominid life. They made the argument that the australopithecines more closely approximated baboon society than did any following hominid form, including the modern humans, which all evolved away from those patterns which make the baboon different while still retaining the essential and pivotal similarity of male centrality.

This 1961 baboon analogy shows Washburn and DeVore determined to "have their cake and eat it too." While they use baboon society to speculate on the behaviour of the proto-hominid, they *also* emphasize that baboons are *not* humans, which on the surface seems a valuable reminder for readers. But this is in fact a very important aspect of analogy; any specific example can be either a positive or a negative case, and often the same analogy will be used to both ends at the same time. When analogy produces results that support the preferred origins story, there are reasonable grounds for establishing resemblances. When the evidence deviates from expected patterns, the limitations of the analogy can be emphasized. The differences simply become codes of the nature/culture transformative stage. Washburn and his students have always been careful that the analogy selected did not become a trap to constrain the heroic tales paleontologists want to construct.

Haraway (1983, 1989) notes that it hardly matters that none of the subsequent, more long-term studies of baboons and other species were able to replicate the results of DeVore and Washburn's early reports. What was important was that the male-centred analogy of the baboon was consistent with wider constructed meanings of the day; thus it was "useful" scientific knowledge. Subsequent researchers often continued to construct primate stories that grew naturally out of Washburn's proposed baboon model of human evolution—focusing, for example, on predation and meat-eating among non-human primates (see Harding and Strum 1976). Most primatologists are well aware that their research will inevitably be viewed through the lens of human origins (Fedigan 1986:25-26), and origins research has largely conformed to Washburn's research agenda, so perhaps it is not surprising that primatology itself also conforms to his several idées fixes.

Alternative Analogies

By the mid-1970s, Washburn's research edifice began to receive increasing criticism. These attacks came from three quarters, and were mostly mounted by former students who endorsed analogy in origins research, but in ways that diverged from Washburn's model. Richard Lee was discovering the social history of the !Kung, DeVore was discovering sociobiology, and feminists were constructing a Woman-the-Gatherer model of human origins (Haraway 1989:227-29). Ironically, Richard Lee's work was to provide the catalyst for the two most damaging of these attacks, the question of the evolutionary role of the female of the species and the issue of cultural unity of forager societies. The Woman-the-Gatherer model, for example, was a direct result of feminist scholars focusing in on Richard Lee's findings on the importance of female gathering to !Kung subsistence. This in turn stimulated new thinking on the issue of gender in origins research.

Adrienne Zihlman was central to this rethinking process. She began her career with a rather conservative approach to the importance of bipedalism in the hominoid-hominid transition. Assuming that a change in physical form was necessarily a response to an adaptive change in behaviour, her thesis argued that bipedality had to have been related to long-distance walking, presumably for provisioning (Zihlman 1967). The accepted notion at the time was that this long-distance walking was probably done for purposes of hunting. Soon afterwards, however, she and Nancy Tanner began to work on another explanation which argued that proto-hominid females were forced to extend their foraging in order to support the higher energy costs of a longer period of infant dependency (Tanner and Zihlman 1976). Female reproductive needs were the key drive towards bipedality. In this approach, Zihlman was consistent with a growing trend among Washburn's other students such as Richard Lee, who had come to view gathering and sharing as basic to the human adaptation.

Zihlman's work had long favoured the chimpanzee, first in her thesis and later in her collaboration with Nancy Tanner where the analogy for proto-hominid behavioural changes was drawn from research on the chimpanzee that was relatively new at the time (Zihlman 1978, 1979; see also McGrew 1981:35). She was central to injecting the chimp into origins stories and she justified her preferred primate analogy by reference to Sarich's (1968) arguments from the molecular data in support of a very recent (5 mya rather than 20 mya) divergence between the human and chimpanzee line. Nancy Tanner, who continued developing this model after she and Zihlman ceased working together, devotes several chapters in her book *On Becoming Human* (1981) to the chimpanzee as an appropriate human origins analogy. She writes: "Chimpanzees, in genetics, anatomy, behaviour, and environment, present a total configuration that provides the best available model for suggesting features of the ancestral ape population" (ibid.:65; see also Tanner 1987).

Their generalized locomotor patterns which sometimes involve a bipedal gait for short periods of time, their use of tools for various purposes, their broad diet which has even been known to include meat, the variability and flexibility of their social groups, their sociability and communicative patterns, the patterns of maternal investment in rearing their young, the sexual interactions between male and female and the various studies of their cognitive and emotional capacities are all said to represent a close match not only to our hominid ancestors, but to anatomically modern humans as well (see comparisons with chimpanzee facial gestures in Tanner 1981:201 and in Haviland 1994:100). Of all of these characteristics, however, the facet of chimpanzee life which probably most engaged feminist interest was the apparent centrality of the adult female. Jane Goodall (1967), for example, wrote about the importance of the matrifocal unit in chimpanzee society and Tanner and Zihlman were able to utilize these findings to postulate new, more central roles for the female in human evolution. They built mixed and mutually reinforcing analogies just as the Man-the-Hunter crowd had, but reached very different conclusions in the process. The use of analogy to construct better stories of human origins had suddenly become contentious and as the number and types of potential primate analogies increased, so did the level of contention.

Analogy Contests: The Gendered Primate

Although the stories of human evolution constructed through Washburn's research agenda were fundamentally androcentric, Haraway (1983:181) observes that Washburn and others did not set out with a conscious goal of subverting the power and status of modern women. Washburn's shibboleth was "the unity of mankind"; the enemy was racism. Androcentrism was neither recognized nor addressed as a problem. But in the years between 1965 and 1985, new influences created an environment suitable for destabilizing androcentrism. As the numbers of women in the field increased and feminists such as Jeanne Altmann, Adrienne Zihlman, Sarah Blaffer Hrdy, Linda Marie Fedigan and others published more widely, alternative interests gained scientific authority. The new focus was on primate reproductive strategies, particularly those of the female. The resulting primate stories explicitly utilized coded commentaries that originated in political contests over the female body and in other Euro-american discourse of the 1970s and 1980s (Haraway 1983:191). At the same time that Western women were struggling to gain more control over their reproductive experiences, for example, primatology was "discovering" the high cost of parenting investments of the female monkey as compared to the male monkey. Jeanne Altmann was using the key metaphors of "dual career mothering," "juggling demands" and "energy budgeting" in her baboon research. An analysis of such language use suggests Altmann's intended audience; for example, consider the word "career" and its middle-class connotations in comparison with the working-class "job" (Haraway 1989:313). For Haraway, Jeanne Altmann's work becomes fully comprehensible only when one knows the "history of discourses on labour in industrial social systems" (ibid.:314). Women were not only decentralizing males by taking careers in the workplaces of industrial society, they were also decentralizing males in academic discourse by successfully pursuing careers in primatology and human evolution. In the ensuing combative atmosphere of sexual politics, structural-functional arguments about the adaptive functions of the supposed behavioural attributes of the two genders multiplied.

The new analogies that attempted to decentre androcentrism did not
go unchallenged. The Woman-the-Gatherer edifice was dealt with in one
of three ways: (1) it was ignored, (2) it was dismissed without serious refu-
tation or (3) it was co-opted (Zihlman cited in Haraway 1989:343-44, see
also chapter 2, this book). Co-optation simply added gathering to hunting
to produce a mixed economy which reinforced the deep antiquity of the
monogamous family and all that that entailed. Alternatively, co-optation
involved accepting gathering tools as an adaptive innovation but one that
was developed by males. As early as 1958, Washburn had presaged this
co-optation when he and a colleague, Virginia Avis, suggested that plant
gathering had been very important at the "pre-transition" phase before
the Australopithecines developed hunting. They also suggested that the
first human tool may have been a device for carrying babies (Washburn
and Avis 1958). But such tools and activities were never considered sufficient cause for the leap towards humanity. Washburn had long argued
that something dramatically new was needed to explain this leap and
only new activities for the male fit the bill (see Haraway 1989:339-40).
This commitment to the androcentric hypothesis was staunchly maintained by many in the face of Zihlman's alternative, probably because of
the insistent demands of narrative-style explanations, demands which
were always the driving force behind analogy. In Zihlman's account,
both hunting and gathering were "repatterned" under conditions of
"constraint and opportunity." For Washburn, repatterning was not
enough—some dramatic stimuli was necessary for the account to ring
true. He and others have responded to Zihlman's work by arguing that
analogy cannot work through overly simplistic constructions of a
"dichotomous opposite" to the hunter model; if the Man-the-Hunter
model ignored female contributions, the damage cannot be rectified by
building a Woman-the-Gatherer model which ignores male contributions. The counter-proposal is that male *scavenging* was the impetus for
the hominoid-hominid transition. Feminists, in turn, feel that these refu-
tations "forget" that Zihlman and Tanner's central premise was based on
four foundations: (1) female (as well as male) physical mobility, (2) social
and behavioural flexibility for all members of the species, (3) the transformative power of the immature members of the species and of the
mother-child relations and (4) the deconstruction of narrative staples in
the hunter hypothesis, including technological determinism (indeed
fetishism), masculinism, male-female sexual bonding, and home bases

for nuclear families (see for example Haraway 1989:345). Despite feminist resistance, this scavenging hypothesis has become the dominant approach in introductory anthropology textbooks.

In this contentious atmosphere of origins research, the sociobiology converts among the primatologists have had a curious role; Donna Haraway has been very critical of this role, particularly given the strange bedfellows it has made for some feminist scholars (1983:194 n 26, 1989:354; see also Sperling 1991). In some ways, sociobiology makes a very nice fit with Washburn's structural functional primatology; both postulate a *progressive* relationship between body, society and environment. As Haraway (1983:193) notes, in sociobiology "all biological structures are expressions of a genetic calculus of interest," with a level of explanation that seeks the "pared down fitness maximization strategy"; it is this strategy that can move the species ahead through troubling times. Primatologists using this approach were able to "discover" that female and male primates could have very different strategies for maximizing their reproductive successes; adaptation did not function at the group level but rather at the level of the "selfish gene." Stories about male contributions to survival of the group were rewritten with an emphasis on male/female conflict in the pursuit of individual genetic maximization. For example, Tooby and DeVore (1987:197, 207, 208) puzzle over the origin of the family, gender-based divisions of labour, the unique human mating system, monogamy and the high male investment in reproduction given that males and females *naturally* have different approaches to maximizing their genetic survival rates. For them, sociobiology and the "strategic reasoning" associated with tight restrictions of scarcity and competition make the Lovejoy hypothesis the best "early transition" explanation around, since it explains both how females maximized their genetic success rate (by co-opting male labour), and how males maximized theirs (by enforcing female fidelity). Such analysis has lately been reinforced by evolutionary psychology, which also actively promotes the notion of the "natural" genetic maximizing strategies of the human male and female psyche (see Wright 1994).

Sociobiological primatology has "recrafting" feminist-inspired primate stories by substituting its own choices for primate analogies of human origins. In the place of the baboon and the chimpanzee they offer the langur. Of particular interest is the langur behaviour pattern of so-called "infanticide" (see Haraway 1983). Male langurs are said to sometimes kill infant langurs when they move into a new troop and dislodge the previous male(s). There are questions as to whether or not such behaviour actually exists, but for those who accept its empirical reality, several alternative explanations are offered, all of which give Haraway (1983) unease, given their implications for Western gender politics. Sarah Blaffer Hrdy, for example, makes a classical sociobiological explanation that the incoming males are behaving in a way calculated to remove rival genes and free up the females for new pregnancies, which is rational given the assumption that ultimate success in life depends on genetic investments in the market of reproduction. *Haraway's* (ibid.:191) comment on the Sarah Blaffer Hrdy story draws attention to its "fit" with capitalist enterprise and the free market system:

> The social origin story of pure liberal, utilitarian political economy ruled; individual competition produced all the forms of combination of the efficient animal machine. Social life was a market where investments were made and tested in the only currency that counts: genetic increase.

Suzanne Ripley, in contrast, writes another kind of story about infant-killing male langurs, one that has a subplot of ecological stress rather than market fitness.

Stress as a motive force has moved the wider evolutionary plot along since the original hunter stories, but Ripley's work is updated to integrate new political anxieties about the consequences of crowding, density sensitivities and population regulation as well as the influence of the ecological movement. Ripley feels that the infant-killing behaviour of langur males serves as a population regulating mechanism to keep langur numbers within ecologically sustainable boundaries, a story that resonates to the abortion debates current in American politics in a way that makes the male central to decisions about population dynamics. In contrast, the Jane Bogess publications offer a different langur story with a stress-subplot (Haraway 1983:197-98). Bogess sees the male behaviour in this instance as purely pathological, stress related but in no way adaptive. Here the outlook on langur infanticide has gone from a more optimistic "population control" model to a less optimistic "canary in the mine" scenario. Langur behaviour, like that of baboons and of chimpanzees, gets written into a number of different stories, all of them important to modern-day sociopolitical debates as well as to arguments about gender.

But sociobiology has never been able to dominate in paleoanthropology as did the earlier Washburn structural functional models. While sociobiology makes good stories, modern academics is a polyphony of voices, none able to completely drown out the others. In primatology, multiple theoretical arguments have meant that either the male or the female can be made central to stories about human origins and our place in nature, but seemingly never both. The work of the two genders must always be separate, although equally "consumed with the topics–and tropes–of the origin of the family, the state, and the individual" (Haraway 1989:288). These same topics and tropes are equally pervasive themes in the second source for analogy in paleoanthropology, that of the forager. And there, too, the polyphonic voices are discordant. In such contests, evoking the authority of the scientist is an important strategy.

Scientific Authority and Analogy: Foragers and the Great Kalahari Debate

Primitives and primates have long been treated as windows onto what is natural and/or unnatural for the human species (Haraway 1988:78; see also Lee 1992:32-33), but since both primitives and primates share an existence in a "field" that is difficult of access, alien and exotic, these windows can only be peered through using proper scientific detachment and methodology. Significant institutional and authorial power is necessary to reach, observe and write about them. And against scientific detachment, both primitives and primates are relatively powerless so that there has been little political cost attached to this "scientific" treatment of them. To enter into "field research" on either has always been to enter into the Western history of "expansion and colonialism" (Haraway 1988). This question of appropriate and reliable science has increasingly become a problem for both origins analogies.

Historically, two models have been perennial favourites in the Western encapsulation and categorization of foraging peoples, the Hobbesian view of life as nasty, brutish and short, and the equally absorbing theme of the Noble Savage. In both models, hunting was viewed as the basic economic prop. Male knowledge of terrain, skill in pursuit, and aggression and fearlessness in the face of the dangers of the hunt were all glorified in classical ethnographies using statements such as: "no other activity of the men can match the importance of hunting" (Holmberg 1969:51), "the Siriono is a master at both stalking and imitation" (ibid.:52), and "their knowledge of the forest is, of course, unsurpassed" (Garvan 1963:67). Warfare was lauded as another significant contribution the males made towards group survival: "The Cheyennes fight to hold the place they have won for themselves on the Great Plains" (Hoebel 1960:69); "Living as they do in an atmosphere of chronic warfare, the Cheyennes, like other Plains tribes, emphasize military virtue" (ibid.). In some ethnographies, warfare, the hunt, and the masculine tools and weapons of the hunt and defence were each emphasized to the point of having entire chapters of their own (see Service 1966 and selected articles in Owen, Deetz and Fisher 1967). While there are also descriptions of women's contributions to survival in such ethnographies, the terminology used and the clear lack of enthusiasm marked such contributions as less theoretically significant. Hunter stories had the widest appeal, and to give early ethnographers their due, were crafted to resist widespread racist perceptions of such societies. And these stories, with their built-in assumptions about male social centrality, became widespread in the popular press and effectively linked to the equally widespread "ubiquitous hunting model" of human evolution (Zihlman 1981:81).

In the context of postwar decolonialization, new studies of foragers emerged which ultimately challenged these older assumptions about male centrality (Zihlman 1981:91). Richard Lee's research on the !Kung was central to this restructured interest which has led some to define Lee as "pro-feminist" (Haraway 1988:108). But Lee's research is not so easily categorized. His real interest was on the economic attributes of foraging societies, particularly on the relative availability of everyday necessities such as food, and this research was done with an eye to expanding the utility of forager ethnographies for origins research. He continues to take the position that foragers are "people who have *historically* lived by gathering, hunting and fishing, with minimal or no agriculture and with no domesticated animals except for the dog" (1992:31, emphasis mine). He also maintains that such foragers are " 'band' or 'egalitarian' societies in which social groups are small, mobile, and unstratified, and in which differences of wealth and power are minimally developed" (ibid.). These are characteristics that he feels are central to their significance as analogies of the proto-hominid life. On the other hand, Lee also demonstrated that at least for the !Kung which he studied in the 1960s, female gathering was the most reliable source of foodstuffs while male hunting provided less of the diet by weight. He characterized !Kung women as significant contributors to the economic well-being of the group, a finding that may have been more palatable given its fit with Western food gendering such that vegetables and starches are feminine while protein, particularly meat protein, is masculine. Also, Lee followed Elizabeth Marshall Thomas (1958) in representing the !Kung as non-aggressive, non-territorial and non-warlike. These were all representations that struck at the heart of the Man-the-Hunter model.

Thus, when Lee's research was subsequently examined under the influence of the feminist critique of "androcentric science practice," the !Kung findings were judged to be compatible with the revisions going on in the primatology realm. This simply demonstrates that both non-human primates and foragers were sufficiently complex as sources of analogy to offer up alternative (pro-feminist) stories towards paleoanthropological model building. And this complexity is probably what allows them to remain remarkably relevant to every new political direction. For example, Richard Lee also interprets foraging cultures as the pristine "original affluent societies" (Sahlins 1982), practising an inherently viable and enduring cultural category of organization which is tied in turn to a sustainable method of survival. Lee argues, for example, that foragers all share "one remarkable organizational principle" which is "the ability to reproduce themselves while limiting the accumulation of wealth and power" (1992:39). The implication is that in the ecologically sensitive future of sustainable development, the foraging societies of the world offer us important insights both into our evolutionary past (to a time when social groups were small, technology simple, surplus difficult and wealth defined by mutually supportive social relationships) and into a future where that lifestyle may again be our best hope of survival as a species. Forager life, like the reconstructed and recast stories of non-human primate societies, thus offers the stuff from which modern-day sociopolitical constructs can be made. The environmentally sound, collective life is cast against the perceived model of the West as rapacious, atomistic and anomistic. Feminists seem to find this Rousseauian vision of the "primitive life"—one of a leisurely existence supported by gathering from nature's abundant offerings—more attractive than the alternative highly competitive, kill-or-be-killed androcentric hunting model. However, this "gentler, kinder" evolutionary past also offers racist and ethnocentric pitfalls.

The joint analogies of chimpanzees and the !Kung foragers, for example, is used in such a way as to suggest a line of evolution from ape to proto-hominid, to primitive and finally to modern man. We see this with Tanner's (1981:143-44) frequent and easy comparisons between proto-hominid, the chimpanzee and the !Kung. This questionable appropriation of and selective storytelling about the cultural practices of foraging peoples was a driving force in the development of the "Great Kalahari Debate" (Kurtz 1994), which primarily turns on the treatment of the !Kung and other foragers as a people without history (Kent 1992:59). This debate turns on the use of several presumed central characteristics of foragers which have been disputed as valid ethnographic information. Grinker (1992:160) writes:

> the characteristics considered central to such societies and to their assumed evolutionary significance—egalitarianism, small residence groups, few exclusive rights to resources, lack of ownership of property, absence of food supplies, and extensive resources sharing, for example—have become increasingly entrenched in anthropological orthodoxy. What began as the evolutionist's search for ethnographic analogy led to the invention of a distinct category of human society.

This distinct category of the forager society has been challenged by "revisionists" such as Edwin Wilmsen (1989), whose focus on ethnographic accuracy rather than on evolutionary significance has led them to challenge the latter as well as the former.

One "fact" the detractors question is that of the supposed immense time-depth of the forager adaptation; if 99 percent of human history has been experienced as foragers, do modern-day examples represent an unchanged continuation of this history? In other words, are foragers closer to human nature, less encumbered by cultural baggage, better able to show us a window on the past? Wilmsen (1989:3) comments on this "nature child" aspect:

> A false dichotomy has crept in, a line drawn between those who produce their means of existence and those who supposedly do not, between those who live on nature and those who live in it, between those whose social life is motivated primarily by self interest and those guided by respect for reciprocal consensus.

He sees Lee's perspective as one viewed through a "lost Eden"-type of rose-coloured glasses. It is precisely this Edenistic view of the !Kung which has made them so popular with human evolution illustrators.

Far from seeing the !Kung as pristine examples of our simpler, happier human past, Wilmsen views them very much as a product of the present. He and others have pursued a line of research suggested by Jean Peterson's (1978a, 1978b) work among the Agta, a Philippine foraging peoples often characterized as "shy" and "elusive" by early ethnographers. Peterson rejected the view that the Agta avoided all contact with their agricultural neighbours and suggested instead that this tribal group lived in an "edge" ecosystem involving a symbiotic relationship with their neighbours. The Agta provided farming peoples with scarce protein through their foraging efforts and in return received carbohydrates which they could not easily procure in the forest. Wilmsen (1989) traces the !Kung historical experiences in the more recent stretch of human history to make a similar argument that they have never been culturally or politically isolated, have never avoided economic interaction with neighbouring non-foragers and have never been unaffected by the sweep of modern human affairs.

This argument is not intrinsically nor necessarily threatening to the forager evolutionary analogy. For example, there is no reason to believe that foragers who came into regular contact with non-foragers would necessarily lose all cultural coherence and thus the resiliency to choose their own historical path. However, the Wilmsen interpretation does not support !Kung cultural coherency and this position was presaged by early criticisms of Peterson's work. Peterson's symbiotic model of forager-farmer relationships was attacked for masking the unequal political and economic status of the two exchange partners. Rather than being tied into a mutually beneficial, farmer-forager exchange system, some analysts viewed the Agta as unwilling clients of abusive patrons who forced the Agta into an economically and culturally untenable situation similar to that experienced by other marginal groups in the Philippines (see Lopez-Gonzaga 1983 and Eder 1987). The Agta were powerless to change this situation which necessarily affected their "culture." Wilmsen's (1989:3) view of the !Kung is similar:

> the current status of the San-speaking peoples on the rural fringe of African economies can be accounted for only in terms of the social policies and economies of the colonial period and its aftermath. Their

appearance as foragers is a function of their relegation to an underclass in the playing out of historical processes that began before the current millennium and culminated in the early decades of this century.

The !Kung foraging lifestyle that we see today, far from being the pattern the human species has enjoyed for 99 percent of our evolutionary history, is instead the cobbled-together, moment-by-moment survival efforts of a powerless and displaced people. This criticism bites deeply into what have become basic conceptual building blocks in anthropology (reciprocal exchange, egalitarian society) and it is part of a larger process of critiquing the traditional ethnographic exercise. In 1982, Eric Wolf wrote:

> The world of humankind constitutes a manifold, a totality of interconnected processes, and inquiries that disassemble this totality into bits and then fail to reassemble it falsify reality. Concepts like "nation," "society" and "culture" name bits and threaten to turn names into things (1982:3).

Recent work "on the margins" of state-local interactions has explored the methodological options that are open to those who accept this assertion. Tsing (1993) for example, uses discourse analysis to document the multiple ways in which such connected processes affect and are affected by Meratus "culture" in Indonesia. In her reading, culture is not a unitary, cohesive "thing" that orders most events within a society and which anthropologists from afar can "observe." She views the Meratus as living an "elaborated marginality" which the state and foreign anthropologists have taken as isolated, primitive tradition (ibid.:29). The notion of "culture" becomes highly suspect from this point of view.

Richard Lee, however, rejects the argument that: "foragers have been integrated into larger regional or even international structures of power and exchange for so long that they can reveal nothing about the hunter-gatherer way of life" (1992:34). Lee and his supporters hold that even given !Kung historicity, we can use them to learn something about our deep past. In a defence which somewhat misses the point, they have attacked Wilmsen's conclusions by attempting to undermine his scientific authority. They challenge his historical accuracy, his understanding of the San language and his victim-oriented concept of forager culture; Wilmsen has returned these attacks vigorously (see Solway and Lee 1990, Grinker 1992, Kent 1992, Lee 1992, Wilmsen 1993). Some people have responded to the debate by attempting to find a middle ground between Wilmsen's negative historicity and Lee's optimistic forager pristine-ness. Susan Kent (1992:59) admits that the problem is tied to "the desire of some anthropologists to find an easy analogue to apply to prehistoric data" but still hopes that studies of forager groups can reveal something about "the nature of foraging cultures and how they are organized." Note that she uses the word "cultures," implying internal coherence, consistent ideology, and a body of unique cultural practice, rather than the word "societies" which perhaps would suggest less. With this language use, Kent positions herself against the more radical position that the forager communal, reciprocal and egalitarian culture may actually be an "invention" of Western ethnographers, who have been motivated by the desire to find a concrete foil to use against neoclassical economic theory with its relentless emphasis on individualism, maximization and rationality.

As the postmodern exercise in self-reflexivity becomes de rigueur in anthropology, the contextualization of knowledge sometimes creates an academic lethargy similar to the mid-life crisis of "What's it all for?" Lee (1992:35-37), for example, argues that if the postmodern critiques of ethnographies are taken seriously, then one must live by the proposition that "Nothing is real." He characterizes such arguments as an example of the prevailing twentieth century malaise, which results in our seeing ethnography through advertisement-jaded eyes, coloured by fears about the invasive powers of the modern bureaucratic institution and that only regimes of power have creative capacity. He argues that if these things were true then perhaps ethnographers would have been reduced to writing fiction, but if "the ethnographers of that not-so-distant era had passed their fiction off as science their readership and their peers would not have stood for it" (ibid.:37). Thus peer review becomes the somewhat naïve vehicle for rejecting the way that cultural studies have contextualized the science product. But that is not the reading that I make of many postmodern arguments.

I think two postmodern questions are important to consider in the origins research context. First, how important are critiques of the scientific authority of different voices in the analogies debate and second, are there any patterns to the way we have dealt with the inherent complexity of subject matter within the discipline? With respect to the first point, it is interesting that attacks on the analogies selected, and the meanings drawn from them, have often been attacked in their turn on the basis of the taint of "political motivation." Feminism or the postcolonial critical stance, according to their deriders, have developed from insidious influences originating "outside" of the scientific exercise. Tooby and DeVore (1987:183-84), for example, argue in favour of retaining primitives and non-human primates as analogies of human evolution by situating the feminist critique as a cultural influence *on* science rather than as an end product *of* science, a characterization that the feminists reject (see Haraway 1989:327). Haraway argues that "outside" and "inside" are inappropriate ways to think about the relationship between science and the wider society. Primatology, paleontology, anthropology and the knowledge they generate are not so much about reality, but about the spin we put on aspects of reality. Both science and sociopolitical processes are "inside" a cultural context and it is important to acknowledge that scientific knowledge be recognized for what it is, a hermeneutical exercise where we generate not so much "data" as "capta" (Laing quoted in Caplan 1988:8) or the captured moments that we have come to consider relevant. Academics are engaged in a semiotic (the science of making meanings) and an hermeneutical (the science of interpretation) exercise, and we can only hope for "a politicized semiotics, where politics is the search for a public world through many socially grounded practices" (Haraway 1988:96). This chapter examines how some capta have been "read" as having significance not only to paleoanthropological reconstructions but to current political struggles, and how those readings have subtly changed over time while retaining several significant themes in common. They create stories about things, people, animals and objects which are contested not because "nothing is real," but precisely because they *become* real, taking on a wider relevance to actions taken both inside and outside of academic corridors. This is vitally important to acknowledge.

This constitutive aspect to society (and to the scientific knowledge it generates) directly leads to the second postmodern point about complexity. Lee and other supporters of the analogy exercise have also missed the point when they defend themselves with the codicil that there are no "easy analogues"; even when acknowledging that the !Kung were never a pristine window on the past and that overgeneralization will always lead to flawed outcomes, they fail to address the more serious problem of the deeply challenged notion of "culture" itself. The question is not whether or not the !Kung live as our evolutionary ancestors did but whether any culture anywhere or at any time had the integrated and functional characteristics that we want to attach to our deep past. Analogy continues to be constructed in such a way as to ignore the increasing evidence for the complexity of the relationship between evolution, change and progress (culture) on the one hand, and the science exercise and resulting knowledge on the other. In both primatology and social anthropology, the use of analogy in origins research has been under attack for being overreliant on flawed basic assumptions and biased findings. Structural-functionalism was falling out of favour even as Washburn and DeVore were using it to construct their early baboon stories. When used to analyze human societies, it was attacked for being generally tautological, ahistorical and for relying on oversocialized actors (see Evans-Pritchard 1950). Adaptationist arguments in biology and primatology, even in various updated versions such as sociobiology, are also attacked for similar functionalist flaws (see the several publications of Gould). And so it is clear that the resilience of these origin models, with their rather reactionary commitment to such analogical approaches, is remarkable and needs to be better researched and understood.

It is important to ask questions, for example, about why the Great Kalahari Debate and the corresponding disputes in primatology are muted in the origins illustrations. The stories told and illustrated for the lay audience in introductory courses and in popularized accounts of origins findings are always simple, unitary narratives. Why is that so important? What messages are being reinforced with this simplicity that could not be conveyed if complexity were to receive the same attention? The answer to this question lies in the way that Western science has constructed its dominant narrative of evolution as one of progress—of a steady upward drive towards perfection and the ideal. Analogy and the illustrations which are developed out of analogy, are designed to reinforce dominant Western tropes of progress and the source of that progress in individual effort, gendered divisions of labour and patriarchal family arrangements.

Summary

The comparisons between proto-hominid, foragers and non-human primates, based on a philosophy of analogy, has a long history, a history of moving back and forth in our interpretations of the meaning of scientific findings. And this history finds its context in the ubiquitous use of scientific data and constructions in Western political discourse, which help shape the scientific information to which we pay attention. Scientific knowledge is constructed, it is contested and it is significant to sociopolitical meanings. Alongside simian orientalism, we must recognize all of the ways in which the West constructs a "significant other" by which to measure (and invent) itself through opposition and emulation (see chapter 5). Gender is a significant other; primates are a significant other; other "races" and non-Western cultures are significant others. Constructing our deep evolutionary past has relied on all of these significant others in order to build a history of "otherness," of a time before "culture." That does not mean that primates, foragers, non-Western cultures and other genders do not exist outside of our imaginations. But it does mean that there are highly selective patterns to the way we pay attention to them, and highly specific goals to that exercise.

In contrasting nature and culture, the Western scientific community continues on a long-standing course of exploring the dynamism of a conceptual duo locked in mutually antagonistic opposition. Haraway suggests that as paired distinctions, male-female and culture-nature are systematically related to each other, in many and diverse ways. She writes (1988:83-84):

> Feminist analysis has frequently erred in assuming that the equation of woman with nature, animal, dark, etc., is the only relationship built into the series of dual terms [nature/culture, male/female]. These dual axes are story operators, ways of structuring relationships. They are not static ascriptions.

This is true, but one traditional way of structuring those dual story operators in origins illustrations is around a masculine-technological and progressive future based on culture versus a feminine and static past based on nature. Thus the overwhelming trend in the illustrations we have been examining has been to link the male with purposive movement, with technological solutions enacted in the wider landscape, with progress and change, and with cultural pursuits, while the female is linked to immobility, stasis in a secure location, biology through the physical aspects of child care and with the drudgery of technologically unmediated contact with nature. Equally important is that male and culture and progress are *endorsed* over female, statis and immobility.

Supportive "data" from the world of non-human primates and from forager societies is selectively used to argue about the distance that male-mediated technology has brought the modern Euro-american.

This chapter has focused on the meaning we give to scientific knowledge, which according to some readings is not fact, but rather contested stories about concepts, categories and classes, of things, people and ideas. This and previous chapters have demonstrated that the stories we have told about human evolution over the past several decades have contained at least two versions which are constructed out of contested knowledge. These stories contain logical flaws, but they are contested not because of their logical coherence, truth value or lack thereof, but because of their relevance to and implication in our group attempts to construct a public space which we all, to one extent or another, must share—if sometimes only by exclusion. What is interesting about this public space is the relentless connections made with the future, with progress and with the Western masculine-technological way we mediate the nature/culture interface. In the next chapter, I turn to this question of progress as the dominant trope in evolutionary research, and investigate the ways in which it is pervasive throughout Western scientific discourse.

CHAPTER SEVEN

Progress: Inevitable as Moral Rewards—
The Ultimate Story Operator

[M]ost of us are still unwilling to abandon the comforting view that evolution means (or at least embodies a central principle of) progress.... Primates are visual animals, and the pictures we draw betray our deepest convictions and display our current conceptual limitations. Artists have always painted the history of fossil life as a sequence from invertebrates, to fishes, to early terrestrial amphibians and reptiles, to dinosaurs, to mammals and, finally, to humans. There are no exceptions; all sequences painted since the inception of this genre in the 1850s follow the convention. Yet we never stop to recognize the almost absurd biases coded into this universal mode. (Gould 1994:91)

There are certain themes that sound and resound throughout the evolutionary discourse; like the leitmotifs of opera they move the story line along and provide drama and suspense. Environmental stress, struggles to survive, competition over resources, all are pervasive in the evolution literature. But underlying all of these is the most pervasive theme of all, a theme that also meets the cultural expectations and narrative demands of a Western audience. The progress motif is expected to be the foundation of all evolution stories. It fuels the persistence of the "adaptation for cause" explanatory mode despite the significant amount of non-adaptationist literature that has emerged recently (see Gould 1977, 1980, 1981, 1984, 1985, 1989; Haraway 1989:322, n 10). Progress and adaptation as major undercurrents in evolutionary thinking create a story field of human evolution which is fundamentally flawed.

These flaws have become obvious as anthropologists attempt to rewrite origins stories to cope with the increasingly complex fossil record. In Richard Leakey and Roger Lewin's (1992) book on human origins research, for example, they make the argument that it is time for paleoanthropologists to reject the old image of the ladder of progress and to replace it with the more data-relevant image of the "evolutionary bush" (ibid.:68-74). Leakey and Lewin address several of the logical flaws that are intrinsic to the ladder model, such as the notion that "initiative and effort are what separated us from the apes" (ibid.:68-69), and that non-human primates are windows on our past (ibid.:72). And yet, they seem incapable of maintaining this advocacy throughout their own explanations of our evolutionary history. For example, there is still a sense of self-satisfaction in their comment that all of the physiological change which gave rise to the human species can best be explained by reference to the "keen pressures" of natural selection (ibid.:83-84). Did other extant primates not respond to keen natural selection pressures as they evolved? Are there "keen pressures" and "not-so-keen pressures" which might explain different patterns of physiological changes among the primate family? Furthermore, Leakey and Lewin continue the pattern of using some non-human primates as prototype hominids. Leakey (ibid.:137) writes: "I have always thought it reasonable to imagine early hominid social life as analogous, in some strictly circumscribed ways, to the social life of the savanna baboon." But it is apparent from the subsequent discussion that as a species we no longer resemble savanna baboons; the intrinsic assumption remains; "initiative and effort" are the main story operators for Leakey and Lewin.

This explanatory conservatism relates to the ongoing reluctance to problematize gender, "race" and progress as themes in origins research. The baboon model remains "reasonable" because Leakey and Lewin have never accepted the need to fundamentally rethink their functionalist view of particular attributes or roles in the narrative of how some genders, species, "races" or cultures were able to "advance" beyond others. Given assumptions about gender attributes and roles, the synchronism of australopithecine fossils of differing size must be interpreted as representing sexual dimorphism, which in turn is tied to gender role specialization, which itself is causal of the ultimate success of the human species over other members of the animal kingdom. Our models have not progressed beyond the early days of origins research.

And why should they? The Leakey and Lewin narrative of australopithecine sexual dimorphism and male centrality makes a very nice fit with the Western obsession with progress stories. Adaptationism makes for such exciting, awe-inspiring tales, stories of struggle, perseverance, near extinction, warfare, conflict and survival against all odds. In contrast,

Haraway has asked: "How do you get a good story out of genetic drift?" (1989:322), although in recent years some very good stories have been constructed out of genetics (see Harpending, Sherry, Rogers and Stoneking 1993). Consider, for example, how mitochondrial DNA sequences are used to support an *Out of Africa* or "strong Garden of Eden" hypothesis of the origins of anatomically modern humans. Such stories are judged as "good" based largely on their ability to satisfy certain cultural expectations. One expectation is that nature and culture are very separate categories and so an important task of any origins narrative is to provide a good "Just So" story to explain how the latter freed our species from the tyranny of the former. A second and somewhat conflicting expectation is that origins stories satisfy our curiosity about "natural" conditions of existence for the human species, especially as these touch on gender roles, family structure, territoriality and violence. Such preoccupations are the driving force behind dollars spent on origins research; origins questions basically reduce down to long-standing twin preoccupations with progress versus the good (read "natural") life.

It might come as a surprise to many people that paleoanthropology is focused more on where the human species is going than on where it has been. Progress is the subplot of all evolutionary discourse that aims us towards the future, as Stephen Jay Gould repeatedly reminds us. Research into human origins is the intellectual exercise of seeking that point in the past which was the start of something that ultimately belongs in the present/future. This exercise is highly visible in the reconstructive illustrations, where a ubiquitous subvoca is predicated on the present and the future. Primitive is defined *in oppositum* to the present and some future reference point is often the context under which viewers read the narrative in these images. Much of what fascinates us about the past is its ability to carry messages considered relevant for the future.

This forward-looking significance of the past is also one reason that Western academic discourse on evolution has proven so contentious. Two core issues have generated the most heat in the debate: classification and the postulated processes of biological change, especially with human evolution. Both of these relate to the degree of separation humans feel that they enjoy from nature and to the crucial designation of humans as something more than animals—not only with respect to the future of our species, but also to the more individualistic concern of persistence after death. Westerners and non-Westerners alike seem to resist the idea that humans belong in a common category with other primates and that the process which ultimately resulted in modern humans (evolutionary changes in physiology and behaviour) is one to which we continue to be subject, along with all living organisms. People are often only willing to accept the applicability of evolution to the human species when evolutionary theory is made in the image of older Western theological and philosophical beliefs.

For example, the modern system of taxonomic classification inherently rests on one of the oldest Occidental conceptions of the "constitutive pattern of the universe," the Great Chain of Being. This presupposition of the larger scheme of things which was dominant in Linnaeus's day, argues that all existing things are linked together in a great chain, connecting the base minerals to the higher organisms, to man and ultimately, beyond to the heavenly hosts (Lovejoy 1936). This is the deep logic behind the panoramic landscape illustrations so important to the history of cartography, geology, paleontology and paleoanthropology. In the time of Linnaeus, this Great Chain of Being was viewed as inherently good, logical and subject to rational analysis, but also as very rigid *and as very hierarchical.* Implicit in the model is the dominance of the upper levels over the lower which allows for that crucial separation of humans from other biological entities despite their commonalities. Along with other eighteenth-century scientists, Linnaeus accepted the three basic principles of the Chain of Being: plenitude (the world was full of a wonderful diversity of things), continuity (these things were all linked together from the least to the greatest) and gradation (there were no gaps in the resulting chain). Subsequently, the Linnaeus system of biological classification was correspondingly linear, rigid, static and hierarchical. It was only at the end of the eighteenth century that the lack of temporality in the Linnaeus system began to be criticized by Voltaire, Johnson and others (ibid.:252-54). By Darwin's time, all three basic principles were under attack. However, the hierarchy inherent in the model has been resilient and today there remain significant echoes of the Great Chain of Being in contemporary evolutionary theory.

For many biologists and anthropologists, the issues of biological change, species development and extinction, and the processes whereby these take place remain inextricably tangled with older ideas of a divinely ordered, upward progression to the history of things (Gould 1974c). Evolution has a direction, and adaptation, together with survival of the fittest, creates a mosaic of life with no distinct gaps. These ideas are ingrained into the fabric of evolutionary theory, which is not surprising since Darwin himself was only partially successful in rejecting them. More than one commentator has noted the correlation between Darwinian evolution and the dominant political and economic ideals of Darwin's day, with their emphasis on individualism and maximization (see Gould 1989:240-91, Levins and Lewontin 1985:1-106; Tanner 1981:5). Darwin especially tended to fall back into conventionality when considering human evolution.

As a consequence, notions about biological change have remained inextricably linked with those of social change, progress and history. This is true no matter how far back we go into the history of evolutionary theory (Ingold 1986). The term "evolution" has held different, if oddly related meanings since the seventeenth century. The Latin *evolvere* means to roll out or unfold something, and the sense of trajectory with its impression of a speed and direction that are implacable are still components of our use of the term. At one point in time, the term evolution was used to refer to the central concept of the theory of preformation in embryology, where every embryo was thought to unfold from a tiny image of itself present in the egg or sperm. Contained within this use is the notion of a predetermined direction to changes which are unfolding according to plan. At yet another time, evolution referred to the idea of a progressive development towards an enlightened future–from homogeneity to heterogeneity. Given these overtones of "an abstract ideal of progress defined by structural complexity," Darwin hesitated to apply the term "evolution" to his notion of "descent with modification" (Gould 1974a:22). Spencer's popularization of the term, however, assured its continued use in ways that did not explicitly acknowledge this accretion of old and new meanings, many of which coexist on uneasy terms with each other.

Several examples from stories of human evolution serve to illustrate this tension. The first example involves the principle of natural selection, which is stuck in the layperson's mind to "survival of the fittest." The glue that binds them seems insoluble. Differential reproduction inevitably becomes merged with a competitive struggle in which there can only be, "tooth and claw" permitting, one survivor. And that survivor, a priori, must be more advanced in the general scheme of things, a direct descendent, by necessity, of the last best-adapted form, who survived by tooth and claw in its day. The ladder of progress imagery as seen in Figure 5 is a direct result of this reasoning and it appears to be very difficult to eliminate or even to limit the notion of a bitter struggle for survival over the history of human evolution; thus, Leakey and Lewin's difficulty in changing their basic origins narrative.

Human origins studies have been able to retain this theoretical conservatism only by systematically ignoring many new developments in evolutionary theory. Paleoanthropologists persist in viewing human evolution as a process whereby a parental stock is transformed over time into something different and progressively better: *Australopithecus* into *Homo erectus* into Archaic man into Modern man. This linear view has fuelled many bitter disputes between paleoanthropologists as to whether or not their specific fossil find represents a direct human ancestor (Lewin 1987); such arguments are basically about whether select fossils are "on the ladder." But this ladder imagery is sadly out of date with a paleontology leaning toward "allopatric" speciation, or the process of rapid, repeated episodes of species change "on the boundaries" of the parental stock range (Gould 1976). In this model, the bush becomes a better metaphor than the ladder, as parental stocks often persist alongside the sometimes very numerous, newer offshoots. The bush model suggests that we should find many different varieties of hominids occupying the African savanna between five and two million years ago, and this is exactly the state of affairs suggested by the fossils. But many paleoanthropologists remain determined to reduce this rich fossil record to simplistic, gender-significant stories (see Johanson 1985 and the critique in Zihlman 1985).

Darwin battled with himself over this tendency to make conservative stories out of evolution. But in the long run, either he was not immune to treating humans as distinct biological entities and thus subject to different rules, or he was astute enough to recognize the high cost to his professional career of flying in the face of every cherished Victorian notion about gender, "race" and progress. Thus, while he emphasized that local adjustment was the most radical aspect of his theory of natural selection, he always downplayed it in human evolution, which he represented as a process of generalized upward progress (Gould 1989). Darwin appeared to endorse the racist Victorian notion that various extant "races" and cultures represented "different stages in the progress of mankind" (Stocking 1968:114). He also had trouble reconciling his theories of sexual reproduction with his notions about human nature, particularly gender roles and attributes. He acknowledged the female role in mate selection in most species but rejected it for humans (see Zihlman 1981:77-78), a position that remains convincing for many today. Primatologists (and one suspects many social anthropologists) often view female subjects as objects, as "passive resources like peanuts or water" (Fedigan quoted in Haraway 1989:323) which are subject to manipulation in male games of power and status.

This Darwinian separation of humankind from the rest of the biological universe sometimes takes the form of omitting selected aspects of his model. For example, "descent with modification" has never been an important organizing principle in paleoanthropology. In Darwin's theory, speciation proceeds from a process of natural selection against a field of phenotypical variation. Variation in the phenotype–the actual anatomy and physiology of an individual–is a product of various forces at work on the genotype–the hereditary factors that make the main contribution to physical form. Those forces include mutation, random genetic drift, and recombination. Ever since Lamarck's ideas were rejected, it has been assumed that phenotypical adaptation, or adaptive biological change which takes place during an individual's lifetime and which is made possible through biological plasticity, is insufficient to produce the variation necessary for speciation. Nevertheless, paleoanthropological explanations of adaptive changes in the human species rarely refer to the processes necessary to produce the expanded field from which specific form(s) survived, nor do they seem able to give good explanations of the selective adaptive pressures which would have created the patterns of survival we see in the fossil record. As the entire hominid fossil record is interpreted as one long drive towards humanity, the essential Darwinian concept of "variability of forms" is obscured by a narrower view of adaptationism. For comparison, imagine an environmental history of the *Equus* family tree written by a race horse. The argument might then be that this evolutionary history was one long drive to create speed and endurance, with the modern race horse at the peak of evolutionary perfection. Of course this conclusion would be one that a zebra might take exception to. Is it any different to imagine, as we routinely do, that the hominid history was one long drive to create intelligence and culture, with humans as the peak of evolutionary perfection?

Yet in sociobiology and paleoanthropology such "adaptation for cause," or the notion that need generates change, is a pervasive and

well-accepted idea (see Sperling 1991). Mandelbaum calls this "the retrospective fallacy" which is "to view earlier events as though they were
controlled by their subsequent outcomes" (cited in Ingold 1986:15).
This fallacy is not only a serious logical flaw, but also gives the history
of the hominids an inevitable character, a pervasive theme in illustrative
material. When students thumb through textbooks or popular articles
on human evolution, they see a ubiquitous progression of images from
"primitive" to "advanced" forms. And given the combined weight of
such illustration fields in many different disciplines, the biological drive
towards progress seems inevitable with no other scenario possible,
much less reasonable. While it is true that natural selection may be
"silent on the future" given that it proceeds on the basis of present conditions (Ingold 1986:15), it is also true that paleoanthropology and
social anthropology are continuously commenting on the future using
the adaptationist stories of the past. The progressive development of
some forms (*Homo sapiens,* white Western males) at the expense of less
fit forms (australopithecines, *Homo erectus,* Neandertals, non-white, non-
Westerners, females) is viewed as inevitable given that the former are
considered superior and in many cases have outperformed their competition. The assumption is that having come this far, *Homo sapiens* (read
white males) will continue to meet new adaptation challenges.

In addition, adaptationism is politically expedient since the model
not only explains success, but also has the potential for explaining, and
even more importantly, for predicting failure. The idea of progress
"involves a synthesis of the past and a prophecy for the future" (Bury
cited in Ingold 1986:15). Culture and nature are opposite faces of the
single wheel upon which these options turn for the human species. The
prognosis for Western technological man is flexible; the same synthesis
of the past may be interpreted either more or less optimistically
(ibid.:16). Sometimes culture will be the solution to future adaptation
problems as it was in the past and sometimes nature needs to be
"returned to" for the species to survive. In either case, pessimists and
optimists are looking to a future they want to comment on today by
seeking patterns in the past that they can project forward through time.

Reading humanity's future is easy in the "boundary sciences"
(Haraway 1988); here culture and nature meet and clash in the exploration
of the human animal. Taking those first steps out of nature in order to
progress into culture are treated as the most important watershed in

human evolutionary history, and a not unimportant corollary of this approach is that the academic career of any individual is assured if they can discover the "origin" of something, especially if this discovery pushes the date into the deeper past. Conkey (1991) discusses the "political economy" of origins research:

> Among the most favoured research problems are those that implicitly or explicitly address "origins": from the origins of hominids to the origins of the state; the origins of agriculture, of ranking, trade, status, fire, art, toolmaking, hunting, the family, gender asymmetry, language, consciousness, symbolism, pottery and so forth (ibid.:104).

The political capital inherent in origins research is tied to the notion that older things (traits, attributes, characteristics) are more natural, and thus immutable, while newer things are less natural and thus easier to change (ibid., see also Haraway 1989:328). Various traits, attributes and behaviours can be moved further back in time, to naturalize them, or closer to us in time in order to make them unnatural. Bipedalism, brain reorganization, masculine tools and technology, and the mastery of fire have all been pushed backwards in time while gendered divisions of labour and fully symbolic behaviours such as language, art and religion move forward or backward depending on alignment with the theoretical politics of paleoanthropology (Conkey 1991:108-11). In both cases, however, previous hominid forms are consistently read as significant markers of our more natural selves before we became hedged in by cultural constraints.

The question of nature versus culture in human evolution is a significant logical problem. How do we reconcile our pride in ourselves as the only culture-bearing animal with our contrary conviction that straying too far from "natural human conditions" may ultimately be harmful? Or to ask another question, how do we reconcile Darwin's model of evolution with our belief in the "rise of culture" as a new and significant force for evolutionary change unique to the human species? Either human culture is something new and unprecedented in evolutionary history, or it is simply an expansion of a natural biological process. In the latter scenario, distinguishing humans from animals becomes simply a matter of degree. We are not *the* culture-bearing animal, but rather *a* culture-bearing animal, with more culture than most. We are not the only conscious, rational animal, but simply the one with the biggest brain (Wills 1993). The latter option is the one Gould (1975a) has argued for. According to him, there is evidence for a steady and general increase in brain size in the mammal record and we have shared in that general increase. What sets us apart is our predator status. We are caught in an evolutionary feedback loop: every time our prey gets smarter, we must also get smarter to continue to catch them. Since humans have a predator relationship with many animals, we have developed a greater than average intelligence. However, as an explanation for encephalization this has one obvious flaw; there is good evidence that the primates (including the hominids) have been preyed upon in turn by leopards and other large carnivores. How "loopy" might this evolutionary process of encephalization be?

Our fascination with this nature/culture conundrum lies in its ability to structure inquiry in ways that serve as a vehicle for political/moral messages. But the structuring of inquiry in this way has its consequences; for example, origins research relies on what Conkey has called the "guarantee of continuity," where we use "the same analytical categories for phenomena that are millions of years and maybe six biological species apart," categories that include social groups, aggression, male cooperation, division of labour, monogamous family units and pair bonding (Conkey 1991:105). The result is that "Origins research has inherited key constructions of the meaning of gender that it perpetuates through its authorial weight" (ibid.:102). It has been obvious since the Scopes trial that human evolution is less about the fossil remains found scattered over the landscape in East Africa than it is about contested aspects of our modern-day lives. Thus it should be no surprise that there is considerable effort expended on controlling the interpretations that can be put on those fossil remains, limiting the damage done by critiques of the resulting logical flaws, and forcing politically expedient conclusions out of origins research.

The Struggle to Control Knowledge in the Evolutionary Field

The origin of the universe, of life, of the dinosaurs, of the mammals and of speciation are issues closely followed in the popular media. One example is the enormous interest shown in the recent revisions to major theories surrounding the biological nature of dinosaurs (were they cold-blooded or warm-blooded?), their way of life (were they social animals that formed herds, did they sometimes nurture their young?) and most importantly, the causes of their ultimate "disappearance" (and could it happen to us?). Another example is the success of "popularizing" science authors such as Stephen Jay Gould, who lectures on biology, geology and the history of science at Harvard University. Gould regularly publishes in a number of mass media educational magazines such as *Natural History*. Many of his essays have been collected in book form (1980, 1984, 1985). In addition, he has published several popular books on related topics (1977, 1981, 1989). Many of these books have been national best sellers, despite the fact that they usually have the rather weighty subject of paleontology as their subject matter.

Paleontology studies ancient forms of life or fossil organisms and topics such as the explosion of life forms in the Cambrian period and the lack of Precambrian ancestral forms that could have given rise to it are hardly the sort of stuff that one would expect to attract so much public attention. And yet, Gould has a way of touching a nerve with his accounts of such scientific practice, perhaps because he is not above narrating these accounts in a rather colourful fashion (see Gould 1974a, 1974b, 1974c). One reason for his popularity is that he challenges widespread values which are reflected in dominant models of the history of life on earth. These models reinforce the relevance of such values to the future of the human species, and in challenging them Gould generates a great deal of media attention. He is not alone in holding up the supposed impartial wisdom of biological theories to closer scrutiny, nor in developing new models for the past/future which, while not having the comfortable ring of familiarity, nevertheless offer exciting possibilities resonating with chaos theory and historical contingency. But he is unique in the level of popular media support that he has garnered over the years.

An interesting aspect of the very public evolutionary skirmishes of which Gould is part is that these skirmishes are highly visual as well as verbal. Gould recognizes the power of visual material in the media and often uses it himself to contest knowledge production in evolutionary discourse. For example, in a recent article, he (1994:91) comments on the "classical representations of life's history" which is usually shown through a series of "incident panels." The particular set of panels he uses as an example were those painted by Charles R. Knight for *National Geographic*. As was discussed in chapter 3, the first Knight panel shows invertebrates of the Burgess Shale, the second shows the evolution of fish, the third brings dinosaurs onto the stage (in this case two *Tyrannosaurus rex* shown fighting), the third panel introduces the rise of land invertebrates, and the final panel shows prehistoric humans. Each of these panels resonates to survival of the fittest, to struggles and tests and to overcoming obstacles. One reason that Gould challenges such views of evolution is because they have some very bizarre consequences in terms of logic (see also Conkey 1991). Paleontological illustrations provide a map of evolution contestation which is easily transferable to the field of paleoanthropology.

Incident panels, for example, are not the only means of telling a highly political story. Consider the charts which are often developed to illustrate discussions of particular "family trees"; as Gould notes, we often see a phylogenic group that is becoming increasingly narrow over time represented as the most successful, upward-reaching branches in a dendritic model. He calls this representation "life's little joke" and comments:

> we are virtually compelled to the stunning mistake of citing unsuccessful lineages as classic "textbook cases" of "evolution." We do this because we try to extract a single line of advance from the true topology of copious branching. In this misguided effort, we are inevitably drawn to bushes so near the brink of total annihilation that they retain only one surviving twig. We then view this twig as the acme of upward achievement, rather than the probable last gasp of a richer ancestry (1989:35).

Fighting battles for control of the wider public mind usually relies on constructing images which burn into the mind and tunnel there, to do the shock troop work of the propagandist while the text does the verbal work of establishing the scientific authority for what are essentially folk views of the universe.

Consider, for example, the difference between the representation of the history of life as a "cone of increasing diversity" and Gould's reworked imagery of the "bush" (see Gould 1989:46). On the surface, there is very little difference between them. The ubiquitous icon for progress-driven models of evolution is a dendrogram, a branching image rather like the mouth of a river or the branches of a tree, as in Figure 4 which I developed for this book from a number of textbook examples.[1] The branching arms of the model depend on a few sturdy

---

1   There are many examples in Gould (1989:264, 265, 266) as well as in introductory anthropology textbooks (Campbell 1982:152-53; Campbell and Loy 1996:188; Haviland 1994:71, 90), and in the media such as the *Washington Post.* (Rensberger 1994: A23).

incoming lines from which they deviate, earlier or later. In this case, a Miocene fluorescence of primate species gradually evolves into the modern-day diversity. But Gould argues that evidence from the total history of biological life falsifies any such notion of evolution as a continuous process of increasing diversification. The biomass present today is not the culmination of a process of continually building on what came before. Instead, while biological life on earth often experiments with more complex forms, these are continually being heavily pruned, leaving the less complex forms to dominate in terms of total biomass (see his illustration, 1994:86).

Furthermore, the heavy decimation of the more complex forms does not often occur as a result of an apparent failure to adapt, but more often for being in the wrong place at the right time, so that if a dendritic model were to be used to represent this, the resulting image would look more like a badly pruned bush than a beautifully swelling tree (Gould 1989:46). The Burgess Shale suggests that evolution has often proceeded by the equivalent of big bangs, followed by massive decimations. Survival in this scenario is not the slow and inevitable unfolding of some inherent superiority, but instead approximates the chance-generated results of a "crap shoot" (ibid.:208. For a critique see D. Briggs, R. Fortey and M. Wills 1992). But if one chooses to illustrate only those branching developments of a highly selective period of evolutionary history, and further, misrepresent the modern end of the scale as more diverse than it is while underrepresenting the diversity of the bottom of the scale, the history of life can look like a cone of increasing diversity. In the Campbell and Loy (1996:188) dendrogram, for example, *Australopithecus* is shown as the ancestor of the *Homo* line, but the australopithecines are represented by only two branches, one of which becomes extinct—a gross underrepresentation of the number of australopithecine species that have been documented. The *Homo* line, meanwhile, flourishes and persists into the present time with six extant branches reaching the category "human" (see also Figure 4). Do they mean to suggest that today there are six existing species of *Homo sapiens*? Or, more insidiously, do they assume that there are "races" of mankind extant today, which occupy different "branches" of the *Homo* family tree? The text under the illustrations says not. It explains the number of branches reaching into the present by the following: "The multiplicity of lines indicates that any evolving lineage contains an unknown number of divergent populations that may or may not be different species" (ibid.:188). However, contrast this with the phylogenic compression at the bottom of the chart where an entire family or genus are represented by a single branch of the tree. These kinds of images are illusion, not a fact of nature.

And yet, the progress model has so many proponents in anthropology, and the "truths" it illuminates seem so self evident, that most people in the field are only dimly aware that the evidence can be interpreted in any other way. This view is often reinforced by the other social sciences, notably economics, where progress and technological innovation are in a causal relationship that is both natural and obvious (see also Conkey 1991:122). Such ontological "facts" are often supported using an epistemological authority borrowed from the biological sciences; an example is Ingold's book on evolution and social life which contains its own visual representations of progress through evolution (1986:21). Ingold notes that it is hard to argue against the apparent evidence for a general pattern of increasing structural complexity in the evolution of animal life; and demonstrates this with a grid image which has three dimensions representing time, structural divergence and levels of general progress. Within the box formed by these dimensions, protozoa are represented as coming forward through time with no structural divergence and a flat level of general progress. In contrast, humans are found at the highest corner of the box, as the culmination of a general upward trend over time, representing increasing structural divergence and the highest level of general progress. These are the sorts of images Gould has tried to counter with his own iconographic representations which show the greater statistical significance of the "structurally simplistic" species in the total amount of extant biomass; structural divergence is definitely the minority case in his representation, suggesting that it can hardly be represented as the highest example of evolutionary development.

Gould is equally critical of the paleoanthropological iconography of human evolution, as when he challenges the ladder of human evolution illustration, calling it the "ladder of predictable progress." Figure 5, in which a linear pedigree is established for a modern form, reflects what Gould calls an "absurd bias" wherein are represented "incarnations of concepts masquerading as neutral descriptions of nature" (1989:28). Gould possesses a wit that is acerbic, and like many feminists, he uses this sense of humour to destabilize the logically flawed evolution story field.

The Progress Convention and Paleoanthropological Conservatism

But how influential has this destabilization been? The illustrative material being produced and/or used in paleoanthropological publications still shows the "progress of man" through key devices such as the development of meat-eating and hunting (which in turn are said to rely on cooperative units such as nuclear families and all-male hunting groups), followed by improved technologies of pursuit and processing of game (weapons, fire, butchering), followed by the development of clothing, shelter and lifestyle "improvements" (ritual, art and other cultural attainments). These developments are represented as stages in the rise of culture, where the hominid line goes from "of nature, not in nature" to "in nature, not of nature." Such illustrations perpetuate the progress convention, however much we may struggle to rewrite the theoretical models.

The ladder-based iconographies of human progress (Figure 5), with their series of male figures striding along from the *left* side of the page (no accident that) to the *right* side, are full of insidious progress messages which rely on several standard devices. In the Jay Matternes example in *National Geographic* (Weaver 1985:574), the stride "speeds up" the action just at the point when the species *Homo* is first represented (mid-frame). Compared to the rather unenergetic gait of the australopithecines which come before it, *Homo habilis* is represented with an exaggerated forward momentum carried through to *Homo sapiens sapiens*. This is a family tree that is going somewhere! In addition, arms go from open-handed and relaxed posture among the figures at the left of the frame (more primitive), to stiffened and purposeful muscularity with closed fists to the right of the frame (more advanced). At each subsequent stage, these fists get held higher, closer to the head as the seat of intellect, while the head itself is elevated on a more erect frame.

Other progress devices are also ubiquitous. In Rudy Zallinger's (Howell 1965:41-45) masculine lineup, rudimentary technology (a sharply pointed stone) is first portrayed in the hand of *Australopithecus*. The "early form" of *Australopithecus* has a suitably thoughtful expression on his face, while the later *Paranthropus* looks rather "dopey," as befits an evolutionary backwater. The "advanced *Australopithecus*" to the right of *Paranthropus,* once again looks thoughtful and carries a primitive club. Thus the *Paranthropus* is bracketed as an evolutionary backwater, a poor distaff relative rather than a direct ancestor. *Homo erectus,* early

Homo sapiens and Solo Man all carry stone tools, while only Cro-Magnon Man has a fully fashioned spear over his shoulder. Thus the presence of (masculine) tools, in addition to stance, facial expression, lack of body hair, colour of skin and hair and beard styles are all used to suggested organizational and cognitive complexity that have increased and refined over time. These visual devices also make a very clear statement about "race" and gender, linking technology to the white male of the species. In this iconographic view, females, other "races," juveniles, and even the criminally insane are evolutionary backwaters whose most useful characteristics are as a measuring stick of the comparative achievements of Caucasian mankind.

When we turn to anecdotal images, the visual devices by which messages about progress and evolution are embedded show many continuities with the ladder imagery. In the australopithecine material, male figures usually hold a weapon—symbol not only of technological skill and of masculine roles, but also of the pivotal nature/culture transition moment of adopting technology-based responses to environmental threats. Here illustrators often borrow from a primatology discourse about rudimentary tool use among primates; use of tools (particularly unmodified tools) is a pattern of behaviour which is not exclusive to humans. This allows illustrators to use the unmodified tool (perhaps a branch or crude rock) to signal an early point in the development of technology, while successively more sophisticated tools indicate progressive stages in the masculine dominance of nature. The ineffective nature of most such "primitive" weapons at the same time allows the self-consciously modern viewer to feel superior. Even at this primitive stage, however, the male usually shows a fully developed sense of his responsibilities and plays the protective/provisioning role written for him in the evolutionary narrative.

The deep past is not only technologically backward, but physiologically backward as well. Hairiness is often a component of creating grotesque images through "the reversal of an expected and pleasing appearance to produce a disturbing image" (Miles 1989:159) of bestiality. We have no physical evidence that the australopithecines had more hairy-looking bodies than we do, indeed, given the current arguments about bipedality, changing behaviour and heat dissipation requirements, it is hard to argue for both a hairy and a bipedal australopithecine, but the convention is very useful as a means of assigning them to their proper place lower on the evolutionary ladder. Nudity and Negroid features have recently replaced hairiness, barrel-chests, and apelike morphology as conventions of primordial beginnings (see chapter 5), but in all such conventions, the message is essentially dualistic; the primitive condition is also one that is free from cultural constraint. Self-satisfaction and a nostalgic yearning for "the simpler life" are present in equal measure in such illustrations.

Thus, illustrations of the australopithecines play on several cognitive borders, between culture and nature, between past and future, between inferior and superior. And in this border zone, another artistic convention, which I call the "Garden of Eden" convention, is useful (see Edey 1972:22-23). It has roots in medieval and Renaissance religious imagery (Clark 1956:52) and has been popular in introductory anthropology textbooks (see Howell 1965:18-19, Campbell 1982:38). In these illustrations, hominids are shown in close proximity to wild animals, who demonstrate no fear of them. The setting is natural and often lush. Lutz and Collins (1994:109-10) talk of this same "halo of green" in *National Geographic* images of non-Western peoples, which are naturalized by exotic locations full of wild flora and fauna that seem to "evoke in readers the nostalgia for an imagined condition of humanity before the industrial revolution and environmental degradation broke the link between humans and nature." The emphasis of the wider frame in such images is usually on landscape and all the figures are placed low or are peripheral. This convention is used to raise the image of natural, primordial innocence or *nuditas virtualis*. As Haraway (1989) has commented, the scientific explanation of human origins still resonates to Biblical mythology, specifically to the expulsion from the Garden of Eden. Paradoxically, while Eden was a safe and secure home, there was no real human progress until we left it; human evolution illustration makes full use of the tensions within this contradiction.

The Jay Matternes "fleeing the volcano" image, where two sets of proto-hominid footprints were shown being left in volcanic ash, is a good example of this Eden convention although the landscape is certainly not lush and green. Nevertheless, many animals are shown travelling across the volcanic ash without concern for the proto-hominids among them, with the exception, perhaps of one jackrabbit running across the path of the male. These individuals are clearly "of nature" rather than "in nature," although if Haraway's reading of this illustration is correct, all of that is about to change. Does the volcano symbolize the expulsion from Eden? What has caused the fall from grace and paradoxically the rise of culture? While Adam and Eve were ejected from Eden for tasting the flesh of the apple of knowledge, the story operator in human evolution places a greater emphasis on flesh than on fruit. In paleoanthropology, the central narrative theme is meat-eating, the ubiquitous stimulus for the "progress of man," whether supply is attributed to scavenging or hunting. The first species to progress beyond the limits of the *natural* primate lifestyle, did so by eating meat. It is probably no accident that most student observers of this volcano image defined the stick in the male's hand as a "club" with all its implications of the hunt.

While a hint of culture is not out of place in the australopithecine imagery, as with the monogamous pair and nuclear family suggested by the arrangement of the couple and child in the Matternes volcano image, the first firm evidence for cultural developments is usually reserved for illustrations of *Homo erectus*. In representing the early members of the genus *Homo*, nature remains dominant but culture begins to emerge in trope-like devices. Zdeněk Burian's early example of the representation of *Homo erectus* is seen in Figure 6. A slightly hairy, central male figure has overly long arms, which denotes primitiveness. However, this male figure carries weapons and/or tools (stick and stone) and stares about him alertly and without fear or nervousness. His place in nature seems less "natural," and the activities of his male companions underscore their increasing ability to travel unmolested across the landscape. The female in the image, in contrast, remains almost invisible, identifiable only because she carries an infant on her back. Maurice Wilson's example of *Homo erectus* appears in Figure 7. In this "freeze-frame," the lone female confronts the two males across a hearth, an explicitly domesticated space. Using grotesque conventions, the female's masculine midriff contrasts with feminine breasts, the aggressive jawline contrasts with the feminine eyes, the overall impression is one of grotesque, primordial femininity. In contrast, the males look very modern and with their activities of flintknapping and hunting, manage to suggest cultural accomplishments. The three figures, together with their environmental context imply that nature and culture are frozen at a point of equilibrium, half animal-half human. Taken together, the cultural symbols of hunt, hearth and home in the scene are contradicted by a grotesque nudity on the part of the female, which has little sexiness attached to it. As Miles

(1989:150-51) points out, the representation of the female gender is the most enduring "grotesque other" by which reasoned, moral and advanced [male] society is to be defined. The illustrator is thus able to convey nature and primitiveness with a jarring suggestion of culture, or perhaps home and hearth with a jarring suggestion of nature. The Stanley Meltzoff *Homo erectus* illustrations found in Howell (1965:90-99), employ similar conventions of grotesqueness including hairiness, elongated fingers and limbs, foreshortened faces, low brows, wide mouths and slicked-back hair. But here, as with the Burian images, *Homo erectus* pursues game, cooks meat over fires and takes part in cultural activities such as ritualized recreations of the hunt.

Thus, illustrations of *Homo erectus* use various visual devices to represent "turning a corner." This species radiated outwards geographically and was found in Asia, Europe and Africa. There is evidence it controlled fire, and perhaps made and used clothing and rough shelters. Once the greater antiquity of bipedality and tool use was established by the East African australopithecine finds, illustrators began to increase the cultural markers associated with *Homo erectus*, modernizing their physiology and cultural accomplishment. One of the changes in their representation, then, has been in that fluid balance of progress with primitiveness. And progress here is especially linked with the rise of consciousness and moral enlightenment so necessary to culture and so admired during the eighteenth century in the concept of the Great Chain of Being (Lovejoy 1936:183). Here, too, is the associated notion that nature is in place primarily to serve man's interests, not by having a separate existence, but by being so intimately bound up with man in the Great Chain of Being, that if man were to cease to exist, "the rest would seem to be all astray, without aim or purpose" (Bacon cited in Lovejoy 1936:187). The use of the gender-specific term in this philosophy is no accident; womankind, as with the rest of nature, would also be lost without man to anchor her existence.

This conception of the universe and man's place in it has the rich symbolic potential for more than one interpretation. As Lovejoy notes, the infinite gradations of creatures, with no gap between them, was considered to extend as far or farther above man (towards the infinitely perfect maker) as it did below him. Man was the "middle link" in that he was at the point of transition "from the merely sentient to the intellectual forms of being"; as the lowest of the angels he was infinitely above the baser creatures, but also infinitely below the heavenly hosts (ibid.:190). The rich imagery of the Great Chain of Being, with its simultaneous flattering and humbling view of "mankind's" place, finds a new expression in the notions of human evolutionary process. This process inevitably places each stage at a significant transition point on the long road from animal to human; each stage is thus a point in the balancing act between being natural and becoming cultural. And each such transition suggests a pattern for future ones, a pattern easily extrapolated into our future.

This point of transition between nature and culture is a major problem when illustrators address the topic of the Neandertals, particularly in older illustrations. In Zdeněk Burian's illustration of a Neandertal community portrayed "at the beginning of the rhinoceros hunt" (Figure 8), the dominant male figure which centres the illustration, as well as the other figures portrayed, are constructed using the conventions of grotesqueness. There is a suggestion of knuckle-walking by the male in the lower left corner and a bent-kneed stance for several others. The central male has a monstrous ear outlined by the shading of his hair, and most figures have a suggestion of a split between their big and remaining toes. Such illustrations have long emphasized the robustness of the Neandertal, and the use of caricature in the treatment of their physique is common (see Figure 10). Everything about them is a little too large including the head, the limbs, and the musculature, which together with the hairiness, semi-nudity and lack of neck, place them firmly in a primitive category. If caricature exposes a "social consensus on what is to be avoided," what is it about the Neandertals that must be avoided? The Neandertal as a species has long presented physical anthropologists with a number of conundrums for the nature/culture divide, many of which remain unresolved despite decades of debate (Rensberger 1981).

Like *Homo erectus*, the Neandertal has gone through a significant revision in recent decades as a result of the new antiquity of the earliest members of the australopithecines. With dates for the australopithecines approaching four or five million years ago, the dates for *Homo erectus* and Neandertal seem very modern by comparison. This has affected the interpretation of their evolutionary place as well as their visual representation (see Stringer and Gamble 1993:17-24). Initially, the great robustness of the Neandertal skeletal remains were thought to prove them a primitive, evolutionary side-shoot of the hominid family. Their fate was to suffer extinction at the hands of the better-adapted anatomically modern humans. Later the Neandertals were thought to have intermingled with in-migrating modern humans such that their genes were submerged in a genetic sea of *Homo sapiens sapiens* (for a survey of changing perceptions of the Neandertal, see Constable 1973, Rensberger 1981, Shipman and Trinkaus 1995, Stringer and Gamble 1993, and Trinkaus 1989). In either case, the Neandertals have offered several scientific enigmas. For example, most introductory textbooks focus on the fact that the steady increase in brain size from the earliest primates until modern human is somewhat disrupted at the Neandertal stage. Some Neandertal finds have suggested a larger overall brain size than fully modern humans, with a range from 1270 to 1640 cubic centimetres (cc), versus 1350 cc on average for modern humans (for comparable discussions of brain size see Stringer and Gamble 1993:82; Haviland 1994:189; Poirier, Stini and Wreden 1994:432,434). Since increases in brain size are linked with increasing capacities for planning, foresight, rational thought, morality and sophisticated culture, this presents us with the problem of whether or not the Neandertal may have been more "well endowed" with these attributes than we are (Constable 1973:52). This problem of Neandertal brain size has been addressed in a number of ways.

For example, it has been argued that the Neandertal brain, while large, is not big in the right places, particularly in the all-important frontal region and thus it probably did not correspond to increased intelligence (see Stringer and Gamble 1993:82). Another argument is that while the brain size is larger, the increase over modern humans is relatively small and can be accounted for by the small sample size of Neandertal fossils, perhaps preselected for archaeological survival by a more robust character than normal for their species. The most recent and popular explanation links the fact that brain size correlates with body mass and the Neandertal were significantly more robust than the modern human (see Stringer and Gamble 1993:82; Poirier, Stini and Wreden 1994:434-35). Still, there is no doubt that the Neandertal figures, even based as they are on an extremely small sample, seem to interfere with a nice progression model of brain advancement.

This larger brain size is also troubling given evidence for a prolonged cultural stability that in turn can be interpreted in either a negative or a positive way. Lack of change can be viewed as static and a consequence of lack of intelligence, or in today's ecologically troubled world, it can be viewed as demonstrating significant adaptive superiority over modern humans who are so rapidly destroying their own habitat. The troubling larger Neandertal brain is linked in some thinking to their particular (some would say peculiar) cultural stability. The Mousterian-like tool assemblage tradition, for example, dates from 166,000 years ago to 40,000 years ago (Haviland 1994:190). Thus, over a time period of roughly 120,000 years, the Neandertal coped with their often dramatically changing environment in a remarkably conservative way. There is no apparent reason for that tradition to have disappeared in favour of the relatively unstable cultures of the anatomically modern humans. If cultural persistence is an indication of successful adaptation, the Neandertal record will not be broken by any modern human population for another eighty thousand years. Of course, as a problem in the progression model of human evolution, even this achievement pales in comparison to the australopithecines, who persisted for upwards of a million years without significant physiological or cultural change. What is better, persistence or change? Given the progress-driven models of human evolution, australopithecines and Neandertals are generally seen as evolutionary losers, unless they can be demonstrated to have changed into us. The third enigma the Neandertals present, their relatively rapid disappearance, lies at the core of this survival-by-evolution question.

And so, are Neandertals directly ancestral to modern humans or aren't they? Given that coeval populations of archaic *Homo sapiens* populations which existed in Asia and Africa never attained the robustness in limb bones and facial features of the European Neandertals, some speculate that archaic *Homo sapiens* in other parts of the world evolved simultaneously into modern humans.[2] These then migrated into Europe and after a brief period of co-existence and perhaps even some interbreeding, replaced the Neandertals by 33,000 years ago, the "hybridization hypothesis." In this scenario, while the Neandertals had certain strengths,

---

2 The various theories regarding the replacement of the Neandertal by anatomically modern humans are numerous and more complex than I can do justice to in this setting. For a concise survey of the various proposals, see Wolpoff 1989. For a good history of the personalities, the theories and the politics surrounding the Neandertal, see Trinkaus and Shipman 1993. For a popular account, see Shreeve 1995.

including the ability to imitate the stone tool technology of in-migrating modern humans, their low level of innovation and their lack of understanding ultimately doomed them (see Stringer and Gamble 1993:201, 207). Or perhaps anatomically modern humans evolved only in one place, in Africa or Asia, and then swept away all remaining archaic forms as they expanded out of this home base, the "total replacement hypothesis" (Wolpoff 1989:101; Haviland 1994:196-97). In either case, the basic story line conforms to the success by conquest, hero mythology of the West. It is obvious that the closer phylogenic proximity of Neandertals, taken together with their different, more robust physiology and their cultural conservatism, make them anxiety-producing for us precisely because they challenge the notion of the Great Chain of Being which has been preserved in some essential characteristics in the progress model of human evolution. In many older illustrations, they are presented as caricatures and as grotesques, but whether that was because they inspired "awe" as male caricature should, or aversion, as female caricature should is uncertain.

Given the general overall progress theme in human evolution, however, cultural advancement conventions are usually found in increasing numbers in Neandertal illustrations, including more effective weaponry, males shown flintknapping, clothing made from furs and produced by females, a domestic space with hearth, ritualized activities including the special treatment of skulls, both human and cave bear, and the sort of family scenes shown in Figure 9. The Lovejoy hypothesis, which places the monogamous couple, the human family and the male provider as central to the evolution of the human species, is often reemphasized in such representation. The Neandertals' greater cultural achievements are masculine and technological in tone, while Neandertal females remain linked to and limited by their natural attributes and reproductive role. The progressive theme of the masculine rise of culture is further entrenched by illustrations which show Neandertal males, however hairy and brutish, burying their dead with tender care and ritual (Figure 10; but see also Constable 1973:99, 102-103).

When illustrators turn to *Homo sapiens sapiens*, cultural symbols are dominant in the construction of the narrative theme. In Figures 11 and 13, we see tents and shelters, domestic dogs, more sophisticated weaponry (knives, bow and arrow, spear), male and female ornamentation (necklaces, earrings), elaborate hairstyles, beards, clothing, belts and drinking vessels. Here, in sharp contrast to the Eden convention, these humans, while "in nature" are definitely not "of nature." There is a significant new theme of cognitive and intellectual development. Aside from the usual male technological (s)kill illustrations, new themes show anatomically modern humans engaged in "high culture," producing devotional objects (Figure 13), works of art, or involved in ritual activities, as with a group of men painting scenes (hunting magic?) on cave walls (Figure 14). Higher consciousness and even moral understanding is conveyed as a uniquely modern human development. Contrast these practices with the hypothesized cannibalism among Neandertals in Zdeněk Burian's illustration in Howell (1965:134). Culture is one thing, true progress is something else.

Exploring Conservatism in the Evolution Story Field

In illustrations covering the many different species including the australopithecines, *Homo erectus*, Neandertals and modern humans, progress themes invite us to congratulate ourselves on our ability to generate and participate in cultural development in order to be survivors in the "race to evolve." In both illustrations and in the paleoanthropological theories that generate them, such ideas are remarkably persistent, despite recent theoretical challenges to the adaptationist model. As an example of a blindness that seems almost deliberate, this conservatism in paleoanthropology can be matched by at least one experience in paleontology. Gould (1989) discusses the Burgess Shale to show how these geological formations presented the paleontological world with two different but related problems, neither of which were recognized as significant challenges to predominant theories of evolutionary history when the Burgess Shale was first discovered in 1909. Nor were these challenges recognized over the subsequent decades and this despite the fact that the Burgess Shale immediately attracted the attention and years of dedicated collection by one of America's foremost paleontologists, C.D. Walcott. The first problem is how did the incredible diversity of the life preserved in the Burgess Shale arise so rapidly and without apparent ancestors, and the second problem is, given the enormous decimation which followed, "what attributes of function, what environmental changes, set the pattern of who would win and who would lose?" (ibid.:227). Researchers have only recently begun to reexamine the Burgess Shale fossils in the more critical light shed by such questions.

Walcott's conservative approach to explaining the Burgess Shale fossils is relevant here, demonstrating as it does the conservatism of evolutionary theory, which also tends to be "fossil proof" (Pilbeam 1980:267). Walcott was able to ignore the Burgess Shale fossils, especially with respect to the lack of survivals among the Burgess Shale body plans, largely by retreating into adaptationism. He viewed the problem as yet another example of the "superior competitive ability" of those organisms that did manage to give rise to modern-day descendants (Gould 1989:234). This idea of survival for cause is both a consequence and a reinforcer of the progress model of evolution. But Gould argues that aside from suffering from the logical flaw of tautology (survival of the fittest becomes meaningless since fitness is defined as survival), this explanation can only be compelling if it can predict the survivors based on an analysis of form, physiology or behaviour (ibid.:236). However, no one working on the plethora of organic forms found in the Burgess Shale can offer good scientific reasons as to why the few survivors were in any way more fit to persevere than their less lucky neighbours (ibid.:239, see also Monastersky 1993).

It is more interesting, given the history of these specimens and Walcott's connection with them, that they failed to generate any debate until recently. The question is, why? An analogy with human evolutionary fossils is hard to imagine. When paleoanthropological discoveries are made, the discoverer has a certain period of time in which to publish interpretations of their significance. During this period, other researchers have been known to have difficulty in gaining access to fossils so that alternative hypotheses have been repressed (Lewin 1987). However, in the case of the Burgess Shale, the Walcott interpretation was not only conservative, but was uncritically accepted for many decades. Once Gould published his interpretations of the significance of the Burgess Shale fossils, debate did develop, but how is it that these fossils failed to give rise to any conflicting interpretations before then? Gould offers two explanations for this situation, one of which is mundane and one of which is theoretically significant. The first problem is that Walcott had onerous administrative duties which restricted the amount of time he could devote to lab work. The Burgess Shale are still yielding up a tremendous treasure trove of material and even Walcott's preliminary collections were enormous. He could not have carefully examined every fossil had he been totally unencumbered with administrative duties, which Gould assures us he was not.

Gould (1989:258), gives a second, more interesting explanation which is rooted in Walcott's scientific philosophy: "Walcott considered himself a Darwinian, expressing by this stated allegiance his strong conviction that natural selection assured the survival of superior organisms and the progressive improvement of life on a predictable pathway to consciousness." For scientists such as Walcott, this survival of the superior form and the subsequent improvement over the history of life was based on conquest and on a model of unstinting warfare between competitors which left a linear trail of evolutionary success. Such a view of evolution was deeply felt although inconsistent with Darwin's progress-free notions of natural selection (Gould 1974a, 1974c). Gould argues that even Darwin was never fully able to resolve this contradiction, consistent as the progress model was with the predominant political, economic and religious orientations of his day (1989:257; see also Ingold 1986:47-48). Darwin delayed publishing his theory of natural selection for twenty-one years, because the careers of some of his peers had been destroyed and papers were repressed by publishers when they propounded an "uncompromising philosophical materialism" (Gould 1974c:69). The social atmosphere which accepted some aspects of Darwinian theory but balked at others explains why Walcott was most comfortable in classifying the Burgess Shale fossils "with a shoehorn" so that they could fit into a conservative model of the cone of diversity. This compression of historically specific, wonderful diversity into a few "laws of nature" has obscured the data presented by the Burgess Shale just as effectively as the hero myth meta-narrative has constrained our interpretations of the hominid fossil records, and with as many implications for the logic of our reasoning.

Logical Flaws in Evolutionary Theories: Functionalism, Presentism, Essentialism and Universalism

Functionalism, presentism, essentialism and universalism are a set of logical flaws which have been generated in paleoanthropological thinking as a result of the progress convention. Feminist scholars have critiqued their presence in primatology (Sperling 1991) and in archaeology and origins research (Conkey 1991). While they are found in many branches of evolutionary discourse, in paleoanthropology each of these flaws is particularly evident and linked to the progress convention.

Functionalism is a pernicious problem in the reasoning behind the supposed "survival of the fittest," and its tautological implications are predominant in origins stories. We seek to explain the rise of particular physiological traits in specific organisms by reference to the function of those traits. In human evolution the focus has long been on those features that are said to mark the emerging hominid line, such as bipedalism. The explanations that we offer for the rise and persistence of such traits all relate in some way to the supposed function they had in enhancing the ability to survive or their "adaptation value." Functionalism assumes, a priori, that such features exist now because they served to further that survival, and then seeks to find the function they performed towards that end. For example, the advantage of bipedality was enhanced survival on the savanna. In the characteristically loopy logic of tautologies, we assume that the trait of bipedalism arose and persisted because it had a survival function, and then explain the continued existence of bipedalism by reference to that supposed function.

Gould has been particularly critical of this "seductively appealing mode of argument about the phenomenon of adaptation" (1984:154). He chastises evolutionary biologists:

> We tend to view every structure as designed for a definite purpose, thus building (in our imagination) a world of perfect design not much different from that concocted by eighteenth-century natural theologians who "proved" God's existence by the perfect architecture of organisms (ibid.).

In another essay in the same book, Gould calls this "the confusion of *current utility* with *reasons for past historical origin*" (ibid.:170, emphasis in original). As discussed earlier in this chapter, future utility, as in the advantages bipedalism was ultimately to confer upon the hominids, cannot be the cause of those adaptive changes nor of their preservation until needed. Adaptation cannot work in advance of the problem it might ultimately resolve. Gould wants to reserve the term adaptation for those structures that evolved for their present use. He prefers the term exaptations for those structures that evolved for other reasons, or for no reason at all, but were then "fortuitously available for other uses" (ibid.:171). Is it possible to speculate, then, that bipedality may have been a random mutation that proved relatively benign until the developments of later millennium resulted in a jackpot utility? All the locomotor experts would reject that assumption out of hand. But it is useful here to reiterate

Gould's main point; we need to question the tendency to see survival
and fitness as necessarily "joined at the hip"; there could be such a thing
as serendipitous survival.

Anatomical changes are not the only traits assumed to have a functional adaptational significance, and the logical flaws which adaptationism draw us into are particularly important to keep in mind given the
rise of environmental psychology and its resurrection of what Sperling
(1991:207) calls: "structural-functionalist models for human evolution
centring on the sexual division of labor, the origins of the family, and the
origins of human gendered behavior." These supposed hominid traits
enjoy a perennial functionalist popularity precisely because they relate to
the unending Western political and social debates about gender, family
structure and social values. Human evolution models project justifica-
tions of "chauvinistic, hierarchical, and warlike characteristics" backwards into time, thus giving them a pedigree based on immutable,
"natural" fact (Tanner 1981:23). Functionalist statements about gender
appear and reappear in the popular press, as in the following:

> The human mind, like any other organ, was designed for the purpose
> of transmitting genes to the next generation; the feelings and thoughts it
> creates are best understood in these terms. Thus the feeling of hunger,
> no less than the stomach, is here because it helped keep our ancestors
> alive long enough to reproduce and rear their young. Feelings of lust,
> no less than the sex organs, are here because they aided reproduction
> directly. Any ancestors who lacked stomachs or hunger or sex organs
> or lust—well, they wouldn't have become ancestors, would they? Their
> traits would have been discarded by natural selection (Wright 1994:30).

But apparently lust does not naturally occur in equal amounts in men
and women. Nature has dictated a difference since women can only
have one offspring a year, while for males, "each new mate offers a real
chance for pumping genes into the future" (ibid.:31). It is "adaptive" then
for males to be more lustful.

The logical flaw in adaptationism is not only one of tautology, but
also that we really cannot offer convincing evidence of the survival function of any trait, physiological or psychological. Survival functions can be
thought of for any existing trait and so long as the explanation makes a
good story, these functions will be thought logical. Only our imagination
limits the functions we are capable of coming up with; bipedalism was
formerly thought to relate to new food-getting demands and resulting

locomotive changes. Recently, however, the popular press has given a great deal of coverage to a new argument that "thermally stressed environments" such as the savanna would have limited the size our brains could achieve without a new cooling strategy. On November 27, 1993, the Toronto *Globe and Mail* reported that: "Men and women walk tall to stay cool" (see McKie 1993 and also Folger 1993:34). The report was presumably based on Wheeler's (1985) theory that bipedalism presented less body surface to the sun which resulted in substantially fewer temperature increases during the day. However, a few months later, another article in the same newspaper reported that evidence from the sediment record on the ocean floor demonstrated that major trends in human evolutionary history, including significant drying trends in Africa, had been precipitated by major climatic "pulses" of severe *cold* (Stevens 1994; see also Vrba 1993). There was no mention of how this evidence would affect the heat dissipation theory. These accounts exist in a story field dominated by adaptationism, and it does not appear to be a problem when they are contradictory, so long as they stress "survival of the fittest." Note too that the "brain super-cooling" theory turns even our biological transformations into technological (read masculine) achievements, resonating to the future predicated on the modern computer era, to cyborgs, to androids and to electric sheep. If we were all walking around with a third arm, one suspects we could justify the survival function of such an appendage with equally plausible techno-stories. On the other hand, we cannot seem to demonstrate how any lack in primate organisms which have not perpetuated themselves is related to physiological or behavioural traits that somehow became maladaptive. Sometimes what we do know about environmental change and species development suggests that other hominid species had a better adaptation track record than our own.

For example, recently a major U.S. newspaper reported the story that the *Australopithecus afarensis* enjoyed an enormous time span of "extraordinary evolutionary stability," which persisted relatively unchanged for approximately one million years (Rensberger 1994: A23). This is all the more surprising given the many abrupt and devastating environmental changes in East Africa during that period, including volcanic, geomorphological and drainage system transformations and resulting shifts in vegetative patterns. Tanner (1981:159) once postulated that it was just these changes that had provided the micro-environmental diversity necessary for the adaptive radiation which ultimately created the many australopithecine forms. It now appears that during at least one million years of just such environmental upheaval, *Australopithecus afarensis* itself remained relatively unchanged. This persistence provides significant support for the allopatric speciation process advocated by Gould, but it seems more telling that it is being highlighted in the public media at a time when environmental concerns are so omnipresent. While functionalist adaptationist stories cannot explain the persistence of the australopithecine any better than they can explain its ultimate demise, the entire field of adaptationist origins stories manages to remain remarkably on target with current sociopolitical debates.

The embarrassing problem with functionalism is that despite Darwin's elegant logic, it tends in other hands to appear rather Lamarckian. For example, although origins stories are often able to identify the adaptive advantage of selected changes once they have taken place (future utility), it seems harder to offer good evolutionary explanations of their development in the first place, except by reference to those needs. The question remains as to how they were accomplished. By random mutation? By genetic drift? Through which of the several processes which Darwin postulated as significant in speciation did these changes come about? Story lines do not address this; they only assume a *need* which precipitates a morphological *change*. Why this should happen for one organism and not another is equally a puzzle, but one that has traditionally been solved with suggestions of superiority. One organism just somehow had the better qualifications over the long run. Survival is not only tied to progress, but to moral, physical and intellectual superiority. This is the origins story version of the West's culturally pervasive "inevitability of rewards for innate superiority" trope. Just as Santa Claus rewards good little boys and girls and the blessed go to heaven, evolution rewards the fittest organisms.

The Lamarckian flavour of such need-based theories and arguments which place behavioural changes as prior to and causal of morphological adaptations are not restricted to one model of human evolution. In proposing her Woman-the-Gatherer model, for example, Tanner (1981: 160) argues that "speciation and therefore the shift into a new niche or adaptive zone almost without exception begin with a change in behavior," which in itself is not a problem. But she then goes on to argue that *anatomical* adaptations followed upon *behavioural* changes which were made necessary by environmental challenges. She makes this kind of argument for bipedality and its superiority as a locomotor pattern for long distance gathering (ibid.:178). Ultimately, the twin need to cover long distances and carry objects resulted in behavioural changes that gave rise to morphological ones. First comes behavioural reorganization followed by morphological elements which can be "rearranged so as to have the same, or similar, function but in a new context or, alternatively, a different function in the same context" (ibid.:160). This would be genetic lability indeed!

In another example of adaptionism, Tanner postulates that the large apelike canine teeth which primitive australopithecine forms inherited from their precursors would have made chewing grass seeds and roots on the savanna rather uncomfortable. She argues that continuing this new type of chewing behaviour *ultimately changed the dentition* and that this hypothesis not only explains both the subsequent loss of the large canines, but also the chipped appearance of the canine in several earlier fossils (ibid.:181, 186). While such ideas could be formulated in a way that explicitly suggests a series of mutations which generate a field of phenotypic variation sufficient to give rise to a different kind of organism, the lack of any obvious need to write such origins stories is a good indication of the demands of the target audience, which is not only fellow scientists conversant with evolutionary theory, but fellow citizens sharing a common cultural discourse of the rewards of innate virtue.

Another clue to the ultimate target audience is that such hypotheses always focus on traits which are currently present in modern-day, "successful" species (presentism). At one time, the adaptive changes considered to give rise to the humans included terrestriality, bipedality, encephalization, and civilization. In the 1950s postwar, suburban environment, Man-the-Hunter models expanded this list to include territoriality, male aggression, male hunting and bonding, male-centred family units and the monogamous marriage. Under the influence of the feminist counter-revolution, the list grew to include female gathering, patterns of child-nurturing and socialization and male-female "friendships." At each stage, the essential definition of "human" has expanded to fit new political demands. Paleoanthropological logic is "presentist" and "essentialist" (Conkey 1991:114), two flaws that are intimately connected.

The understanding of presentism owes much to the British historian H. Butterfield (1965). Butterfield was interested in what he called "the psychology of historians" which he argued produced certain undesirable results in written history. In describing his own work, he wrote:

> What is discussed is the tendency in many historians to write on the
> side of Protestants and Whigs, to praise revolutions provided they had
> been successful, to emphasize certain principles of progress in the past
> and to produce a story which is the ratification if not the glorification of
> the present (1965:v).

This produces accounts which are judgmental rather than exploratory,
that address narrow interests rather than encompassing the richness of
detail on past lives, that overdramatizes and oversimplifies in order to
meet present-day prejudices, and which downplays the unintended consequences of the application of human will.

In commenting on Butterfield's work, Stocking (1968:3) writes about
history in a way that rings equally true for paleoanthropology. The historian practises presentism when confronted with the "massive complexity
of historical particularity." Rather than deal with this complexity, the historian abstracts and judges historical facts apart from their context and
practises a form of reductionism which measures the importance of the
past against a yardstick generated by the present. In origins research, the
present offers us just this sort of template for deciding which features or
traits were adaptive and thus which were essential to the emergence of
humanity.

Essentialism as a logical flaw promotes the definition of selected
phenomena on the basis of their putative essential features, and in doing
so ignores a significant constellation of other traits which are not considered essential. At one time the essential feature of the hominid line was
the ability to create an artificial response to the environment in the form
of culture. From this perspective, "tool making" was assumed to be the
essential definition of humanity, and tools were a significant pictorial
code of modernity. A related assumption was that bipedality and tool-
making emerged together. Thus, in early illustrations of the "progress
ladder of mankind," tools were a signifier of the anatomically modern
human. By the mid-1970s however, the fossil record was pushed back
in time to two and then three million years ago and the lack of tools at
that time depth reduced their overall importance. Tools became notice-
ably absent in the illustrations, which turned instead to other signifiers
of modernity, including a modernization of the physical form. An erect
and modern-looking bipedality became the essential feature, and the
first evidence of bipedality became vital evidence of direct ancestry.
The appearance of tools over a million years later was confirmation of

that ancestry. Other features which the early australopithecines shared with close phylogenic relatives, of dentition, of molar shape and function, of brain size, and perhaps of behaviour, on the other hand, were downplayed as less important to explain. Only those features essential to separating human ancestry from the primates receive continued attention. The essential traits are those found in the present and the present traits are there because they had adaptive significance on the road to evolutionary progress.

But essentialism strips any phenomenon of its inherent complexity, just as the psychology of historians tended to strip history of its richness of detail. I earlier discussed the fact that paleoanthropology tends to be *Homo*-centric. The entire history of the hominid family tree is reduced down to an exercise of finding those species who had the essential traits that eventually led to humanity as well as when and where they emerged. In Stocking's (1968:3) terms, *Homo*-centric origin research "moves forward in time by tracing lineages up to the present in simple sequential movement." The entire history of the human species is boiled down to the development of bipedal locomotion, of encephalization and of the rise of culture, and thus the sum total of modern humans is reduced to several highly selective component parts such as bipedalism, speech, symbol and opposable thumbs. Having decided on the quintessential human, the rest of the hominid family are then reduced to ancestors or side-branches. And even the essential traits are stripped of their complexity: does bipedality necessarily appear in only one form and towards only one purpose? Does tool use? What degree of encephalization is essentially human? This raises the issue of yet another logical flaw: whenever researchers have focused on such a narrow field of a few essential traits, they have inevitably fallen into the tendency to universalism.

Most of the traits which paleoanthropology considers essential tend to test even the rather generous limits of the guarantee of continuity (Conkey 1991:105), where the same analytical concepts are used across vast distances in time, space and species boundaries. Is female the same category when speaking of australopithecines, modern baboons and anatomically modern humans? Is bipedality the same morphological and locomotor complex in the several different fossil species in which it is found? In the same way as racist administrators in the United States once treated "blackness" as an "all or nothing phenomenon" (see Lutz and Collins 1993:157), paleoanthropologists have tended to treat "humanness" as either present or absent in the fossil record. Further, wherever there are the signifiers of humanity, bipedalism, tool use, encephalization, then the universal categories that the West associates with humanity, pair bonding, nuclear families, mother-child bonds, must also exist.

The list of essential human traits has particularly related to and endorsed our Western values and conceptions of gender, "race," progress and culture. Universalism springs from this narrow focus. Woman, as a universal category spanning millennium and a wide variety of species, is a weak, nurturing, dependent creature wherever and whenever she is found. Although feminists reject the universalizing concept of womanhood as promulgated by the Man-the-Hunter crowd, female traits in some of their theories often look very little different. It is simply a matter of putting a different spin on them. Or alternatively, female traits may begin to look alarmingly like the older models of male traits. Feminist-inspired research on primate females specifically focused on attempts to redress the preceding androcentric bias which they felt had seriously distorted the discipline (Fedigan and Fedigan 1989; see also chapter 6 of this book). But their models equally naturalized selective female traits which one suspects were developed specifically to challenge the older models of passivity and subordination. Males were not the driving force behind social cohesion. Instead, females became the social hub, selecting mates for sexual partners from among those males "wise" enough to establish special friendships with them. These females then socialized the resulting offspring into maternal-centred social groups (ibid.:49). Females, not males, were the paragons of cooperative social skills. But this rarely shifted the older models to any significant degree, for although females here are social hubs, they are still stereotyped as needing to solicit assistance from males and as using feminine (including maternal) wiles to build up enduring social bonds.

Such feminist explanations relied on quite traditional-sounding "feminine skills," which they argued should be respected in the world of science. Fedigan and Fedigan (1989:45) write:

> Several scholars in the social studies of science (e.g., Bleier 1984; Fee 1983, 1986; Gilligan 1982; Messing 1983) have suggested that Western women scientists tend to be holistic and integrative thinkers, who, as a result of differential social interactions, may be more attuned than men to the complexities and subtleties of social interactions, and less satisfied

with reductionist principles of analysis (Keller 1983, 1985, 1987). They argue further that the values *traditionally defined as feminine* may lead women to be generally more persistent and patient, willing to wait for the material to speak for itself rather than forcing answers out of it, and envisioning themselves as more connected to the subject matter than in control of it (emphasis mine).

Fedigan and Fedigan feel that a survey of female primatologists and their work could be interpreted as offering some support for this argument.

This position is criticized by Sperling (1991:218), who argues that some feminists have actually reinforced older androcentric models by endorsing the attributes of femininity contained in them and by conforming to "a biological essentialism at the heart of human behaviour." She is also critical of the other trend, which is to replace the central male actors with female actors who behave in much the same way: "The new female primate is dressed for success and lives in a troop that resembles the modern corporation: now everyone gets to eat power lunches on the savanna (ibid.)." Sperling calls for a "deconstruction of all functionalist models, including sociobiological ones, of sex-linked primate behaviours" (ibid.).

One of the first steps in such a "house cleaning" would be to expunge all universalistic concepts which are really a set of unexamined preconceptions about the nature of the (gendered) universe. But is it possible to move beyond our cultural influences in constructing models of primate social behaviour, past and present—or for that matter, can we move beyond them in constructing models of evolution in general? There is consistent and persistent resistance. Sperling comments on gatekeeping to the published word and cites Gould as having "written of the frustrations involved in critiquing adaptationism," based on the barrier of "what is privileged as publishable" and notes that these same frustrations attend on critiquing genderism in evolutionary research (Sperling 1991:221). This has rendered functionalist-reductionism in primatology "immune to sophisticated arguments about evolutionary epistemology in other disciplines" (ibid.). Although postmodern critiques of evolutionary models have ignored the question of "good science versus bad science," their analysis of "primatology as text" has been revealing of central cultural meanings (ibid.:223): "the life and social sciences in general, and primatology in particular, are story-laden.... Facts are theory-laden; theories are value-laden; values are story-laden. Therefore, facts are meaningful within stories" (Haraway 1988:79). As political and cultural winds shift, so do the weather vanes of our theoretical propositions, which demonstrate the extent to which the past interests us mostly as legitimations and indeed as naturalizations of the present day. Sperling tells us that we can construct an "epigenetic approach" to evolutionary biology, which will accept and explore the complicated and problematic history, diversity and persistence of gender dimorphic behaviours. Gould (1989) also supports the drive to construct new "possible worlds" by challenging traditional ways of looking at the data. In the field of paleoanthropology and the illustrations that accompany it, this new construction will first require that we become sensitive to the hidden meanings conveyed in illustrative conventions and learn to critically deconstruct the illustrations that have dominated in the past.

Summary

Evolution is not the history of the rise of consciousness and of inevitable and unending biological progress where innate virtue has its rewards. The patterns in evolutionary history are not ladders of upward progress nor are they ever-expanding cones of increasing diversity. There are no essential features which define a species or a historical moment in biological evolution more than do other traits present before, after and during that time. Individual (read "male" or "female") pursuit of excellence (in either "hunting" or "gathering" or "nurturing") has not been the motivating force in an upward drive to human status and civilization. Gender attributes and roles are species-specific, context-specific, history-specific and cannot be reduced to essential, universal categories. Cultural and behavioural attributes must similarly be de-universalized. The present should not be taken for a template of what to look for in the past and the past should not be continuously used as a mirror to reflect the aspirations or realities of political patterns of the present. But these and other patterns have characterized the pursuit of paleoanthropological knowledge in Western science and will probably continue to do so in the future, unless we learn to deconstruct the increasingly complex codes of meaning used to perpetrate them.

CHAPTER EIGHT

Lucy as Barbie Doll: Eroticism in the Human Evolution Meta-Narrative

RECONSTRUCTIVE ORIGINS ILLUSTRATIONS have changed in recent years. There has been a subtle shift which developed soon after the rise of the Woman-the-Gatherer debate in paleoanthropology. In its content, this shift is consistent with similar patterns of representation which developed during periods of history when gender roles (particularly female social roles) came under dispute. In the sixteenth and seventeenth centuries in Western Europe, for example, a protracted struggle began over attempts to curtail women's rights and public roles (Miles 1989:127). There were attempts to limit female roles in the public sphere and to isolate them in the private world of domestic life and these coincided with a shift in the representation of women, particularly with a fetishism of female nakedness in the visual realm. Art increasingly associated the female with evil, particularly through witchcraft. At the same time, however, the visual arts became more sensual, with overtly sexual postures, particularly for females and "the damned." In general, an inverse relationship seems to exist: where females have power and responsibilities in the public realm, these are logically incompatible with representations of the female body as erotica—that is, as a visual object designed to reinforce the role of the female body in arousing sexual pleasure in males. On the other hand, where females are restricted to a non-public social role, erotic representation of the female is particularly evident.

When Adrienne Zihlman (1989) summarizes the Woman-the-Gatherer debate in human evolution and offers several course components which could integrate this debate into introductory anthropology courses, she raises the issue of how female representations are changing in reconstructive human evolution illustrations. But her assessment of this change is rather different from mine:

> There are historical changes. The most positive depiction of women's
> activities are found in the November 1985 cover story "The Search For
> Early Man." These reconstructions of early hominid social life can be
> used for comparison with some earlier and more negative ones
> (ibid.:39).

I find Zihlman's comments curious and quote them here for several reasons. First, I disagree with her positive assessment of these 1985 illustrations. Second, I find the terminology of the *National Geographic* article
she cites, with its emphasis on "Early Man," an example of the tendency
to androcentrism in paleoanthropology and I am surprised that it did not
draw comment from her. And finally, her conflation of "women" with
females of the proto-hominid species is unfortunate. Despite a tendency
which Haraway (1989:292) notes among some female primatologists to
intentionally "blur" the boundary between themselves and the female
animals which they study, to intentionally use the term "women" to refer
to female primates is unacceptable. It is exactly this conflation of all
things feminine into a single universal category which must be resisted.
In this chapter I explore another universalizing image of woman which
has been utilized to achieve a subtle but disturbing change in the visual
field since the introduction of the Woman-the-Gatherer model.

In the last few chapters I have argued that "race," gender and
progress have been mixed together over the years in a potent brew of
visual tropes designed as much to reinforce politically constructed viewpoints of the present day as to educate on the past. This use of illustration, whether consciously motivated or not, is one that must be
deconstructed in order to make way for a more positive use of the illustrator's art. However, what has been happening to the representation of
gender in human evolution illustrations in recent years presents a new
problem. Since the early 1980s, there has been a small but marked trend
towards eroticization of the female gender in illustrations, even as the
numbers of and roles provided for females in illustrative material has
increased. Furthermore, there is evidence to suggest that students read
these newer illustrations in ways that seriously undercut the feminist critique. This returns us to the problem of the relationship between illustration production patterns (artist's intent) and viewer interpretation
(readerly autonomy). I begin a discussion of this issue with a focus on
eroticism in this chapter and in the next I raise the related problem of
the commodification of evolutionary illustrations.

Undulating Women–Reaffirming the Meta-Narrative

In more recent introductory textbooks, the chapters addressing human evolution are strikingly devoid of the type of illustration which were so popular one or two decades ago. Compare, for example, John E. Pfeiffer's 1978 *The Emergence of Man*, with Staski and Marks's 1992 *Evolutionary Anthropology*. However, in the quasi-educational media such as *National Geographic, Newsweek, Time, Nature, Discover, Natural History* and other magazines, the illustrative conventions I explore in this book are still used, probably for reasons of commercial viability (see chapter 9). In this popular media field of illustrative material, the trend to eroticism is clear, although it does also occasionally show up in textbooks.

I first noticed this trend in exactly those illustrations which Zihlman cites when referring to improvements to the old androcentric illustrative patterns, including several Jay Matternes images published in *National Geographic* in 1985. What are the significant differences that lead her to see an improvement in these illustrations? In one, we see "members of an afarensis group forage for figs in a mountain forest (Weaver 1985:595)." Several things are immediately apparent, especially as relates to gender. For example, there is no single, forward-frame, dominant male figure occupying the centre of attention. The central image in the Matternes "foraging for figs" image is the female in the middle distance, although she is of smaller size than the male in the lower right foreground. Her importance relates to the fact that she is not only central in the frame, but also in that the artist's play of light draws viewer attention to her first. She is shown standing erect in the full frontal posture which was previously reserved for males and which has long marked the masculine body as important and powerful. Furthermore, for the first time we see a number of male figures occupying low or crouching positions–and even more surprising, in close proximity (although hardly attached to) some juveniles. According to Zihlman (1989:39), this is a good example of a more "positive depiction of women's activities." But what activities is Zihlman specifically referring to?

The central female in this "foraging for figs" illustration, as one of perhaps two in the entire frame, is standing with an infant on one hip. She holds a handful of figs in the opposite hand. She looks down field in the frame, perhaps looking at a male in the lower field of the image, and she does not engage the viewer's eye. Her facial expression is focused but enigmatic. Her stance is neither tense, fearful, nor particularly relaxed. A quick look at the frame would suggest that her activities do not appear to be substantially changed from previous depictions of female gender roles, visually connected as she is to child care and food. How do her activities compare to the male ones portrayed? First, males still dominate numerically. There are at least four adult males in this image. In terms of the low/high placement in the frame, it is certainly true that the central female is neither crouching nor placed lower frame. However, the highest figure in the frame is a male, and he is also the most active in that he looks up the tree with a rock in hand—preparing to knock down more figs. Another male stands behind and to the left of the central female. He holds an armful of figs and is also active as he is busy eating them. The lowest figure, again a male, is placed in the lower right-hand corner and is the largest figure in the frame. He crouches with his own armload of figs and has another in his mouth. He appears to be interrupted in his eating as he looks off frame alertly. Although he has juveniles close by, one eats figs and ignores him while another looks rather apprehensively at him while reaching down protectively to a lesser horde of two figs. The main activity here seems to be eating, and the many males in the image are doing more of it than are the females.

Nevertheless, it is the centre stage female which draws the viewer's eye and perhaps this should be seen as an improvement. But how does the viewer read this centrality? One thing that has interested me from the beginning of this research is the way that students are often inadvertently vocal in their reactions to the illustrations which flash up on the projector screen during class discussions. Inevitably, when this image appears the class is interrupted by a few students laughing. Why? Students admit that their eyes are immediately drawn to the female figure first. What is humorous about her? For one thing, unlike her hairy and therefore brutish male counterparts, the artist has presented her with a relatively hairless torso *and* with a set of round, high and pointed breasts which are very human in their appearance. Given that Jay Matternes is very adept at the realist style, students are embarrassed by her nudity and release their tension through laughter.

Why should this naked female torso embarrass more than the other female torsos in previous illustrations (see Figures 7 and 9)? The reaction has to do with the difference between nudity and nakedness. The difference is in the artist's intent such that nakedness is not embarrassing in the same way that nudity is. As Hollander (1978:88) writes: "Since the erotic awareness of the body always contains an awareness of clothing, images of bodies that aim to emphasize their sexual nature will make use of this link." The image of this female figure is erotic because it resonates to clothed female bodies of our stylistic period, to the way that we represent our bodies in the public sphere for public consumption as the body of a sexual being, or more importantly, to how our bodies are co-opted for the display of consumer goods which suggest patterns and ways of consuming our physical representation. Lutz and Collins (1994:93) demonstrate the ways that the exotic dress, ornamentation, hairstyles and body postures are used in *National Geographic* photography to make the physical bodies of non-Western people more sexually alluring, or more stylistically palatable to Western tastes. This makes it more likely that Westerners will then "consume those bodies" through the act of subscribing to a magazine which portrays them that way (see chapter 9).

The use of light in creating this centre-stage female image in the "foraging for figs" illustration is an example of Hollander's (1978) observations on "invisible clothing." As was discussed in chapter 3, this form of nudeness transforms the female body into a titillating object of male desire through the simple device of drawing the body as if it were wearing "ghostly clothing" (ibid.:85). Details based on the way bodies look in clothing are used to "make the nude look 'realer' for its epoch and therefore sexier and more nude" (ibid.:88). The breasts which Matternes drew on the central female are unaffected by gravity and are pert enough to refract light, as if encased in a bra. Further, they are placed in a rather feminine context, unlike those of the female image in Figure 7, for example, where the breasts are found on a classically male midriff. In comparison to the females in earlier illustrations, this australopithecine female is less hairy and has less of a barrel chest or protuberant belly to detract from the very rounded shape of her breasts. The overall effect is much sexier. Another article of invisible clothing for this female image was spotted by a male student and is suggested by the shading of the fur around the pelvis. This "G string" shading was not something I had noticed in preparing the lecture. Miles (1985a:196) has argued that in uncritical or nonreflective viewers the choice of what to pay attention to in an image relates to congruency with their particular interests. Other aspects will be ignored, and perhaps go unrecognized. Certain aspects of this illustration are obviously less apparent to women than they are to men. Miles may be overstating the relationship here, however, since a critical stance and a selective viewing are not mutually exclusive; the male student who noticed the G string was practising a newly critical stance at the time. On the other hand, despite my developed critical stance, I had failed to observe it!

Ghostly clothing has appeared in earlier illustrations and it has never been restricted solely to female representation. It is apparent in the slightly too-broad shoulders of the heroic male images such as those in Figure 11 where military epaulette-style shoulders are found on the central male figure as well as on several of his male companions. Eroticization can also affect male images in origins illustrations. In the March 1996 *National Geographic*, artist John Gurche's *Australopithecine afarensis* group consists of extremely dimorphic males and females foraging through juniper and olive trees (Johanson 1996). The two large males placed prominently in the forward frame both have pronounced "body-builder" physiques. But this use of eroticism and of invisible clothing is directed to both the males and females in the audience, as a template for the desirable male physique. The central female in the Matternes "foraging for figs" drawing is directed exclusively to a male audience. The result is a highly eroticized image.

Another clue to the eroticism taking place in the "foraging for figs" illustration is the relationship between the central female figure and her infant. One of the female's breasts is being cupped by her infant into prominent display. And yet, the infant is not being carried in a nursing position nor is it actually nursing. This act of cupping the breast forward seems an obvious imitation of a famous sixteenth-century painting by Hans Baldung entitled *The Fall,* in which Adam does the same thing with Eve's breast (Miles 1989:127). This image of Eve is one example of the eroticization of the "evil" attractions of the female common to historical periods of gender role upheaval. It seems a rather strange convention to have reappear in human evolution reconstruction illustrations, but Matternes has recreated it not once, but at least twice, as it also appears in his end paper illustration for Johanson and Shreeve's (1989) book *Lucy's Child.*

There is yet another subtle convention in this illustration, which sends a message about the proper place of the genders. Two male figures "bracket" the central female in their "active gaze" in a way not seen in pre-Woman-the-Gatherer illustrations. In her analysis of several Degas paintings, feminist art historian Carol Armstrong (1985:229) identifies this kind of "male gaze" as a device to "objectify" the female body. Why do these two males gaze fixedly at the central female? The narrative theme of the illustration does not suggest an explanation for their behaviour, but the female in the image clearly is rendered as the passive object upon which the male gaze acts. Another disturbing aspect with respect to the artist's treatment of gaze is that none of the figures engages the eye of the viewer. Their eyes are all directed away from the viewer in a "closing out" which has been historically used in representations of females to suggest to the male viewer a lack of common ground, as well as coyness and inscrutability. In this "foraging for figs" illustration, such inscrutability is used to build up a more complex message which simultaneously suggests universal "natural" gender roles and sexuality as well as an unfathomable alien freedom from cultural constraint which can be voyeuristically enjoyed by the viewer. The feeling created is one of watching unobserved while natural behaviour unfolds before you. Meanwhile, the text annotation links the visual field to "figs," which leads the mind on to "fig leaves" and nudity and from there on to the first redesigned ancestral female (Eve) who lured a male (Adam) into a patriarchal provider role. Was Matternes (consciously or unconsciously) responding to the Lovejoy (Love-Joy) hypothesis in crafting this illustration? One has to wonder if the eroticism in this image was directly related to an attempt to discredit or to co-opt the Woman-the-Gatherer model.

A second Matternes illustration from the same *National Geographic* article is equally troubling. In this picture, a nubile female is found centre frame with an upraised digging stick in one hand. She is kneeling on the ground digging tubers and the action has thrown dirt over her bare thighs. Her youngster sits beside her and reaches out to beg for whatever it is she has uncovered. While she is certainly active, she is still associated with child nurturing and food. She too wears ghostly clothing with full round and pert breasts, and with G string shading in the fur of her lower torso. A large male figure stands off centre and behind the digging female, tugging vigorously at the upper branches of a bush. Further behind in the distance a larger group of australopithecines appear to be sitting on the ground eating something. They are the only evidence that the foreground cluster is not a domestic grouping based on an incipient nuclear family. In this "digging for tubers" image, Matternes has crafted a female that resonates to the Western cultural trope of the woman as fertile earth (duBois 1988). The association of female, fecundity, and the masculine plowing of the earth to sow the seed, creates a female image as allegory for human sexuality.

These Matternes images of australopithecine females remind me of Haraway's (1989:191) observations on Lucy, the fossil most often seen lovingly laid out on red velvet like priceless jewels. Haraway writes that Lucy is the Biblical Eve incarnate, "the Barbie doll of a high-tech culture, which would clothe her in the latest fashions of flesh and behaviour." If we contrast such "Lucy" figures with earlier illustrations of bare-breasted females, we can see the extent to which older illustrations used physique to convey gender without eroticizing body parts in a manner suggesting "pornographic disintegration" (Miles 1989:161). As Haraway (1989:191-92) notes, fossils are the ultimate disintegration, "rebroken and reformed at will" by the scientists who would use their reconstruction to tell tales of female traits three million years old or older. Thus, the disintegration of their reconstructed bodies in "reconstructive" illustration should not surprise us. Crafted and recrafted over time to tell different stories, breasts, upper arms, thighs, bellies and buttocks are powerful indicators of natural gender attributes. This is especially true of newer illustrations, which subtly recraft the female body as stimulant for the male gaze.

Perhaps such sexy evolution imagery partially explains the failure of the Woman-the-Gatherer model to gain wider public acceptance. Consider Tanner's (1981:196) attempt to visually reconstruct the behaviour of Woman the Gatherer. In her image of the australopithecines which was designed in consultation with the artist Dee Anne Hooker, female figures are shown as active, capable and aggressive as they attempt to drive a leopard away from a juvenile. Two females from a group of australopithecines are already attacking the leopard while two males in the background prepare to join in. Females not only outnumber the males in the illustration but despite being encumbered by offspring, also outperform the males. The representation is definitely not sexy and definitely not erotic. The central female is presented in a full-frontal and erect posture, but unlike those discussed above, she wears no ghostly clothing. Tanner's collaboration with the artist has managed to redesign the female to avoid stereotypical or allegorical imagery.

Reading the Eroticism Message

But what reading do students make of these contrasting representations of the female gender? In interviews, students were asked to compare and contrast the "fighting off a leopard" image by Tanner with a second illustration drawn from the Howell (1965:74-75) book which shows a violent confrontation between *Paranthropus* and a more advanced australopithecine species. Both images explicitly deal with environmental threats that confronted the evolving australopithecines and at the same time make implicit comment on the division of labour by gender. In the former case, the threat is predation by carnivores which females are helping to deal with, while in the latter "warfare" image, the *Paranthropus* females are running away while several of the males stay behind to confront their clearly superior attackers. Students were encouraged to comment on both their interpretion of the main story line in the two images and on the plausibility of that story, but they were not asked direct questions about the suggested gender roles unless they themselves raised the issue. Their responses clearly indicate that they found the warfare image straightforward and unambiguous, but that in a number of ways, Tanner's illustration both confused them and was generally less appealing.

Student language use was much more hesitant when describing the Tanner scene, with more pauses and self-corrections. Several criticized the artistic merit of the leopard attack representation, complaining of the lack of colour and realism. Many didn't notice the body of the juvenile, half hidden in the grass beside the leopard, until they had been looking at the image for a few minutes. Once the body was discovered and students felt more certain of what they were seeing, there was still a sense of confusion over the best way to read the story line. One student commented that there was "a lack of adult males" in the image, but when pressed, veered away from gender and began talking about the realism of the confrontation between leopard and hominids. He commented that it was realistic because "we couldn't always have been at the top of the food chain." A second student made a similar comment: "when people are confronted with something like that, they do have to ... you know, they would attack it like that, however they could grab things." Another student expressed uncertainty as to whether the central figure was a male or a female, despite the depiction of breasts, because the threatening display the figure was making with a weapon seemed a more masculine type of behaviour. When asked to contrast the leopard image with the warfare one, more than half of the students interviewed commented that the main theme in both images was "a sense of community" which allowed our ancestors to cooperate in fighting off an environmental threat. On occasion, students referred to the division of labour when making this point. In reference to the leopard image one student said: "The women are right up there, doing things. They're more like a group that doesn't have any particular specialization of jobs or tasks. Just functioning as a group." Only two students explicitly critiqued the leopard story line, arguing that it would be very difficult to drive an animal off with only sticks as weapons: "blatantly attack a big cat like that? That doesn't make sense to me!"

What struck me in talking to students and in listening to the interview transcripts was the extent to which students were more ambiguous about images which contained female figures placed uncharacteristically central to the narrative. In another illustration by Jay Matternes, for example, showing Neandertal "preparing a kill," the old shambling grotesque Neandertal is gone (Weaver 1985:599). The most prominent male figure has a good physique with broad shoulders, muscular chest and arms and long lean calves. The women are also well proportioned although short in stature. Everyone has a neck. Contrast these Neandertals with those in Figures 8 and 10; in the more recent depiction, the Neandertals have definitely been "humanized." Another change is that we see women and juveniles dominating numerically in the foreground, although many males sit in the rock shelter in the indistinct background. Females are also in more prominent placement and are active participants in the scene. One stands in centre frame holding the edge of a hide which she is in the process of skinning. A second female stands off centre and forward frame, speaking and gesturing with her hands. Most of the individuals in the illustration are listening to her, including a male who has paused in his flintknapping in the opposite corner of the frame. All the females in this image are much more active although they conform to the traditional female placement within a base camp setting. Females as central to the story line of the illustration is a new representation and perhaps Zihlman's positive assessment of these illustrations relates to this fact. And yet, as was discussed in chapter 4, students often read the females in these images as lacking authority, as "trying" to "maybe" explain a story or do some activity, while their companions "sort of" listen or watch. Male centrality was never interpreted in such a wishy-washy fashion.

And when these images are examined closely it becomes obvious that despite the new centrality of the female figures, little in the gender roles has actually changed. In Matternes's updated Neandertal image, the female which commands the attention of the others has a child grasping her from behind. Another female kneels in the centre frame, beside a juvenile who is playing with the ears of the dead animal. A third female with her back to the viewer tends a fire in the background while still another brings more firewood. In terms of their activities, then, females are still tied to stereotypical activities such as dressing game and tending children and fires, while males are shown making the stone tools that women use. At best we are getting a mixed message with a slightly improved position for women. In the worst case scenario, there is ample evidence that the women in this image will be seen primarily as sexual objects.

Here again, the disturbing pattern of eroticization is clearly present. As with the australopithecine example discussed above, these Neandertal females are wearing invisible clothing; their breasts are large and full while their upper arms, bellies and shoulders are attractively rounded. While all of this contrasts with their heavy brow-ridges and jaws, hairy muscular legs and large bony feet, the overall impact is still one of nudity rather than nakedness. Matternes has also chosen to combine these adult and womanly upper bodies with pigtails, a hairstyle we associate with youth. And while this illustration is full of females, it is also true that given the use of light by the illustrator, the first thing the eyes are drawn to is the bare breasts of the central female. The gender attributes of these females have been eroticized, while the gender roles have not been seriously rewritten. This pattern of eroticizing women is consistent with that occurring in other areas of mass culture, including advertising and television roles. Female images in advertising, for example, went from "women as domestic royalty" in the 1950s and early 1960s, to women posturing in explicitly sexual ways over the next few decades (Lutz and Collins 1993:176).

Eroticism and the use of invisible clothing was sometimes useful in pre-Woman-the-Gatherer illustrations, as can be seen in Figure 13, a Zdeněk Burian illustration produced before 1965. The central figure here is a seated male who worships his own artistic efforts in the form of a clay

Venus figurine. Directly behind him stand the suggested inspiration for his efforts, three females each of whom is bare breasted. The central female is buxom and her breasts are heavy, suggesting fecundity as does the child that stands beside her. One of the other two women is younger and has pert, nubile breasts. All three are represented with the Victorian trope of voluminous, unrestrained long hair to signal unrestrained sexuality. These women are obviously meant to represent the assumed function of the Venus figure as fertility symbol and their sexy qualities are an integral part of the narrative theme, which is not the case with the eroticism in the post-Woman-the-Gatherer Matternes illustrations. Another Burian illustration published in Howell (1965:156-57), shows a woman mourner at a funeral who sits on the ground between two men, leaning back on one hand while her clothing slips down off one shoulder in the classical "slipped chiton" style. This image also holds an erotic quality, although I would argue it is quite subdued in comparison to the Matternes examples discussed above. The difference is a subtle one, as Miles (1985b:203) notes, when she argues that representations with an element of nudity will always carry a sexual message for Westerners. The use of nudity or suggested nudity "intensifies the narrative, doctrinal or devotional message ... by evoking subliminal erotic associations" (ibid.). But Miles also argues that in order to make the message and not the nudity the dominant theme, the nudity must be artfully portrayed so that it evokes interest without overwhelming other goals of the artist. We have to ask ourselves what it means when the nudity appears to have been devised to dominate.

As another example of the latter situation I have included Figures 15 and 16, which I first saw in an advertising flier mailed out to academic departments in 1991. This flier promoted a book called *Grain Collection. Humans' Natural Ecological Niche* by Sergio Treviño (1990). The illustrations appear in the book itself on Plate 1 and Plate 2. In a manner reminiscent of *Playboy* or Vargas Girls, these illustrations are a very blatant example of the "undulating" Eve. In Figure 15, female curves are brought to an almost anatomically impossible extreme in the manner of the "dirty" French postcard. This simultaneously symbolizes female seductive power and the male prurient fascination with selective parts of the female anatomy. The ghostly clothing is apparent on both the female breasts and waists as well as on the male shoulders. A number of females carry cherubic children, and the females all look like children themselves. Only the front and centre male figure in Figure 15 looks fully

mature (bearded) and serious-minded. A juvenile male in the right
frame, like the women, has long free-flowing hair. In Figure 16, we see
this same Victorian trope of unrestrained and voluminous hair taken to
extremes on both the male and female figures, "dressing and undressing"
the body (Michie 1987:100) in a fashion reminiscent of Lady Godiva.
This illustration also utilizes the Garden of Eden convention, with wild
horses grazing unconcerned in the wider landscape. In both illustrations,
the males and females portrayed are harvesting grain from tall grasses.
But it is only if you look closely that you can see the chipped stone harvesting blades in their hands. This book argues the hypothesis that the
hominid ecological niche was a grasslands one and that grain seeds
would have formed a dietary staple from an early point in our evolutionary history. But none of the students involved in my study recognized
the intended message in these male and female images. The grain suggested cultivation and the horses reinforced the theme of an agricultural
lifestyle. Students were mainly puzzled by these illustrations in that they
could not "fit" the nudity of the figures into a post-agricultural adaptation. The sensuality of their representation has completely obscured the
message about their lifestyle.

Summary

Many authors have drawn attention to the fact that representations of
gender and sexuality (particularly of the female sex) are transformed
during periods when gender roles come under dispute (see Miles 1985b,
1989:127; Nead 1988, 1990; Warner 1985; Michie 1987; duBois 1988;
Sydie 1992). For example, when feminine public roles are contested, the
erotic Eve-based imagery becomes more common in female representation than the demure Madonna-based imagery. As I have demonstrated,
this trend is apparent when one examines the relatively short history of
illustrations accompanying texts on human evolution. Until the 1980s,
the representation of gender roles and the connection of those roles to
progress and the "rise of civilization" closely replicated the largely
androcentric theories of human evolution. Representation of the female
nude largely conformed to Hollander's (1978:89) observation that: "The
degree to which a nude image in art departs in form and line from the
influence of its implied absent clothing is a good index of its aim to
appear primarily non-erotic." There is little or no invisible clothing on

the females in early illustrations of the australopithecines. However, illustrations done to represent the same fossil group by the same artist at a later date suddenly contain the ghosts of invisible clothing–they are not naked, but nude.

Following the publication of gender-specific challenges to androcentric narratives of human evolution (particularly Dahlberg's *Woman the Gatherer* in 1981) a subtle but significant shift developed in the way that gender was portrayed. Despite earlier publications (Linton 1971, Tanner and Zihlman 1976 and Tanner 1981), serious reconsideration of the androcentric model was slow to develop. Once this challenge did emerge as a threat to the male hunter model, it was variously co-opted to male-dominant models or undercut by reworked pair-bonding arguments (the Lovejoy hypothesis). In this environment, it would appear that illustrators and publishers found it both useful and possible, in tandem with advertisers and other agents of Western culture, to employ more complex messages about the two genders.

While females are portrayed in different ways–often in larger numbers and in more activities, their roles and attributes still orbit around the constellation of stereotypical Western female codification. Male roles, on the other hand, have also increased as many illustrators have added gathering or scavenging-style activities and tools to the masculine roster. One example is the Matternes end paper for Johanson and Shreeve (1989). While elephants wallow in the shallow water at lakeside, a group of australopithecines forage for food on the shore. Males make tools, dig for roots, teach juveniles and stand guard down the beach. Females nurse children, dig for roots and watch children play in the water. One of the females is eroticized, with an infant cupping her breast up for display and with smoothly rounded upper arms and thighs. This female, in her bodily encapsulation of female gender roles, is simultaneously food, sex and fecundity. Her body is made erotic through devices such as invisible clothing, the play of light on breast and thigh and her passive stance in the face of the male "active gaze." This eroticization subverts the other messages contained in these illustrations, of the less passive if still procreatively encumbered female of the species. That subversion may be a sufficient goal and explanation for the eroticism we see, or perhaps other processes are at work. I explore the latter possibility in the next chapter.

CHAPTER NINE

The Commodification of Human Evolution: Selling a Story Field through Illustrations

WHEN PEOPLE WILE AWAY the hours in doctor's offices or hospital waiting rooms glancing through magazines such as *National Geographic*, *Nature*, *Science Digest*, *Discovery* or *Natural History*, they probably never stop to think that in the act of looking at the illustrations or reading the articles, they are being consumers. Even in the act of passing a magazine stand and glancing at the cover illustrations, people are consuming images pre-designed to convey certain kinds of messages. Illustrations have the power to pass into the mind and lodge there, consumed whole with little thought or criticism of producer motives. Even in the highly consumer-oriented culture of the West, illustrations are rarely suspected as poor value by the people who regularly consume them. And yet, as commodities, illustrations are capable of all the same sorts of manipulations as other consumer goods. And as a significant component of the "popularization of science," those manipulations can be quite damaging (see Burnham 1987). So why are there no "Lemon Reports" on educational and quasi-educational illustrations? One reason is that educational artwork has received so little attention that its production, distribution and consumption are little understood.

As consumer goods, illustrations must be viewed as a form of commodity. A basic definition of commodities is "goods produced for sale" (Polanyi 1968:133) and the tendency is to assume that their exchange value is the single most important attribute to analyze. However, the anthropological understanding of commodities and commodification has long borrowed from Marxism, which recognizes the many levels on which commodities exist and operate in capitalist economies. For the Marxists, commodities are first and foremost "abstract social labour" (Hart 1983:108), which is to say that the "social use value" tied up in commodities is put there by human labour, making the structural arrangements by which human labour is organized a critical component of the study of commodities. This view of commodities has been strongly influenced by the French structuralists such as Godelier and Meillassoux (Hart 1983:123-28). Appadurai (1986:8) recognizes these debts and influences, but argues that we need to return to the exchange attributes of commodities; specifically, we need to follow them through the "total trajectory from production through exchange/distribution, to consumption" in order to better grasp their "socially relevant features" (1986:13). He (ibid.:6) draws attention to several avenues of research: the paths and diversions that commodities follow, the short- and long-term patterns in commodity circulation that show how consumption is mediated by political control and redefinition, the relationship of commodity value to knowledge and of both of these to politics, and the means by which politics controls exchange. Basic to all of the above is the need to better understand the concepts of "desire and demand" (ibid.:29). This is not incompatible with another influence on the analysis of commodities which is that of semiotics (Barthes 1957). This approach focuses on the "freight of meaning" commodities can carry. The relationship between images as signs and signs as commodities has been explored by people such as Baudrillard (1975, 1989, 1990) and Taussig (1992). I find all of these approaches useful in the following discussion where I address the following questions: Who produces human origins illustrative commodities and in what form and why? Who controls the distribution of these commodities and towards what ends? Who consumes them and towards what interpretive understanding of their content?

Illustrations as Commodities

Illustrations are commodities. They are the "thingification" of illusive images of the imagination; once captured on paper, images of people become things and things (images) begin to have the power of people (Taussig 1992:4). When Taussig (ibid.) quotes Marx on fetishism, he could be speaking of the sort of illustrations we have been examining: "The productions of the human brain appear as independent beings endowed with life, and entering into relation both with one another and the human race." The individual images found within a single illustration enter into relations with one another, such as masculine provider and feminine caregiver, or as common members of a nuclear or extended family, or as superior and inferior species struggling to compete against each other in the race for survival. But these images also enter into relations with those of us who view them, as our ancestors, as the signposts of the natural life or as indicators of how far we have evolved. The viewer also enters into a relationship with the total body of illustrations, where the latter "stands for" or represents science and the kinds of knowledge produced by scientists. This science sign can be consumed relatively critically or uncritically depending on the viewer's context, but the relationship between the two is one of scientific authority to the uninformed (but see Whitley 1985). The images also stand in various kinds of relations to the text in which they appear, including (1) merely adorning it, albeit in culturally loaded ways; (2) reinforcing assumptions underlying the textual argument and leading the viewer to absorb certain messages in the text and to ignore others or even to draw conclusions which cannot be openly stated in the text; or (3) replicating the visually oriented thought process by which the scientist arrived at his conclusion (in what Shelley (1996) calls "demonstrative visual arguments"). Finally, using the language of signs, these illustrations allow unseen people to relate to us, speaking to us through imagery in ways that make it hard for us to discount the message (Barthes 1957).

Illustrations are commodities in other ways too. They are produced by artists, who like other labourers, are "absorbed into a homogeneous mass of labour power" (Taussig 1992:4), and who are thus largely invisible to us. Illustrator motivations, backgrounds, religious beliefs and loyalties are treated as irrelevant to the production process, when in fact they are quite relevant. Science illustrators earn a living through the capitalist production process, a process of production that is constrained not only by the income-earning potential of artwork, but also by artist training, knowledge, inclinations, objectives and, particularly in the context of illustrations, the cultural context of employment. Finally, the output of this artwork enters with other commodities into a marketplace where it takes on a life of its own, being used in ways for which it was never designed and competing with other illustrations for space in the public world of evolution discourse.

Illustrations are produced in a social matrix which is extremely complex. That complexity does not diminish if we consider each of the stages through which illustrations as commodities must pass. As a market chain, the illustration industry is not a simple line from producer to wholesaler to distributor to retailer to consumer. Many institutions, and subsequently many motivations, intervene in the process and the process itself can continue for decades. For example, an illustrator may produce a diorama on human evolution as a staff member of an organization such as the American Museum of Natural History. A staff photographer may catalogue the diorama when it is discontinued as a display in the museum, thus imposing his artistic image of the illustrations through cropping, lighting and other attributes available through photographic technology. The image produced by the photographer may then be catalogued and held in the image library for use by anyone willing to pay the reproduction and publication fees assessed by the Museum. Or the copyright/ownership of the thing that is an image of imagination may remain with the artist. In either case, an image produced in the early 1950s, to provide a backdrop to an educational presentation on human evolution based on the knowledge available at the time, may ultimately find its way into a popular magazine of the 1990s, to be represented there as current scientific knowledge. Illustrations can take on a life of their own extending beyond the control of the artist, and in many cases beyond their lifetime too. Maurice Wilson's 1950 illustration of Peking Man (*Homo erectus*) in Choukoutien Cave (Figure 7), for example, has reappeared in several recent textbooks and in one it is used to illustrate the Neandertals in Europe.

The Power of Erasure

Taussig (1992:128) has commented on the power of a "totem" (image) by writing: "[It] would exist and be effective *precisely on account of erasure*–of the erasure locked into the commodity in its exchange-value phase ensuring its dislocation, it being prized apart from the social and particularist context of its production" (emphasis in original). Totem, or icon, illustrations operate effectively only through such erasure. For example, in the "ladder of human evolution" (Figure 5) we see the erasure of the environmental, historical and behavioural context of each of the represented forms. They are stripped of almost all of their real context and thus become vehicles to convey a very narrow message. Because of our *Homo*-centric interest in them, the images have but *one* message to convey, the meaning that each of the represented species has for understanding human evolution. All other aspects of their existence are of little importance. No information is offered to us on topics such as the relative persistence of each of the species over time, the habitat that they would normally be found in, the social lives they engaged in and the behavioural patterns associated with locomotion and food getting. In fact, in some instances these aspects become grossly misrepresented in the construction of the totemistic message, as when quadrupeds are shown attempting a bipedal gait. Each figure becomes warped to fill the iconographic function of one of several stages on the road to humanity.

But beyond this erasure, there is another erasure wrapped up in the icon/totem and that is the erasure of the economic, social and political context of the production of the image. Such erasure is the primary concern of this chapter. It makes invisible not only the illustrators, but also the science authors and the publishers. Illustrators produce an image, often of startling realism and clarity, and the image is then presented in a format which allows it to be stripped of the context of both the producer and of the act of production. This erasure acts to endorse the realistic image as science fact; downplaying the artistic context of its production makes it seem more like reality–a freeze-frame out of the past, rather than a social construct. What motivates the artists to tolerate this erasure? And what about the science author who combines the illustrative material of the artist with their own scholarly text? One motivation may simply be the desire to have their material read; there is no doubt that a colourful illustration will draw the reader's scanning eye into an article and that the scholarly text can benefit from this initial attraction if it can continue to hold the reader's interest. There is also an element of seeking public endorsement for one's research and for the public funds spent on the topic through research grants. Illustrative material has no doubt sustained an interest in paleoanthropology, archaeology and human evolution that would not have been there to the same extent without it.

It is precisely because of the erasure of their economic and political context of production that these images have this power to benefit the discipline; generating public support for origins research relies to a significant extent on representing the science exercise as altruistic. This question of motivation reaches beyond the artist and author role to explain the erasure of the publisher. It would be naïve, for example, to ignore what might be called the crass economic motivations behind the publication of origins illustrations. If pictures speak a thousand words, they also sell a thousand copies. Publishers in the popular media cannot afford to ignore this aspect of illustrations. On the other hand, the erasure of such crass motives is also important to the power of the image. Any critical analysis of illustration must uncover and understand the influence of these motivations. They should not remain invisible as they have in the past. In this chapter, I discuss some possible reasons for these forms of erasure by focusing on the motivations of artist, science author and publisher.

Some Thoughts on Publisher Motivations

Publishing houses exist in an intense, complex and competitive economic and political context. Moreover, this context has not remained static over the past several decades; the expansion of multinational corporations at the expense of smaller publishing houses, the effect of free trade on national protectionism and cultural content laws, and the erosion of the print media with the rise in popularity of the electronic media are but a few indications of the stresses the publishing world confronts. In this milieu, economic survival is a driving motivation and one that may explain much. Consider, for example, an anecdote related by Haraway (1989:337, n 11). Zihlman and Cramer (1976) were publishing an article on bipedality in the magazine *Natural History*. Given the Woman-the-Gatherer model, Zihlman had selected an illustration of a !Kung woman, heavily pregnant, carrying a toddler on her shoulders and a full load in her gathering sack, striding along in the Kalahari. To Zihlman, this image epitomized the ergonomically and reproductively stressed, highly mobile, female provisioner hypothesized in the gathering model. However, without consulting Zihlman, the editors of the magazine substituted two images of white, male American football players, one with an outline of bones superimposed on his hips and upper legs and a second player shown throwing a pass with the major muscle groups of the body outlined. Were the editors simply calculating that most readers were likely to be male and to relate better to masculine examples? Did these football players make for better sales than an African tribal woman would have? Perhaps so, but the reasons may be more complex than a simple gender bias. Certainly the advanced pregnancy and heavy burdens of the woman might create uncomfortable associations, but so might the racial and regional background of Africa and of Third World conditions. Lutz and Collins (1993:132) found that *National Geographic* reader surveys indicated Africa as the least popular topic for articles in that magazine. The publishers of *Natural History* may have been aware of similar kinds of reader preferences/prejudices, or they may simply have assumed that illustrations of (Western) males involved in a typical (Western) male activity would better reflect the target audience interests.

To what extent do publishers rely on economic motivations linked to assumptions about reader interests to control the production, selection and use of illustrative material? Lutz and Collins note that in the production of *National Geographic*, the corporate executives severely constrain what will appear on the magazine pages. And considering that this magazine has a huge circulation worldwide, this translates into a tremendous power to control the visual images the reading public sees; any such gatekeeping power is well known, and feared, in the "publish-or-perish" world of academia. This does not mean total control over what Lutz and Collins (ibid.:13) call the "looking practices" of the reading public. Intentionality or communicative intent is not the same as consequence (ibid.:52). Indeed, there are many stages along the production and consumption process which could subvert the intentions of the producers of illustration commodities: the production process may fail to produce the desired image; the "looking practices" of the wider audience may not be correctly anticipated or properly understood by the producers; the public may read things into an image that were never intended. Nevertheless, given the gatekeeping power of publishers, their goals are particularly important to consider when questioning what the viewing public has available for consumption.

The guidelines which direct the production of illustrative material for *National Geographic* are one indication of the types of considerations given priority throughout the popular quasi-educational publication world. At *National Geographic*, those principles include: "fairness, veracity, and positive outlook: [pictures] were to be beautiful (aesthetically pleasing), artistic (embodying certain conventions of highbrow forms of art), and instructive (realistic in representation)" (Lutz and Collins 1993:27). I would argue that these rules of conduct apply in equal fashion to university textbooks and scientific journals. Even a brief examination of a series of introductory anthropology textbooks shows to what extent publishers (and perhaps authors) prefer to publish attractive or sanitized-by-distance images of the "other." Lutz and Collins found that the management staff of *National Geographic* regularly sample their readership for feedback on the popularity of their articles and illustrations. In this way, the staff is kept aware of the socio-economic profiles, religious beliefs, political convictions and prejudices of their audiences. They walk a careful tightrope between influencing the values of that audience and catering to them. Given the competitive textbook market, publishers in that field must make similar judgments to make sure that their books appeal to the target audience, the professors who will select books for use in courses and the students who will chose whether or not to buy them.

These marketing goals are achieved by rigorously controlling the various stages of the production process. In the *National Geographic* way of doing things, the story does not come first to be embellished by photographic images; instead, the images come first. The staff writers provide the photographer with a set of themes and then produce an article around the resulting photographs. While the sorts of illustrations I discuss in this book are not photographic representations, nevertheless photographer and illustrator share a similar context of production in that they must both please their buyers. Thus, the two concepts of a "charge" and a "brief" which Lutz and Collins (1993:53) discuss in relation to the photographer are useful here as well.

A charge is some kind of a prompt to action, either internally or externally generated. The charge that illustrators by and large respond to is a commission, which in turn guides two components, the form the artwork will take (in this case an educational illustration) and the representational content of that artwork. The latter component takes the form, among other things, of a set of social expectations. In the case of an illustration about human evolution, illustrators may be under significant pressure to produce in a realist style, particularly for outlets such as *National Geographic,* and to fill that illustration with evolutionary codes well-recognized by the story editors and conforming to their expectations about the reading public. The way the artist responds to this charge can be comprehended better through the concept of a brief, which comprises the list of constraints, influences, and the artistic reaction to these, all of which go into making up the artist's "probable intention" (ibid.). Briefs include the immediate task confronting the artist, the training and experience that (s)he has, local expectations about the ultimate form of the product and the physical constraints of the media, as well as aesthetic considerations.

One can imagine then a scientific illustrator being confronted with a charge (commission) from *National Geographic* to produce a highly coloured, realistically styled, reconstructive illustration of two hominids walking across a volcanic plain. The artist does research on the archaeological excavation and the fossil finds, the geography of the find site, and the inferences about the ecosystem at that site at the postulated time the fossil was laid down. This is followed by preliminary drawings to be run past the story editor(s), who may request changes. For example, given that *National Geographic* survey research shows that an important market segment of the readership is conservative Christian in orientation (Lutz and Collins 1993:56), one can imagine the story editor suggesting softening the evolutionary aspects of the narrative (i.e., to repress "ape man" imagery) and highlighting instead the natural antiquity of sexual and reproductive practices endorsed under Christian family values (pair bonding, nuclear family, maternal gender roles for women). I do not know if this is what happened with Jay Matternes and the "fleeing the volcano" illustration, but given the context of illustration production, it is a possibility. One question is the role of the science author who is to have their text illustrated by the artist. In the case of the Matternes "fleeing the volcano" image, what role did Mary Leakey play?

One could postulate that much of the imagery considered acceptable in evolutionary reconstructive illustration may be responding to just such market-driven forces. Family values and their hard sell in evolutionary illustrations is certainly a suggestive combination. The family as a concept stands at the centre of an incredible swirl of social debate in the 1990s. The role of the family in the production of socially responsible and responsive individuals, the extent to which divorce and resulting dysfunction in families plays a role in the generation of various social evils, the natural gender roles of both males and females in the nuclear family structure, the possibilities and threats inherent in non-bisexual partnerships, the history of family arrangements and the social forces that bring about changes in the family are all contested topics. Given the variability of social forms that could be labelled as "family," the representation of the family in paleoanthropology is remarkably monotonous, based as it is on a monogamous pair, masculine provisioning and authority, and female child care. Can this monotony be attributed to readership surveys and socioeconomic profiles that determine what definition of "family" must be adhered to?

One can imagine these influences being felt from more than the Christian subsection of the readership of any particular publishing outlet. University students in the United States, for example, are primarily middle- and upper-class individuals who are young and economically dependent. They are a rather jaded audience, just sophisticated enough to recognize the manipulative elements of advertising and political posturing, but also vulnerable to guilt and anxiety about their place in the wider world. Lutz and Collins (1993:38) argue that *National Geographic* has long pushed a positive, upbeat, progressive image to the parents and grandparents of these students, one that allows them to avoid the more unpleasant connotations of Third World poverty, neocolonialism, and American militarism (i.e., Vietnam) and jingoism in the postwar conditions of ascending U.S. economic and political dominance (see also Bloom 1993). This is not surprising in a mass media outlet such as *National Geographic*, but it should surprise us in the textbook world where that same upbeat, guilt-reducing style prevails. There are many possible reasons for this, including the pressure to compete and make sales, the fear of backlash by political interest groups, and the desire to keep the text accessible to as wide an audience as possible.

Another motive that must be considered at the publisher's end of the production process is the cost of obtaining, reproducing and publishing illustrations which, particularly in the textbook industry, can represent a significant proportion of the costs of publication. For an organization such as *National Geographic*, with its enormous subscription rates, tax-exempt status in the United States, and general revenues, this is less of a problem than it is for other magazine and book publishers who produce works on the boundary between learning and entertainment. This has given *National Geographic* a significant edge in dominating the world of educational representation; it can afford to use original reconstructive artwork by people such as Jay Matternes and to reproduce these in four-colour, expensive and high-quality formats (i.e., fold-out pages). Other magazines which regularly publish on origins research tend to utilize less expensive, existing illustrative resources.

As a general indication of the costs involved in reproducing existing illustrations, I can turn to my own experience in publishing an article on the topic of reconstructive illustrations (Wiber 1994) and in preparing this book. One significant cost is the research hours spent in tracking down the sources of and the copyright holders for illustrations I wanted to reprint, but the largest expense involved acquiring the rights to reproduce those illustrations. Copyright holders range from the illustrators themselves or their heirs, to public or semi-public organizations such as the American Museum of Natural History, the Smithsonian Institution and the Natural History Museum of London, to publishing houses whether academic or commercial. Some of these sources charge substantially more than others for the rights to reproduce an illustration.

The laborious process of acquiring reprint permissions usually begins with an image search by the agency that often involve hourly research rates. Once the illustration is located, it must then be converted from the negative on file in the agency library into a reproduction-ready form and for this you pay another fee depending on size of print and on whether a black and white or a colour print is desired. You may wish to have a mural or diorama in a museum photographed for use as an illustration; most museums have photographers who do such work; fees for this will vary, depending on whether you want flat work or three dimensional images. Finally, once you have the image(s) you wish to use, you must pay for permission to reprint. Reprint fees in turn depend on the ultimate planned use (print versus television or electronic publishing), the medium (black and white versus colour) and the level of rights to be obtained (one language, one country, up to all languages and world rights). Many agencies take the circulation levels of the published work into consideration. For example, an image to be reprinted in a medium with a distribution level of five hundred thousand copies would cost significantly more than one with a more limited distribution.

To illustrate the way that such fees can mount up for a single image, assume a one-hour search time by museum staff, a normal textbook distribution level with world rights, and a colour reproduction. If such an image were to be obtained from the American Museum of Natural History, the total cost could be in excess of three hundred and sixty dollars.[1] Reproduction in an electronic outlet could cost in excess of five hundred dollars per image for one cycle of distribution. Multiplying

---

1 Figures quoted here are in American dollars and are cited from the American Museum of Natural History information sheet dated 10/92.

these costs by the numbers of illustrations often found in textbooks, films, educational books and magazine articles gives some indication of the production costs faced by publishers. Some agencies, artists or institutions charge less for the use of illustrations over which they hold copyright than do others and so it is not surprising that some illustrations reappear over and over again in various kinds of publications while others never reappear. Reprint permissions are extremely variable and context specific, an aspect that makes the "gatekeeper" function of copyright difficult to predict.

In my own case, I experienced very different reactions when soliciting reprint permissions from various agencies and individuals. For example, in 1994 when I published my original article on this topic, I was charged a fee to reprint some images held by the American Museum of Natural History. The same images for this book were granted without paying any additional fee. On the other hand, *National Geographic* allowed me to reprint a Jay Matternes image for the 1994 article and then later denied access to that same image for this book. Some publishing houses granted reprint permissions gratis while other agencies charged very high fees. The more commercial agencies expressed a reluctance to sell the rights to their commissioned work to a "media competitor." When I requested permission to reprint Rudy Zallinger's ladder of human evolution (Howell 1965:40-45), for example, Jack Weiser of the Time-Life organization responded that their illustrations were not available for reproduction as "our commissioned work helps to give our books a unique experience which we wish to preserve." While this unique product argument is understandable, critical studies of these images are made very difficult in the process. On the other hand, perhaps the critical nature of the publication in which I was engaged was also a factor; publishing outlets such as Time-Life and *National Geographic* probably are reluctant to have their unique product devalued as a result of such scholarly critique.

The relationship between increasing legal control of published images and scholarly critique of them is a complex and intriguing one. The "visual culture" of Western society has been increasingly subjected to cultural critique at the same time that the producers of widely consumed images have been exerting tighter control over their production and dissemination. Rosemary Coombe (1996) for example, points to the politics of intellectual properties such as trademarks—where battles swirl around ownership, protest, domination and resistance. She notes that as widely disseminated visuals, trademarks are at one and the same time "shared in a commons of signification" and "jealously guarded in exclusive estates" (ibid.:203). Their former status makes them important targets for the "objectified" and "othered," whether colonial (racial) or internally dominated (gendered) in source. Their latter status, however, results in fierce commercial struggles to defend and extend their influence. Time-Life is probably well aware of the postcolonial discourse which challenges the unique visual product that they market (as is *National Geographic*, see Lutz and Collins 1993). On the other hand, they are also aware that highly coloured visual components that are "saturated by signs of social difference" make their products the particularly marketable commodity that they are. This contradiction is but one aspect of the increasing commodification of images, of the "consumption of commodified culture" (Coombe 1996:202-203). Copyright over illustrative material, and its maintenance of the "exchange value of texts" (ibid.:206) in the face of fierce criticism, is another indication of the level of politicization involved in the commodification of images.

On a purely practical level, copyright over origins illustrations may be extremely difficult to track down, especially in cases where the original artist has died or copyright-holding agencies have ceased to exist. The Czech artist Zdeněk Burian is a case in point, as copyright over his material has been difficult to trace since his death, the end of socialist government publishing houses in Czechoslovakia and the dissolution of that nation.[2] Even with their international resources, *National Geographic* had difficulties in searching out Burian copyright, according to Fern Dame, former illustrations permission officer with *National Geographic*. After many months of contacting anyone who had ever published a Burian illustration and asking for help with permissions, I managed to reach Artia Publishers in the Czech Republic who put me in touch with Burian's daughter in Prague. She sent me permission to use her father's images in the initial article, but it arrived too late for them to be included. When I began collecting the permissions for this book, I discovered that she had since died and her son now claimed control of his

---

2 I had similar problems with the "attacking a leopard" illustration which was a collaboration between Nancy Tanner and Dee Anne Hooker, as Tanner is now deceased.

grandfather's copyright. These sorts of search problems may make Burian illustrations more difficult to reprint in the future and the associated cost will continue to act as significant checks on critical analysis of the illustrative exercise. It will also be a factor in the gatekeeping practices of publishing houses, as to who gets to use existing illustrations and where they will be published. This gatekeeping aspect is an important area for future research.

Possible Artist and Author Motives

Some of the most popular science illustrators, including Jay Matternes, Maurice Wilson, Zdeněk Burian, Rudy Zallinger and Stanley Meltzoff have been drawn to the field of human origins research. Their motivations in being there are clear on one level and very unclear on another. While science illustration is obviously paid employment, why would artists tolerate the erasure of themselves which is common to the marketing of their product as "science product"? There are indications that artists find compensations over and above the financial. In an interview in 1956, Stanley Meltzoff spoke to this question when he addressed his own need to reach a wider audience than "gallery painting" would have allowed:

> When I spend my creative energy and time on a picture I like to know that I am working for some useful purpose. The things I am doing now, while commissioned by a corporate client, will be seen by hundreds of thousands of people; the painting is a sharing of ideas among artist, client, and public (Watson 1956:25).

Matternes, on the other hand, speaks of the artistic demands of going beyond the limitations of classical training to challenge the Greek ideal of human beauty by faithfully representing the primate in all of its diversity (Rensberger 1981:43). Interviewing human origins illustrators more directly on their production process would be an interesting avenue of future research, but one that might have several limitations including the tendency to distortion when discussing images produced years and perhaps decades before, the fact that some of the more interesting illustrators such as Maurice Wilson and Zdeněk Burian are now dead and that some others seem hostile to the exercise (see below). Nevertheless, this could provide a level of information beyond that found in the artistic conventions employed in the images. These conventions speak volumes about the messages that illustrators intend to send, as the past several chapters have demonstrated, but say nothing of why the artists felt those messages were important to convey.

Copyright, as a form of trademark, "provides both a generative condition and a prohibitive obstacle" which together are a wonderful locus for the exploration of mimesis and alterity (Coombe 1996:206 exploring Taussig 1993). As Coombe (ibid.) writes: "[Copyright] manages mimesis (authorising true copies and distinguishing between legitimate and illegitimate reproductions) while it polices alterity (prohibiting the resignifications of others)." The difficulties I experienced in gaining illustration reprint permissions are sometimes suggestive of this second policing aspect of artist motivation. For example, both in the initial article I published on this topic and in this book, Jay Matternes refused to allow reproduction of any illustrations held under his copyright under any circumstances. He also refused when I offered him space in this book to rebut any interpretation that I had placed on his work. I can only speculate on his reasons since he provided me with none, but considering that other illustrations by him have since appeared in glossy popularizing publications such as Tattersall (1993), I suspect that he wishes to exercise control over the type of text found in association with his images. Perhaps his motivations are similar to those of Time-Life; he may fear that his future income could be jeopardized by any critical stance taken on his former work. No one would want to have their work defined as "politically incorrect." Or he may feel that taking images produced as long ago as the early 1960s and subjecting them to a critical eye which is the consequence of the intervening thirty years of theoretical development is inherently unfair. Whatever his reasons, gatekeeping is the practical effect of his refusal. Since his illustrations are a significant component of the origins illustration market and have been for several decades, his position left a rather large gap in the illustrative material included in this book which I was powerless to fill except by the clumsy device of verbal description.

The author of the written material which is illustrated with these images is another important source of information as to the guidelines employed in the production and use of illustrations. Selling copy may be one important author goal, others decidedly exist. Whitley (1985), for example, argues that popularization as an activity by scientists is often downplayed in the halls of academe and thus has low institutional support and professional status accruing to it. This has to do at least partially with the perception that science "facts" are merely conveyed to an undifferentiated audience, comprising atomistic and uninformed receivers of knowledge. But Whitley argues that the science exercise itself is highly differentiated, the science product is often disputed, the audience of the scientist's popularization efforts is actually a significant source of support for highly contested knowledge and the publishing effort will in a real sense be a product of the interaction of scientist and the ultimate consumers of science knowledge. As one example of this interplay, Whitley points out that funding agencies are staffed by members of the public and are influenced by the public perception of a field of science which in turn is based on popularization efforts. Science author motivations can be contextualized within this framework. Those who participate in popularization may be calculating the end benefits as more important than the loss of prestige among their colleagues. This may make them more susceptible to significant influences from the heterogeneous target audience. But there is no evidence that other science authors, publishing in other sorts of venues, are immune to pressures from the wider public.

The relationship between research funding and science popularization, and the use of "grandstanding" to obtain more funding, has been explored in paleoanthropology only to a very limited degree (Lewin 1987). Those who widely and successfully popularize their origins research are often rewarded by attacks on their research professionalism, perhaps because those who are most successful at popularization are usually also most successful in cornering a lot of research funding. The images produced in the heat of such battles are difficult to judge on the basis of scientific merit alone–the opportunity to use their rhetorical capacities to convince must be acknowledged as a significant factor. The rhetorical content of the images is a window onto such author motivations, but should be supplemented by research methods which go directly to the author as a source of information.

The relationship between author motivation and outcome can be quite complex as well. For example, consider the highly eroticized images found in Figures 15 and 16. Here a group of naked, anatomically modern humans, including a number of buxom, curvy females, are collecting grass seeds in a field with a scenic vista behind them. Based on the artistic conventions and on the suggested narrative, we would be justified in assuming that the author's intention was directly linked to the eroticism of the female form and perhaps therefore to a rebuttal of the feminist critique. But in fact, Sergio Treviño may have had something else in mind when he gave his instructions to the artist. In a recent letter to the American Anthropological Association Newsletter (1995, Vol. 36(1):8), Treviño hypothesizes that humans are "victims of their own intelligence." He argues that intelligence may have led us astray from the "natural" life, one where we would be "living in nature, belonging to nature and enjoying life as our ancestors did." Anthropologists, he argues, have an obligation to guide humanity towards the happiness that could be ours if we would only abandon all of the false trappings and pursuit of progress into which intelligence has (mis)led us. Given these strong feelings about progress, Treviño's use of these types of illustrations takes on a whole different meaning. Furthermore, his instructions may have misled (inspired?) the artist to make his own call on what that happy and natural life would look like. There is always the possibility of miscommunication between author and artist, or of limitations in an artist's background and training, which could result in compromise illustrations that are not exactly what the author intended.

The pitfalls of the image production process may generate other significant limitations. Lutz and Collins (1993:70) comment on the tremendous choice that story editors have when using photographic images in *National Geographic*. Literally thousands of slides are produced by photographers on assignment and editors then cull through these to select the choice few that will appear in a story. It is safe to assume that illustrators cannot work that way. The tremendous cost and time involved in producing original artwork by hand must result in a much more detailed charge at the outset. The illustrator probably only produces a few rough mock-ups to be used in narrowing down the final illustration content. Another significant problem for future research, then, is the opportunities and constraints connected to this more limited production process. For example, do publishers and authors collaborate to provide as detailed a charge to the illustrator as possible? Is the artist more constrained than the photographer? Are there more opportunities for miscommunication or compromise because of the cost of redoing things? Does a reputation as a high-quality "scientific illustrator" allow some artists more latitude than others and thus more power over the final product? And is that latitude (if it exists) justified by extensive training and research on the part of that illustrator?

Looking Practices of Viewers

Another important question concerns the consequences of illustrations. After asking questions about the intent of authors, illustrators and publishers, we need to question the impact of the illustrations as a commodity, which might very well be different from that intended. In examining the looking practices of readers, it is important to remember that readers have their own autonomy in selecting images for consumption and in interpreting what they have chosen to consume. Throughout my study of origins illustrations, students have surprised me by their ability to see things differently. For example, the burial finds at La Chapelle-aux-Saints, Le Moustier and La Ferrassie where Neandertals not only buried their dead, but often did so in a bower of flowers, have spawned a whole set of Neandertal "graveside" images. On occasion, however, when students were shown such images (see Figure 10) they failed to recognize the artist's intent. Instead, they interpreted the story line as an attack scene, with the action frozen just after the victim was struck down. In a similar fashion, many of the students examining the Vargas girl imagery of Figures 15 and 16, never explicitly focused on the eroticized nude females but instead found the nakedness of the group as a whole questionable since the figures seemed to represent agriculturalists with domesticated horses.

There is also some evidence that the looking practices of readers may be inherently conservative. When illustrations portrayed higher numbers of females in more central narrative roles, student responses indicate that they had trouble accepting that female centrality. The central females were sometimes incorrectly identified as males, there was often a degree of hesitancy in interpreting the narrative, and students continued their pattern of describing the *males* portrayed first, even in such images. The Jay Matternes illustration of a group of Neandertals which was published in *National Geographic* (Weaver 1985:599) is a good example. Seven Neandertals of assorted age are in the foreground, clustered around a dead animal. Two women are standing while a third crouches beside the animal with a cutting tool in her hand. A male sits off to the side making stone tools. Several adolescents and children are present. One of the standing women is speaking and gesturing with her hands while the other adults listen and look at her. Of the eight students who described this illustration, one avoided any mention of gender by simply describing them as "a group," one explicitly described the talking female as a male, one failed to mention the women at all, another noted that three women were present in the picture and then went on to discuss the flintknapping activities of the male, two discussed the male first before mentioning the females briefly, and only two described the females first and specifically mentioned that a female was speaking and all the others were listening to her.

The two students who described the talking female and ascribed narrative importance to her, did so in a very hesitant way. They used several qualifying terms such as "sort of," "almost," and "seems to be." One student offered a very sharp contrast when asked to comment on this Neandertal image right before commenting on a second illustration with a traditional-style central male figure. The descriptions offered in the two cases were striking. In the Neandertal image, the female was: "trying to explain to a group something with her hands" but in the second image, the male was "wise because they are all listening to him." What is particularly striking about this student's comments is that the second illustration is the Burian image seen in Figure 13. Here, a central male figure in the foreground is shown facing the viewer and gazing down at a small Venus figurine set on a boulder. While there are three women standing behind him and watching him, he is not speaking to them.

Students seemed particularly to resist the narrative in cases where females were shown playing a role usually associated with males in evolutionary theory. The Tanner-Dee Anne Hooker collaboration which was published in Tanner (1981), for example, shows three females and two males attempting to drive a leopard away from a juvenile it has attacked. Two females lead the attack with heavy sticks raised overhead. Students could accept the possibility of australopithecines defending themselves against leopards, but they clearly had more difficulty accepting a female lead role in that defence. Several respondents expressed doubt about that role until they noticed the figure of the supine adolescent hidden in the grass at the foot of the crouching leopard. At that point, they revised their estimation of the female involvement by saying that they could see females acting this way if they had to, *in defence of their young.*

There are several ways we could explain such conservatism on the part of viewers. They may be culturally programmed to see males as more important no matter how the illustrators try to "recraft" narratives of human evolution. This may explain why they selected the males in any image to describe first, going so far as to label active females as male in their viewing practices. And it also may explain why they relied on the code of infants to ascribe female gender to any figure associated with the very young: "They must be females because they are carrying children." An alternative explanation of viewer conservatism, however, may be that illustrators have never really made a serious attempt to craft females as important, despite surface appearances. The highlighted and pert breasts of the women in the Neandertal grouping described above, for example, may operate to undercut their centrality and erode their authority through the simple device of eroticism. Viewer conservatism may arise from the correct interpretation of that eroticism as a signal to ignore the apparent centrality of the female images.

Authors and editors attempt to constrain the independence of reader looking practices through text and captions which Lutz and Collins (1993:76) call "lyrical fixative." They cite Barthes in describing the "anchorage" function of captions, which direct the reader to one possible interpretation out of several, anchoring them to a stripped-down version of the narrative field. According to Lutz and Collins (ibid.:77), captions have "an inherently repressive value" which has the effect of directing the reader towards some meanings and away from others. One graduate student came to me with an excellent example of lyrical fixative in an origins illustration. In this image, a female figure reclines against a tree with an infant on her lap. She stretches out a hand towards a male who sits nearby holding some roots. Without its caption, this illustration could easily be read as an effort to naturalize the Western sexual division of labour. However, the caption attempts to fix the reader's attention on the development of language by stating:

> Australopithecines, prehuman creatures with relatively small brains who lived some 2.5 million years ago, almost certainly could not speak, but they could probably make simple tools and communicate with gestures and vocalizations. In an artist's imaginary view, a female Australopithecine successfully communicates her needs to a male companion (Hicks and Gwynne 1994:280).

Here the attempt is to constrain the reader from seeing other meanings in the image and to guide them into considering the "dawn of language use." However, both the looking practices of viewers and the fixative nature of captions should not be taken for granted.

To be better informed of the constraining nature of such lyrical fixatives, we need more research into how often people read the captions and how easily they discount the captions if their looking practices lead to different interpretations. Lutz and Collins (1993:76) found that as many as 53 percent of *National Geographic* readers did not read any text *except* the captions. But we do not know how many people actually pay close attention to what they are reading in the text accompanying illustrations, or in those captions placed directly under them. The utility of lyrical fixatives, furthermore, must be evaluated in the wider context of the total package of illustrations found in a magazine article or textbook. In the above "dawn of language" illustration, for example, the lyrical fixative may not restrain the sexist interpretations of the viewer if this is but one of a number of illustrations in the textbook which privileges the evolutionary role of the human male. This question of how readers consume packages of images when they appear in a larger context was not addressed by either my research strategy, nor that of Lutz and Collins. This is a future arena of research that is full of possibilities. Origins articles in the popular press often emulate the "landscape of life on earth" model and attempt to show freeze-frames over time, demonstrating how a number of different human ancestors may have looked and acted. This allows them to build presumed evolutionary progress into the images as well as into the text. Similarly, museums which provide entire halls of dioramas on the evolution of the human species present a collection of images which are viewed and interpreted as a group. Future studies might examine how students respond to such a body of freeze-frames both with and without the captions.

The consequences of the commoditization of illustrations has apparently been consistent with other factors affecting the illustrator's art. The visual codes which have come to dominate in human evolution are regular enough to be highly visible to an audience which has the tools to deconstruct these images. There is an obvious pattern of sanitizing the significant other, whether people of colour from extant cultures, or ancestral hominids in our evolutionary past. In making them safe and less threatening, they are also trivialized, recrafted to fit our expectations, or eroticized and manipulated to appeal to our cultural sensibilities. In making them meaningful, the images are riddled with elements of style and cultural consciousness (Ewen 1988). In making them politically useful, they are universalized, made presentist and stereotypical on the basis of essential traits and then presented as objective interpretations of the scientifically established truth. And all of this together makes them an easy sell.

Summary

Educational illustrations are commodities, and this aspect of their existence and use requires more thought. Artists create illustrations through an act of labour and release them as commodities into a market where knowledge is contested and sociopolitical contests provide one important context of knowledge dissemination. Illustrations not only sell copy but also often help to finance the operations of large cultural institutions who also have political motivations and agendas (see Baudrillard 1989 on American museums). Illustrations have a market life and a market pattern that is extremely complex, which is consistent with their position as markers of several kinds of boundaries in human thought; between information and entertainment, between fact and story and between signifier and signified. Yet most of this is invisible to the casual consumer of illustrations.

The consequences of the economic life of illustrations are important. They earn income for various kinds of people and institutions and as "science knowledge" this makes them vulnerable to manipulation based on monetary considerations. For example, the copyright attached to them allows the copyright holder to grant or withhold permission to reprint, and to attach whatever conditions to reprint that they wish. Copyright earns the holder income from the images, independent of the context of production. Indeed, the context of production must apparently be stripped from the images in order to protect their income-generating abilities. Those individuals or organizations which hold copyright can act as gatekeepers over their publication and thus ultimately over their use. These motivations and restrictions play a significant role in the cyclical nature of the use of some images. However, the commercial life of an image may sometimes be largely unintentional; artists and institutions often do not have the resources or inclination to monitor all the subsequent uses to which origins imagery is put, nor can they ensure that it is never used in ways that reinforce misinformation, stereotypes or racism.

Since commodities exist to be sold, it is also important to examine the influence that consumption patterns may have on the images that are produced and published. It may be that illustrators rely too much on Western artistic tropes in order to convey their own (mis)conceptions about gender, "race," progress, evolution and human prehistory. But it is far more likely to be the result of pressure to please the ultimate audience, the viewing public, whose standards and tastes may severely constrain the artist. This is the commodity aspect of illustrations coming into play. We could argue that it is up to the editors and/or authors of the textual material to redirect the artist's efforts in ways which challenge common stereotypes of "race," gender and progress. But editors and authors are subject to their own commercial pressures and the historical result has been a collective dismissal of the sexist, racist and theoretical implications of these illustrations. If the looking practices of the viewers are never challenged through education and criticism of the conventions in use, the results will continue to have significant effects on the thinking of layperson and specialist alike.

In future, I hope to direct more research into a whole host of questions, including the way that author, editor and publisher goals come together and result in the use of certain types of illustrations; the ways that these goals are not convergent and the impact that has; the outcome of publishing such illustrations; the role that context (of publication and of captions) plays in restricting reader autonomy and the role that reader background ("race," gender, socioeconomic level) plays in the looking practices of the various members of the public and on the resulting consumption patterns of origins illustrations. We need to know more about what role the commodity aspect of illustrations plays in their deployment as educative and quasi-educative materials. We need to know more about the ways that illustrations are selected for use in educative and quasi-educative popular publications. We need to know more about how illustrators set out to construct a narrative tale in the form of a visual illustration; what motivates them and what theories and/or assumptions they are making use of and why. We need to know more about the way that readers consume these images and the ideas that they generate. Once we begin to better understand these issues, then we can begin to deploy origins illustrations in ways that open up new avenues of thinking, instead of confining us to well-worn patterns of thought.

CHAPTER TEN

Conclusions and Future Directions for Research

EXAMINING THOSE EDUCATIONAL and quasi-education illustrations which convey in visual form many complex ideas about the appearance and lifestyle of our evolutionary ancestors has opened the proverbial Pandora's box on the stinging issues of gender, "race" and evolutionary progress. Those who teach anthropology, and those who popularize it for the mass media, must begin to critically reflect on the form educative illustrations have taken in the past, and should take in the future. This in turn requires that we develop the tools necessary to deconstruct the extremely dense and rich meaning contained within them. Unpacking this meaning involves several interwoven themes including the many contested theories about human history and origins, the way that Western artistic conventions are useful in sending very complex messages, the use of analogy in reconstructing our distant past, the underlying problems in evolutionary theory in general, and the way all of the above comes together in the art of the scientific illustrator. A number of different fields are required to develop the tool box necessary for the job, including art history and feminist criticism, paleoanthropology, paleontology, primatology, scientific illustration and the social anthropology of foraging societies. I have been able to only touch on the importance of each of them. My goal has been to begin a process of critical evaluation of paleoanthropological educational illustrative material, to report some early findings based on this process, to suggest some fruitful lines of future research and to encourage other researchers to consider them.

Unpacking Pandora's Box: Educative Illustration and Critical Deconstruction

While feminist art critics have long examined trends in the Western visual representation of gender and sexuality among the "fine arts," educational illustration as a mass-consumed branch of visual representation is under-represented in the feminist analysis. When we examine the representation of gender found in origins illustrations using the tools of the feminist critique, however, we find that prominent ideas about human evolution, gender and "race" have all been mixed together into a potent brew of visual tropes. This brew requires expanding the feminist perspective to incorporate several different conflated themes, including "natural" gender attributes and roles, racial stereotypes and a distorted message of evolution as "progress over time." The imagery links the (white) male with the changeable, the progressive, the technological, the cultural, the ascendant, the future; in opposition, it links the (dark) female with the immutable, the limited, the natural, the static, the past. These messages have been maintained in paleoanthropology despite recent, feminist-inspired challenges to the old, androcentric theories of human evolution. Indeed, the messages have been retrenched by a subtle shift in recent years, involving an increasing "eroticization" of the female image. This shift developed soon after the rise of the Woman-the-Gatherer model in paleoanthropology and is consistent with similar patterns of visual eroticism during periods of Western history when female gender roles have come under debate. Explaining the use of these conventions and the patterns of eroticism observed requires a better understanding of the role of illustrations as commodities, and of the relationship between the intent of the author, artist, publisher and of the consequences for reader understanding of human evolution research.

Contested Story Fields

There is no doubt that visual imagery is produced in a social context, and as such often reflects, comments on and subverts messages pertinent to the wider theological, political and economic debates of the day.[1] Following Nead (1990:326), I would argue that we cannot separate the significance of these illustrations from the "historical discourses" to which they relate. Nead (1988:4) defines a discourse as a "particular

---

1 I have not addressed the extended literature on the semiotics of artistic expression, and the even more extensive literature on the politics of the public sphere. For those interested in this topic I recommend beginning with the journal *Semiotica*, which published several articles on these topics in 1990 and 1991 in particular.

form of language" with its own rules and conventions. Certainly origins research forms a significant discourse (see Conkey 1991) or "story field" (Haraway 1988) in Western society, one which shows interesting patterns of change and continuity. Since the late 1980s, for example, proponents of the Woman-the-Gatherer stories have "raised the costs" of defending Man-the-Hunter stories of evolution, forcing the discipline to rethink and reconstitute some of the narrative staples of the hunter approach. The environment that shaped our species was transformed from a harsh, hot and dry grasslands to a kinder, gentler ecological mosaic; the pedigree of the natural human family changed from a patriarchal, monogamous institution of great antiquity to a matricentric, nurturing, multi-generational social unit; technological determinism went from "stones and bones" to carrying net and digging stick. A whole host of tropes became downplayed if not eliminated: male-male competition, male bonding, home bases and the male master of tool and weapon.

However, Woman the Gatherer never completely banished Man the Hunter from the stage, and some narrative staples remained resilient. The feminist critique has been submerged by attempts to meld together the less challenging aspects of the Zihlman-Tanner model with the more appealing parts of the Tarzan theory. In this new scenario, meat is still considered central to human evolution, and male technology is still seen as the primary avenue to meat acquisition. What we are left with in the discipline is an heterogeneous mix of ideas that are not functionally integrated into a logically consistent and coherent model. As a result, introductory textbooks have become much more tentative in their discussion of human evolution. The various theories concerning the rise of bipedality and encephalization, of speech and culture or of gender dimorphism are discussed in a way that represses their political context and contested nature. The mass media presents an even more simplistic, science-boosting perspective. Students and laypersons are often confronted with contradictory notions from various sources which they have trouble resolving in a meaningful way. They construct their own coherency using the resources with which they are most comfortable and in this effort the illustrative field becomes an important resource.

But perhaps this merely results from a confusion under which the experts themselves are operating. This is clearly a contentious period in the production of scientific knowledge on human evolution, with a number of experts being firmly entrenched into opposite camps while others are unsure who to support. Periods of contention in history, particularly in arenas affected by sexual politics, have always generated a subtext within the dominant discourse. Illustrations are a way of narrativizing this subtext, a way of deploying arguments not openly made, perhaps not even acknowledged at a conscious level. Their deployment into the social arena is a political, educative, scientific and cultural strategy of great power. The power to deploy narrative illustrations is the power to speak authoritatively in a "science" voice in order to comment on the nature of being human and to popularize this topic for wider consumption. Coombe (1996:210) argues that trademark in the U.S. culture of the late nineteenth century had a lot to do with nation-building and the forging of a national identity through a set of contrasts and powerful syntheses (barbarism, conquest and servitude, for example). But it may be that in popular culture, "nation-building" has been recently bypassed for a larger audience. For example, consider how the image of the evolutionary lineup, with its successive stages of problem-solving, technology-wielding, highly adaptive males, has been so widely and successfully disseminated that it appears on magazine covers in the Middle East and the Far East as well as throughout the West (see Gould 1989:33). Origins images have been marketed globally, through movies, books, magazines and even video games. Their messages are given an impeccable pedigree through the "science" status of the origins discourse. The dominance and dissemination of the Western visual imagery of human origins has been powerful enough to forge a nearly global perception of the Western story of the history of our species. This global perception constitutes white Western males as the peak of evolutionary perfection. All other marked categories can only occupy a subservient (or subversive) position in their shadow. And to resist this construction of our human past is to resist science.

But is science in the driver's seat? One consequence of this global deployment of imagery is that the discipline of anthropology has become trapped in a very limited view of human evolution, one which it participated in making, one which has since gone beyond its control and one which now conspires to continually remake the discipline in its own image. Paleoanthropologists have collaborated in generating this particular and image-rich discourse, and even illustrators have had more than a passing knowledge of the discipline in order to do their work in the field. But the relationship between origins discourse and the visual illustrations embedded in it are complex. While prevalent views of human evolution are mirrored both in the visual field and in the accompanying text, much of what is suggested in the visual field is never directly stated in the text, and furthermore, is sometimes contradictory to that text as is the case with the Matternes illustration of the Laetoli footprints. Deconstructing the illustrations then, forces us beyond the apparent meaning constructed in tandem with the written text. And beyond the textual meaning lies a world of meaning accessible through the artistic conventions employed by the illustrator.

In the West, art represents, creates and recreates, stimulates, narrates, signifies and leads by example. There is no doubt of its influence or importance and no doubt that the past serves as a significant context for present art production, where it impacts on the mind of art producers, whose intentions and motivations are multiplex and most probably deliberately opaque. The artistic conventions employed by Western illustrators play on several dominant wider cultural themes: the contrast between nudity and nakedness and between the femininity codes of Mary versus Eve, as well as the obsession with the Greco-Roman *nuditas virtualis* and male aesthetic athleticism, the Medieval "grotesque other" and the post-Renaissance revival of classical themes. Understanding the conventions used in Western art is an important window into embedded meanings and into the means of changing those meanings.

Miles (1989:179) argues that the overwhelming weight of tradition in the visual representation of the nude in Western art is such that we will never be able to reinvent it in any other form, an observation that is suggestive about the future of paleoanthropological illustration. Reconstructive illustrations of human evolution have leaned heavily on the codes associated with the representation of gender in Western art, but they have also, given assumptions about the late development of clothing in human history, leaned heavily on Western artistic conventions of the naked human form. While this representation of gender and of nakedness has not remained static, it has maintained a continuity of hierarchy. One change in recent years has been to move the female form to a more front and centre location in the frame, while simultaneously transforming it from an essentially non-erotic and somewhat grotesque imagery into a more blatantly erotic representation. This has maintained the essential role of the female in origins illustrations, where along with the primitive, the non-Caucasoid and the juvenile, they play the role of "significant other." This transformation was easily accomplished using the Western codes of nudity, rather than of nakedness. But if it was possible to make this effort, then surely it will be possible to go in other directions. Until we make the commitment to attempt a recrafting of the codes of nakedness, of primitiveness, of gender roles and attributes, we will not be able to fully explore the myriad of physiological and behavioural possibilities that may have played a role in our evolutionary history. The first step is raising our awareness about some of the deeply embedded meanings found in illustrative material and the second is to discover how readers are interpreting them.

Raising the awareness of people within the discipline implies, however, that there is no malice aforethought in some of those illustrative messages. Androcentrism in the meta-narrative of human evolution flourished before the feminist critique. It is clear how this androcentrism was played out in illustrations prior to 1981. But what is more important is the illustrative response to the Woman-the-Gatherer model. The use of eroticism to destabilize or even overwhelm any new messages about a larger role for females in human evolution is curious if we postulate an objective illustrator provided with a charge and brief which were linked only to apolitical scientific knowledge production. Somewhere between the producers of contested scientific knowledge and the brief of the artists, sexism, racism and ethnocentrism have been allowed, maybe even encouraged to develop. There are a number of possible explanatory approaches. The first and easiest is that we lay blame and view many reconstructive artists and science authors as sexist and racist.

The question of who is at fault in the production of sexist imagery underlies a great deal of the feminist critique of cultural artifact production. Many feminists reject "high art" as an "edifying, moral and privileged form of cultural" venue (Nead 1990:329) and instead focus on the patriarchal institutions of a largely masculine public world which produce this material as part of a hegemonic control over sexual politics. But this indulges in what van Benthem van den Bergh (1986) calls "blame orientation." Blame orientation has in common with many other modes of thinking an inclination to personalize the interactions between events. It tends to see events as having been planned by someone, it tends to ask "who" instead of "how," and it views as causal the relationship between purpose and outcomes. It is part of a larger ethos of attempting to control events rather than to understand them. Blaming is

linked to an oversimplistic view of life where answers to complex problems are easily arrived at since the remedy is automatically suggested by
the identification of the culprit. If underdevelopment springs from neocolonialism, for example, the exploitative character of the West must
change (ibid.:115). This tendency for oversimplification is a major impetus for bad social science (ibid.:119). Since it is rare for any phenomenon
to have a single cause, or to exist in a simple unidirectional relationship
with another phenomenon, blame orientation tends to repress knowledge. Once the culprit is identified, all attempts to continue the search
for other explanations can cease.

If we blame masculine artists and science authors, then we can cease
to look any farther for explanations of the patterns we see in origins evolution. But to do so ignores a much larger context of educational publications. Other explanatory options exist. We could argue that these
masculine purveyors of a distorted evolution message were simply misled themselves, thereby disconnecting intention and outcome and
absolving the authors and the artists. But to do so would fail to situate
multiple and multiplex motivations and even more complex patterns of
outcome, into a wider framework of understanding. Illustrations tell an
ageless story. That story changes very little no matter what the theoretical winds of change. Eroticism is a small blip on that horizon, and one
that is consistent with a larger pattern of recrafting the other to make
them palatable to our tastes (Lutz and Collins 1993:89). And tastes
change, although basic values are more conservative. I think it no accident that the taste for eroticism is more imperative during a period of
heightened dispute about the public roles of women and men, but I see
no conspiracy underneath the patterns.

Dancing with Dualities: Western Discourse Analysis

In propagating Western stereotypes about gender attributes and roles,
origins illustrations also convey subtle messages about culture and
progress, about "race" and Western superiority. Perhaps these spring from
the Western obsession with dualities. Various authors in cultural studies
and in discourse analyses have demonstrated the operation of these dualities: female and male, nature and culture, private and public, layperson
and scientist, entertainment and information, primitive and progressive,
body and mind, black and white, others in contrast to ourselves (see

especially Haraway and Lutz and Collins). I follow Haraway in seeing these dualities not as narrowly defined and mutually reinforcing immutable "stacks," but rather as "turnstiles," which twist and turn in the winds of politics, to let different meanings through. While these meanings may change, the turnstile itself remains in place.

Thus, for example, in Victorian England, the elite female was associated with culture and the male was seen as sullied by his closer association with base natural instincts. On the other hand, the working-class woman was not the paragon of cultural virtues that her elite sister was, and working-class men were even lower on the animal side of the scale. Class and socioeconomic position allowed specific males and females to pass through the turnstile and convey different, context-specific meanings about gender attributes. Masculine and feminine characteristics have the same ability to transmogrify under various conditions in ways that are not perceived to be logically inconsistent. In a similar fashion, the environment can be viewed from various perspectives today. As a participating unit in the female/nature trope, the environment can be seen as a dangerous entity, only subdued by masculine technology, or it can slip through the turnstile and take on slightly different meaning as a feminine entity badly abused by male rapaciousness. Perhaps it is this very slipperiness which gives such tropes their enduring ability to fascinate the Western mind. When an artist uses these tropes in his or her illustration production, his or her goal may be as limited as creating images which the audience, trained to Western standards of aesthetic beauty and to Western conventions of appearance and demeanour, can recognize and acknowledge.

When we deconstruct such images, we must do so with these complexities in mind. Deconstruction can be deep and critically evaluative as in semiotic research, or it can be accessible and geared to a wider audience, as in general art critique. In either case, an important objective is that no one receives preconstructed messages as uncontested fact. This is as true of the feminist messages as of those they seek to replace. The most important aim should be to develop a self-reflexive stance. We need to reflect on why certain ideas and models appeal to us at a gut level and we need to encourage an academic environment in which theoretical ideas can go beyond our comfort level. This environment should employ the talents of artists in different ways, in creating alternative options that can challenge us to think more critically about the phenomenon being investigated. This can only happen if the illustrative world receives increased attention.

Although visual anthropology is a field of growing interest to members of the discipline, the use of photographs, films, drawings and reconstructive illustrations in the field has a long history compared to the work that has been done to critically reflect on how this material is used and what messages may actually be apprehended by the viewing audience. For example, consider the photographs that to a great extent have replaced the artist's conception in many introductory textbooks. What sort of photographs are selected for the covers of anthropology textbooks? How many introductory textbooks in socio-cultural anthropology have a nubile young female on the front cover (see the example on Jolly, Plog and Bates 1980)? How does the respective "science" contributions of the two genders within the discipline find visual representation? What is the relative representation of males and females as authoritative scientists in the photos of field sites and laboratories? And what about the non-narrative illustrative material? Must the hands of the flintknappers always be masculine in appearance? When students are taught in what order flakes are struck off a stone core, must they also absorb spurious notions about the techno-hierarchy of gender?

Illustrations that appear sometimes bear less relevance to the science or to the popularizing text than they do to concerns of commodification. Sometimes the affordable alternative is relabelled or reworked so that it becomes relevant to a particular text when that was never the artist's intention, as when Choukoutien Cave *Homo erectus* illustrations are reprinted as an illustration of European Neandertals. In such a situation it is dangerous to rely too much either on the accompanying textual material or on the artistic conventions utilized by the artists to interrogate or deconstruct the purpose behind the particular form the illustrations take. Deconstruction must be fixed in the complex social matrix of which illustrations are a part.

It is ironic that one of the more interesting features of the commodification issue is the extent to which the utility of the illustration relies on *oversimplification* through erasure—the erasure of most of the complex physical and social contexts of the illustrated biological entities; the erasure of the production context surrounding the work of the artists and their collaboration with scientists and publishers; the erasure of alternative models of human evolution; and most importantly, the erasure of

scientific conjecture in favour of a narrativized discourse. It is ironic
because it is this very erasure which must be reversed in a critical deconstruction. It is also important to ask about reader autonomy, and to
explore the ways in which readers interpret illustrations, perhaps in spite
of the lyrical fixative which attempts to limit their interpretations along
the lines suggested by the text. And finally, it is important to ask questions about the feedback relationship between audience demands
(expressed through sales figures, readership opinion surveys, image popularity and levels of funding support) and science popularization,
whereby science is actually constrained by the narrative themes
demanded by the popular audience.

To better understand the trend in gender representation in origins
illustrations or the more recent eroticism of the female in these illustrations, for example, we need to develop a stance that explores complexity,
that resists simplistic personalized explanations, and that prepares us for a
deeper understanding instead of an attempt to control or change events
on the basis of incomplete information. As an example, if we broaden our
view on eroticism, it becomes apparent that the trend in paleoanthropological illustrations is part of a larger trend in Western society. Advertisers
have increasingly turned from images of women as mothers and home-
makers, so common to the 1950s, to women represented in horizontal
stances of allure and sexual invitation. There has been a general "inflation
of sexualized images of women in the culture at large" (Lutz and Collins
1993:176) with the rather sterile, television family mothers of the 1950s
(Lucille Ball, Laura Petrie) turning first into the emancipated, single working women of the 1970s (Mary Tyler Moore and Rhoda) and finally into
the more gritty, single working-class moms of of the 1990s (*Grace Under
Fire*). Eroticism may be consistent with disputes over the position of
women in society, but at the same time the turnstile has allowed for an
increasing permissiveness bringing with it a general liberalization of rigid
roles for both genders. Does the more explicit sexual behaviour of a character like Grace in *Grace Under Fire* represent a tendency to eroticize and
thus repress women, or an attempt to liberate female gender roles from
limiting stereotypes of traditional motherhood? Western gender conventions allows it to be both at the same time.

Masculine conspiracies *may* be at work in the flow of these events;
however, I would agree with Haraway (1988:96) that: "There is no conspiracy of capitalist patriarchs in the sky to create a science of animal

behaviour to naturalize the fantasies of twentieth century American white men, no matter how tempting the evidence sometimes seems." No patriarchal conspiracy underlies the periodic swings in values that result in increasing permissiveness, new standards of dress or undress in the public view, new imagery of women which draws on the Eve codification rather than the Mary; this is too simple a causal relationship to explain what has been an extremely complex socio-political period in history. However, we can explore the coming together of a number of societal and political forces which along with the change in social values, allows this increasingly eroticized view of women to be useful in contesting scientific knowledge. It is difficult to discover if illustrators knowingly construct more erotic visions of female hominids, or if the scientists who use these illustrations select them for those qualities, but we can interrogate the social circumstances that make it possible for them to do so, including investigating the relationships between illustrators, authors, editors, publishing houses, museums and their boards of trustees, archives, variable copyright laws across national boundaries and other players in the game of educative illustration. There is no point in holding illustrators accountable for misinformation, subtle messages and ulterior motives. Illustrations come from many sources, including museum displays, archives, libraries, older textbooks or popular books and work commissioned by editors, particularly in textbooks. The ubiquitous "artist's conception" covers many tracks. Illustrators cannot be expected to be well-versed in all the academic disciplines they may illustrate, nor can they always control the subsequent places their illustrations end up. Nor is it fruitful to blame the authors or the publishers of the written material with which these illustrations are found in association. But we *can* demand a more conscious practice of illustration in the future.

This requires that we be more conscious as an audience, since we consume these origins myths as readily as the world of science and quasi-education publication produces them, and train others to do so as well. In discussing the goals and utility of a feminist science, Haraway (1988:81) has written that it is not a mechanism for "replacing false versions with true ones" but rather works through "altering a 'field' of stories or possible explanatory accounts, by raising the costs of defending some accounts, by destabilizing the plausibility of some strategies of explanation." Thus the Woman-the-Gatherer model is no more "the truth" about hominid evolution than was the Man-the-Hunter model

which predated it. It has many of the same theoretical limitations as the
Hunter story, suffering as it does from presentism, essentialism, functionalism and universalism. The science product, whether feminist or not,
participates in a wider cultural context which cannot fail to influence
what scientists do and believe as well as what they produce. On the
other hand, the Woman-the-Gatherer model *did* begin the process of
problematizing the origins discourse by drawing attention to androcentrism. It *did* destabilize the origins narratives so that we could ask different questions and ask them differently. The same destabilizing outcome
could result from a cultural analysis which questions the illustrations
found in association with origins texts.

There seems reason to hope. I have stated that colleagues tended to
respond to the illustrative material discussed here in one of two ways.
The first response was that the visual representations of gender and
progress, much as the "politically correct" might deplore them, are
grounded in "natural facts" and are thus inevitable, representational and
inscribed in male and female biology (see also Miles 1989:219). Other
comments were that these androcentric and ethnocentric models have
long been under critical attack and are in the process of being dislodged,
as is their illustrative material so there is nothing to worry about. But in
many cases, these same colleagues later returned to me with new illustrations of which they were now highly critical. Our cultural expectations
are influential, as are narrative demands, preconceived notions and prejudices, which are contained in the scientist as they are in the layperson.
However, these influences need not be straitjackets. People can be
alerted to their own prejudices and proclivities of thought and can force
their thinking beyond them.

Landau (1991:178) writes of the constraining nature of the narrative
format which has held paleoanthropology captive, limiting it to telling
the same kinds of stories over and over despite changes in the data base;
illustrations have played a similar constraining role. It is up to us to critically deconstruct the limiting stereotypes of gender, "race" and progress
in our models of human evolution; if we do not challenge them wherever they are found, origins research will remain captive to their limitations. But Landau argues that constraint can turn into liberation, by
using narrative approaches to imagine "the full set of possible arrangements" that may have played a role in our evolutionary past. Perhaps
grappling with the "artistic conventions" common in paleoanthropology

(and indeed in anthropological illustration and/or photography) will ultimately lead to theoretical growth. As more research and critique is done on the way visual illustrative material is used in educational discourse of all kinds, we can turn this "edifying tool" to more constructive purposes. Illustrations could provide scope for one to imagine many alternative pasts and this can only help challenge the dominant narratives of human evolution, and perhaps of the human experience in general.

Looking to the Future

Various themes then, of the illustrator's art, of evolution and human progress, of male and female gender roles and of primate and primitives as analogies of early human evolutionary stages, are brought together in this book in an attempt to deconstruct the deep meanings available to the viewer of educational and quasi-educational illustrations in paleoanthropology. We can look at these illustrations in a critical way, to find their cultural messages and meanings which are really points of view, as well as to investigate the means by which their creation and publication are given authorial weight as "science-product," and therefore as fact. We can be more alert to these messages and challenge them in the classroom and in textbooks and quasi-educational publications where they are given scientific authority. But we need to take care in doing this, both in the classroom and in the wider public. Alienating the non-specialist with highly public acrimonious debate is not constructive for the discipline. And alienating students is also a possibility. How can we teach students and the public to be more critical of the messages contained in these illustrations, and to make a point of mentally challenging them without undercutting their faith and interest in anthropology?

I think the answer to this last question relates to the many directions research on this topic could take in the future. We need to gain a more sophisticated understanding of the process of production and dissemination of contested knowledge and we need to interest future anthropologists in this research task. Understanding origins images requires investigating a larger cultural context, including but not limited to gender and racial politics, epistemological issues of knowledge generation, and the interaction between institutional power and knowledge dissemination. Future research might further investigate the circulation of these illustrations as commodities in the publishing world. How is scientific knowledge marketed, to whom and why? What are the power relationships in society which have contributed to the development and use of certain primate and forager society analogies? How can we reprogram our scientific effort to challenge our cultural patterns of thinking about evolution and the related themes of "race," progress and gender? And further, how can we go beyond the comfort zone of our mass audience and encourage them to exercise their imaginations when applied to our human past? Only when we have answered these questions will it be possible to construct different images of the past which challenge us to "imagine differently" the potential past lifestyles, gender attributes, gender roles and evolutionary directions of the hominid line. This would indeed be using illustrations to educate.

Figures

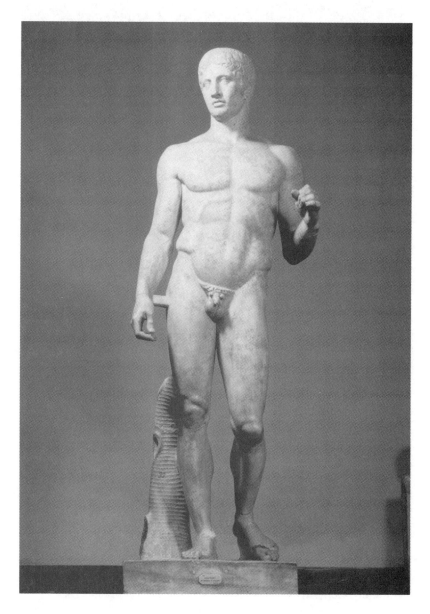

FIGURE 1. The Greco-Roman Classical Male, the template for aesthetic athleticism. Polykleitos, c. 540 B.C. Doryphoros. Museo Archeologico Nazionale, Naples, Italy. Courtesy of Scala/Art Resource, NY.

FIGURE 2. Erect Man/Undulating Woman; a fifteenth-century example. Jacopo della Quercia's Adam and Eve panel on the Baptismal font in the Chapel of S. Giovanni, Duomo, Siena, Italy. Courtesy of Alinari/Art Resource, NY.

FIGURE 3. The Gothic Nude Encased in Invisible Clothing. Woman as if made from some viscous material. Detail of Eve from the Ghent Altarpiece by Jan van Eyck, Cathedral St. Bavo, Ghent, Belgium. Photo courtesy of Scala/Art Resource, NY.

Prosimians   Monkeys   Gibbons Orangutans Gorillas Chimps Humans

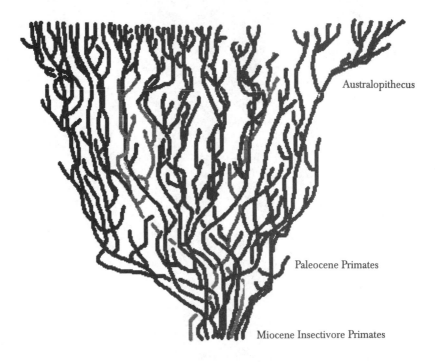

FIGURE 4. A Typical Dendrogram of Primate Evolution, with diversity com-
pacted at the bottom and artificially inflated at the top to create the cone of
increasing diversity.

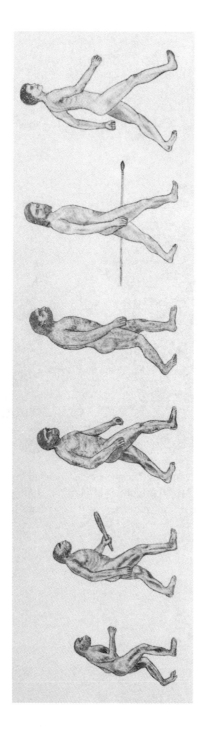

FIGURE 5. A Typical "Progress Ladder" of Human Evolution, showing well-muscled and healthy males of the hominid family. Interpretive illustration rendered by H.T. Dignam, 1996.

FIGURE 6. Male Centrality among *Homo erectus*. Published in Josef Augusta and
Zdeněk Burian, *Prehistoric Man* (London: Paul Hamlyn, 1960), plate 2, and entitled: "*Homo erectus* foraging in the wilderness of Java perhaps half a million years
ago." Artist is Zdeněk Burian. Courtesy of Jiří Hochman.

FIGURE 7. *Homo erectus* and the Beginnings of Culture. Peking Man–360,000 years ago, Choukoutien Cave, China. Artist is Maurice Wilson. Courtesy of The Natural History Museum, London.

FIGURE 8. The Neandertal as Grotesque Other. Published in Josef Augusta and Zdeněk Burian, *Prehistoric Man* (London: Paul Hamlyn, 1960), plate 8, and entitled: "Neanderthal Man: home base, limestone shelter, at the beginning of the rhinoceros hunt." Artist is Zdeněk Burian. Courtesy of Jiří Hochman.

FIGURE 9. The Neandertal and the Prehistoric Patriarchal Family. *The Neanderthal Family.* Artist is Maurice Wilson. Courtesy of The Natural History Museum, London.

FIGURE 10. Neandertal Burial Imagery Showing Male Masters of Ritual. Published in Josef Augusta and Zdeněk Burian, *Prehistoric Man* (London: Paul Hamlyn, 1960), plate 18, and entitled *The Le Moustier Burial.* Artist is Zdeněk Burian. Courtesy of Jiří Hochman.

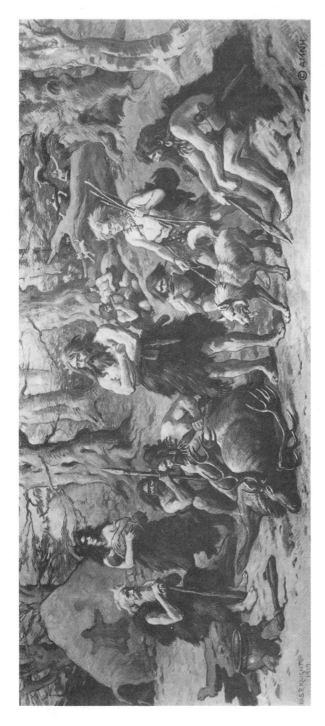

FIGURE 11. *Homo sapiens sapiens*–Just Below the Angels. Neolithic Man of the Campignian Stage. Artist is Charles R. Knight. Neg. no. 37952. Photo by Julius Kirschner. Courtesy Department of Library Services, American Museum of Natural History.

FIGURE 12. Archaic Humans Done with Aesthetic Athleticism. Hunting party at Swanscombe 250,000 years ago. Artist is Maurice Wilson. Courtesy of The Natural History Museum, London.

FIGURE 13. The Male-Sponsored Rise of Religion. Published in F. Clark Howell, *Early Man* (New York: Time Inc., 1965), 155, and entitled: "One of the world's first artists, a hunter is portrayed here kneeling before the product of his labor, a Venus made of clay." Artist is Zdeněk Burian. Courtesy of Jiří Hochman.

FIGURE 14. Male Technological Prowess as the Inspiration for Art and Ritual. Artists in the cave of Font-de-Guame. Artist is Charles R. Knight. Neg. no. 2A21479. Photo by AMNH Photo Studio. Courtesy of the American Museum of Natural History.

FIGURE 15. Anatomically Modern Humans in the French Postcard Genre. Published in Sergio Treviño, *Grain Collection. Humans' Natural Ecological Niche* (New York: Vantage Press, 1991), plate 1, and entitled: "A group of naked men and women trying to survive in the long-grass savanna." Artist is Angel Martin. Courtesy of Vantage Press.

FIGURE 16. The Victorian Trope of Unruly Hair. Published in Sergio Treviño, *1991 Grain Collection. Humans' Natural Ecological Niche* (New York: Vantage Press, 1991), plate 1, and entitled: "A group of naked men and women trying to survive in the long-grass savanna." Artist is Angel Martin. Courtesy of Vantage Press.

References Cited

Andrews, Peter J., and Chris Stringer
    1989 *Human Evolution. An Illustrated Guide.* Cambridge: Cambridge University Press.

Anthony, Piers
    1993 *The Isle of Women.* New York: Tom Doherty Associates.

Appadurai, Arjun
    1986 Introduction: Commodities and the Politics of Value. In Arjun Appadurai, ed., *The Social Life of Things. Commodities in Cultural Perspective,* pp. 3-63. Cambridge: Cambridge University Press.

Ardrey, Robert
    1966 *The Territorial Imperative. A Personal Inquiry into the Animal Origins of Property and Nations.* New York: Dell Publishing.

Armstrong, Carol M.
    1985 Edgar Degas and the Representation of the Female Body. In Susan Suleiman, ed., *The Female Body in Western Culture. Contemporary Perspectives,* pp. 223-42. Cambridge: Harvard University Press.

Auel, Jean
    1980 *The Clan of the Cave Bear.* New York: Crown Publishers.

Augereau, Jean-Francois, and Jean-Paul Dufour
    1994 New Views on the Origins of Man. *World Press Review* 41(8):42.

Augusta, J., and Zdeněk Burian
    1960 *Prehistoric Man.* London: Hamlyn.

Barthes, Roland
    1957 *Mythologies.* Translated by Annette Lavers. London: Jonathan Cape.

Baudrillard, Jean
    1975 *The Mirror of Production.* Translated by Mark Poster. St. Louis: Telos Press.
    1989 *America.* Translated by Chris Turner. London: Verso.
    1990 *Revenge of the Crystal.* Edited and translated by Paul Foss and Julian Pefanis. London: Pluto Press.

Bloom, Lisa
    1993 *Gender on Ice.* Minneapolis: University of Minnesota Press.

Bolger, Diane
    1996   Figurines, Fertility, and the Emergence of Complex Society
            in Prehistoric Cyprus. *Current Anthropology* 37(2):365-73.
Boserup, Ester
    1970   *Women's Role in Economic Development.* New York: St. Martin's
            Press.
Brain, C.K.
    1974   A Hominid's Skull's Revealing Holes. *Natural History*
            83(10):44-45.
Brettell, Caroline, and Carolyn Sargent
    1993   Biology, Gender, and Human Evolution. In Caroline Brettell
            and Carolyn Sargent, eds., *Gender in Cross-Cultural Perspective*,
            pp. 1-5. Englewood Cliffs, NJ: Prentice Hall.
Briggs, D.E.G., R.A. Fortey, and M.A. Wills
    1992   Morphological Disparity in the Cambrian. *Science* 256:1670-73.
Burnham, John C.
    1987   *How Superstition Won and Science Lost. Popularizing Science and
            Health in the United States.* New Brunswick, NJ: Rutgers
            University Press.
Butterfield, Herbert
    1965   *The Whig Interpretation of History.* New York: Norton.
Caird, Rod
    1994   *Ape Man. The Story of Human Evolution.* With Dr. Robert Foley.
            New York: MacMillan.
Callender, Charles, and Lee Kochems
    1983   The North American Berdache. *Current Anthropology* 24:443-56.
Campbell, Bernard G.
    1982   *Humankind Emerging.* 3rd Edition. Boston: Little, Brown and
            Company.
Campbell, Bernard G., and James D. Loy
    1996   *Humankind Emerging.* 7th Edition. New York: Harper Collins
            College Publishers.
Caplan, Pat
    1988   Engendering Knowledge. The Politics of Ethnography (Part 1).
            Anthropology Today 4(5):8-17.
Caws, Mary Ann.
    1985   Ladies Shot and Painted: Female Embodiment in Surrealist
            Art. In Susan Suleiman, ed., *The Female Body in Western*

Culture. Contemporary Perspectives, pp. 262-87. Cambridge: Harvard University Press.

Chard, Chester, S.

1975   *Man in Prehistory.* New York: McGraw-Hill Books.

Clark, Kenneth

1956   *The Nude. A Study in Ideal Form.* New York: Pantheon Books.

Conkey, Margaret W.

1983   On the Origins of Paleolithic Art: A Review and Some Critical Thoughts. In E. Trinkaus, ed., *The Mousterian Legacy: Human Biocultural Change in the Upper Paleolithic*, pp. 201-27. Oxford: British Archaeological Reports International Series

1991   Original Narratives. The Political Economy of Gender in Archaeology. In Micaela di Leonardo, ed., *Gender at the Crossroads of Knowledge: Feminist Anthropology in the Post Modern Era*, pp. 102-39. Berkeley: University of California Press.

Constable, George, ed.

1973   *The Neanderthals.* The Emergence of Man Series. New York: Time-Life Books.

Coombe, Rosemary

1996   Embodied Trademarks: Mimesis and Alterity on American Commercial Frontiers. *Cultural Anthropology* 11(2):202-24.

Cowling, Mary

1989   *The Artist as Anthropologist. The Representation of Type and Character in Victorian Art.* Cambridge: Cambridge University Press.

Dahlberg, Frances, ed.

1981   *Woman the Gatherer.* New Haven: Yale University Press.

Darwin, Charles

1930   *The Descent of Man.* Part I. The Thinker's Library No. 12. London: Watts and Company.

Day, Michael H.

1971   *Fossil Man.* New York: Bantam Books.

Desmond, Adrian

1989   Lamarckism and Democracy: Corporations, Corruption and Comparative Anatomy in the 1830s. In James R. Moore, ed., *History, Humanity and Evolution*, pp. 99-130. Cambridge: Cambridge University Press.

DeVore, Irven
   1962   The Social Behavior and Organization of Baboon Troops.
          Ph.D. thesis, University of Chicago.
   1965a *Primate Behavior: Field Studies of Monkeys and Apes.* New York:
          Holt, Rinehart and Winston.
   1965b Male Dominance and Mating Behavior in Baboons. In
          Frank A. Beach, ed., *Sex and Behavior*, pp. 266-89. New York:
          Krieger.
Diamond, Jared
   1993   Sex and the Female Agenda. *Discover* 14(9):86-93.
Dickason, Olive P.
   1984   *The Myth of the Savage and the Beginnings of French Colonialism
          in the Americas.* Edmonton: University of Alberta Press.
di Leonardo, Micaela ed.
   1991   *Gender at the Crossroads of Knowledge: Feminist Anthropology
          in the Post Modern Era.* Berkeley: University of California Press.
Dronfield, Jeremy
   1996   The Vision Thing: Diagnosis of Endogenous Derivation in
          Abstract Arts. *Current Anthropology* 37(2):373-91.
duBois, Page
   1988   *Sowing the Body. Psychoanalysis and Ancient Representations of
          Women.* Chicago: University of Chicago Press.
Eder, James
   1987   *On the Road to Tribal Extinction.* Berkeley: University of
          California Press.
Edey, Maitland A., and the Time-Life Books Editors
   1972   *The Emergence of Man. The Missing Link.* New York: Time, Inc.
Elkins, James
   1996   Cultural Representation and the Methodology of Close
          Reading in Archaeology. *Current Anthropology* 37(2):185-226.
Ember, Carol
   1983   The Relative Decline in Women's Contribution to Agriculture
          with Intensification. *American Anthropologist* 85(2):285-304.
Errington, Shelly
   1990   Recasting Sex, Gender, and Power. A Theoretical and
          Regional Overview. In Jane M. Atkinson and Shelly
          Errington, eds., *Power and Difference. Gender in Island Southeast
          Asia*, pp. 1-58. Stanford, CA: Stanford University Press.

Evans-Pritchard, E.E.

1950 Social Anthropology: Past and Present. *Man* 198:118-24.

Ewen, Stuart

1988 *All Consuming Images: The Politics of Style in Contemporary Culture.* New York: Basic Books.

Fedigan, Linda

1986 The Changing Role of Women in Models of Human Evolution. *Annual Review of Anthropology* 15:25-66.

Fedigan, Linda, and Laurence Fedigan

1989 Gender and the Study of Primates. In Sandra Morgan, ed., *Gender and Anthropology. Critical Reviews for Research and Teaching,* pp. 41-64. Washington, DC: American Anthropological Association.

Foley, Robert

1988 Hominids, Humans and Hunter-Gatherers: An Evolutionary Perspective. In Tim Ingold, David Riches, James Woodburn, eds., *Hunters and Gatherers,* pp. 207-21. Oxford: Berg Publishers.

Folger, Tim

1993 The Naked and the Bipedal. Anthropology Watch. *Discover* 14(11):34-35.

Foucault, Michel

1978 *The History of Sexuality.* Vol. 1: *An Introduction.* Translated by Robert Hurley. New York: Pantheon.

Fox, Robin

1967 *Kinship and Marriage.* Baltimore, MD: Penguin Books.

Garvan, John M.

1963 *The Negritos of the Philippines.* Edited by Hermann Hochegger. Horn, Wien: Verlag Ferdinand Berger.

Geertz, Clifford

1995 Culture War. *The New York Review of Books,* Vol. 42 (19):4-6.

Gero, J.

1991 Genderlithics: Women's Role in Stone Tool Production. In M. Conkey and J. Gero, eds., *Engendering Archaeology: Women and Prehistory.* Cambridge: Blackwell Publishers.

Gifford-Gonzalez, Diane

1993 You Can Hide, But You Can't Run: Representations of Women's Work in Illustrations of Palaeolithic Life. *Visual Anthropology Review* 9(1):23-41.

Goodall, Jane [van Lawick]

  1967   *My Friends, the Wild Chimpanzees.* Washington, DC: National Geographic.

  1971   *In the Shadow of Man.* Boston: Houghton Mifflin.

  1986   *The Chimpanzees of Gombe: Patterns of Behavior.* Cambridge: Harvard University Press.

Goody, Jack

  1983   *The Development of the Family and Marriage in Europe.* Cambridge: Cambridge University Press.

  1990   *The Oriental, the Ancient and the Primitive.* Cambridge: Cambridge University Press.

Gore, Rick

  1996   Neandertals. The Dawn of Humans. *National Geographic* 189(1):2-35.

Gould, Stephen Jay

  1974a Darwin's Dilemma. *Natural History* 83(4):32-39.

  1974b The Great Dying. *Natural History* 83(8):22-27.

  1974c Darwin's Delay. *Natural History* 83(10):68-70.

  1975a Evolution and the Brain. *Natural History* 84(1):24-26.

  1975b Catastrophes and Steady State Earth. *Natural History* 84(2):14-18.

  1976   This View of Life. *Natural History* 85(4):24-31.

  1977   *Ever Since Darwin.* New York: W.W. Norton.

  1980   *The Panda's Thumb.* New York: W.W. Norton.

  1981   *The Mismeasure of Man.* New York: W.W. Norton.

  1984   *Hen's Teeth and Horse's Toes.* New York: W.W. Norton.

  1985   *The Flamingo's Smile.* New York: W.W. Norton.

  1989   *Wonderful Life. The Burgess Shale and the Nature of History.* New York: W.W. Norton.

  1994   The Evolution of Life on the Earth. *Scientific American* (October):85-91.

Grinker, Roy Richard

  1992   History and Hierarchy in Hunter-Gatherer Studies. *American Ethnologist* 19(1):160-65.

Hager, Lori D.

  1991   The Evidence for Sex Differences in the Hominid Fossil Record. In D. Walde and N.D. Willows, eds., *The Archeology of Gender*, pp. 46-49. Proceedings of the 22nd Annual

Chacmool Conference. Calgary: The Archaeological Association of the University of Calgary.

Hall, K.R.L., and Irven DeVore
1965 Baboon Social Behavior. In Irven DeVore, ed., *Primate Behavior*. New York: Holt, Rinehart and Winston.

Hallowell, A. Irving
1956 The Structural and Functional Dimensions of a Human Existence. *Quarterly Review of Biology* 31:88-101.
1961 The Protocultural Foundations of Human Adaptation. In S.L. Washburn, ed., *Social Life of Early Man*, pp. 236-55. Chicago: Aldine Publishing.

Haraway, Donna
1983 The Contest for Primate Nature: Daughters of Man-the-Hunter in the Field, 1960-1980. In Mark E. Kann, ed., *The Future of American Democracy*, pp. 175-207. Philadelphia: Temple University Press.
1988 Primatology Is Politics by Other Means. In Ruth Bleier, ed., *Feminist Approaches to Science*, pp. 77-118. New York: Pergamon Press.
1989 *Primate Visions. Gender, Race and Nature in the World of Modern Science*. New York: Routledge.

Harding, Robert S.O., and Shirley C. Strum
1976 Predatory Baboons of Kekopey. *Natural History* 85(3):46-53.

Harpending, H.C., S.T. Sherry, A.R. Rogers and M. Stoneking
1993 The Genetic Structure of Ancient Human Populations. *Current Anthropology* 34(4):483-96.

Hart, Keith
1983 The Contribution of Marxism to Economic Anthropology. In Sutti Ortiz, ed., *Economic Anthropology*, pp. 105-44. Society for Economic Anthropology, Monograph Number 1. Lanham: University Press of America.

Hatch, Elvin
1973 *Theories of Man and Culture*. New York: Columbia University Press.

Haviland, William A.
1979 *Human Evolution and Prehistory*. New York: Holt, Rinehart and Winston.
1994 *Anthropology*. 7th Edition. New York: Harcourt Brace.

Hicks, David, and Margaret A. Gwynne
    1994   *Cultural Anthropology.* New York: Harper Collins College
            Publications.
Hinde, R.A.
    1975   The Comparative Study of Non-Verbal Communication.
            In Jonathan Benthall and Ted Polhemus, eds., *The Body as a
            Medium of Expression,* pp. 107-42. London: Allen Lane.
Hoebel, E. Adamson
    1960   *The Cheyennes. Indians of the Great Plains.* New York: Holt,
            Rinehart and Winston.
Hollander, Anne
    1978   *Seeing Through Clothes.* New York: The Viking Press.
Holmberg, Allan R.
    1969   *Nomads of the Long Bow.* New York: American Museum
            Science Books.
Hosken, Fran P.
    1982   *The Hosken Report: Genital and Sexual Mutilation of Females.*
            Lexington, MA: Women's International Network News.
Howell, F. Clark
    1965   *Early Man.* New York: Time, Inc.
Hrdy, Sarah Blaffer
    1981   *The Woman That Never Evolved.* Cambridge: Harvard
            University Press.
Ingold, Tim
    1986   *Evolution and Social Life.* Cambridge: Cambridge
            University Press.
Isaac, Glynn L., and Elizabeth R. McCown, eds.
    1976   *Human Origins. Louis Leakey and the East African Evidence.*
            Menlo Park: Benjamin/Cummings.
Johanson, Donald
    1985   The Most Primitive Australopithecus. In P.V. Tobias, ed.,
            Hominid Evolution. Past, Present and Future, pp. 213-20. New
            York: Alan R. Liss.
    1996   The Dawn of Humans. Face-to-Face with Lucy's Family.
            National Geographic 189(3):96-117.
Johanson, Donald, and Maitland Edey
    1981   *Lucy. The Beginnings of Humankind.* New York: Simon and
            Schuster.

Johanson, Donald, and James Shreeve
:   1989 *Lucy's Child. The Discovery of a Human Ancestor.* New York: William Morrow.

Johanson, Donald, and T.D. White
:   1979 A systematic assessment of early African hominids. *Science* 203:321-30.

Jolly, Clifford J., and Fred Plog
:   1986 *Physical Anthropology and Archaeology.* New York: Alfred A. Knopf.

Jolly, Clifford J., Fred Plog and Daniel Bates
:   1980 *Anthropology. Decisions, Adaptation, and Evolution.* New York: Alfred A. Knopf.

Jolly, Pieter
:   1996 Symbiotic Interaction between Black Farmers and South-Eastern San: Implications for Southern African Rock Art Studies, Ethnographic Analogy, and Hunter-Gatherer Cultural Identity. *Current Anthropology* 37(2):277-306.

Kent, Susan
:   1992 The Current Forager Controversy: Real Versus Ideal Views of Hunter-Gatherers. *Man* 27:45-70.

Kessler, Suzanne, and Wendy McKenna
:   1978 *Gender: An Ethnomethodological Approach.* New York: John Wiley and Sons.

Kinzey, Warren, ed.
:   1987 *The Evolution of Human Behavior: Primate Models.* New York: State University of New York Press.

Knauft, Bruce M.
:   1994 Pushing Anthropology Past the Posts: Critical Notes on Cultural Anthropology and Cultural Studies as Influenced by Postmodernism and Existentialism. *Critique of Anthropology* 14(2):117-52.

Knight, Charles
:   1942 Parade of Life Through the Ages. *National Geographic* 81(2):141-84.

Kottak, Conrad
:   1994 *Anthropology. The Exploration of Human Diversity.* New York: McGraw Hill.

Kurtz, Donald V.
  1994   Winnowing the "Great Kalahari Debate"; Its Impact on
         Hunter-Gatherer Societies: A Review of Current Literature.
         Polar 17(1):67-80.
Landau, Misia
  1991   *Narratives of Human Evolution.* New Haven: Yale University
         Press.
Lancaster, Jane
  1989   Women in Biosocial Perspective. In Sandra Morgan, ed.,
         *Gender and Anthropology. Critical Reviews for Research and
         Teaching,* pp. 95-115. Washington, DC: The American
         Anthropological Association.
Langness, L.L.
  1993   *The Study of Culture.* San Francisco: Chandler and Sharp
         Publishers, Inc.
Leakey, Mary
  1979   3.6 Million Year Old Footprints in the Ashes of Time.
         National Geographic 155(4):448.
Leakey, Richard, and Roger Lewin
  1992   *Origins Reconsidered. In Search of What Makes Us Human.* New
         York: Doubleday.
Lee, Richard B.
  1969   !Kung Bushman Subsistence: An Input-Output Analysis. In
         P. Vayda, ed., *Ecological Studies in Cultural Anthropology,* pp.
         47-79. Garden City, NY: Natural History Press.
  1992   Art, Science, or Politics? The Crisis in Hunter-Gatherer
         Studies. *American Anthropologist* 94(1):31-54.
Lee, Richard, and Irven DeVore, eds.
  1968   *Man the Hunter.* Chicago: Aldine Publishing.
  1976   *Kalahari Hunter Gatherers: Studies of the !Kung San and Their
         Neighbors.* Cambridge: Harvard University Press.
Leibowitz, Lila
  1993   Perspectives on the Evolution of Sex Differences.
         In Caroline B. Brettell and Carolyn F. Sargent, eds., *Gender
         in Cross-Cultural Perspective,* pp. 5-13. Englewood Cliffs, NJ:
         Prentice Hall.
Lemonik, Michael D.
  1994   How Man Began. *Time* 143(11), March 14:38-45.

Levins, Richard, and Richard Lewontin
  1985 *The Dialectical Biologist.* Cambridge: Harvard University Press.
Lewin, Roger
  1987 *Bones of Contention. Controversies in the Search for Human Origins.* New York: Simon and Schuster.
  1993 Paleolithic Paint Job. *Discover* 14(7):64-70.
Lightman, Bernard
  1989 Ideology, Evolution and Late-Victorian Agnostic Popularizers. In James R. Moore, ed., *History, Humanity and Evolution,* pp. 285-309. Cambridge: Cambridge University Press.
Linton, Sally
  1971 Woman the Gatherer: Male Bias in Anthropology. In S.E. Jacobs, ed., *Women in Perspective,* pp. 9-21. Urbana and Chicago: University of Illinois Press. Reprinted under Sally Slocum. In Rayna R. Reiter, ed., *Towards an Anthropology of Women,* pp. 36-50. New York: Monthly Review Press.
Lopez-Gonzaga, Violeta
  1983 *Peasants in the Hills. A Study of the Dynamics of Social Change among the Buhid Swidden Cultivators in the Philippines.* Diliman: University of the Philippines Press.
Lorenz, Konrad
  1966 *On Aggression.* New York: Harcourt Brace Jovanovich.
Lovejoy, Arthur O.
  1936 *The Great Chain of Being. A Study of the History of an Idea.* Cambridge: Harvard University Press.
Lovejoy, C. Owen
  1981 The Origin of Man. *Science* 211: 341-50.
Lutz, Catherine, and Jane L. Collins
  1993 *Reading National Geographic.* Chicago: University of Chicago Press.
Lyons, Harriet
  1981 Anthropologists, Moralities, and Relativities: The Problem of Genital Mutilation. *Canadian Review of Sociology and Anthropology* 18(4):499-518.
Marcus, George E., and Michael M.J. Fischer
  1986 *Anthropology as Cultural Critique. An Experimental Moment in the Human Sciences.* Chicago: University of Chicago Press.

Marshack, Alexander
  1996 A Middle Paleolithic Symbolic Composition from the Golan Heights: The Earliest Known Depictive Image. *Current Anthropology* 37(2):357-65.

McDermott, LeRoy
  1996 Self-Representation in Upper Paleolithic Female Figurines. *Current Anthropology* 37(2):227-75.

McGrew, W.C.
  1981 The Female Chimpanzee as a Human Evolutionary Prototype. In Frances Dahlberg, ed., *Woman the Gatherer,* pp. 35-74. New Haven and London: Yale University Press.

McKie, Robin
  1993 How Mankind Became Upright, Naked and Brainy. *The Globe and Mail,* Saturday, November 27.

Mead, Margaret
  1928 *Coming of Age in Samoa.* New York: William Morrow and Company.

Merchant, Carolyn
  1980 *The Death of Nature: Women, Ecology, and the Scientific Revolution.* New York: Harper & Row.

Michie, Helena
  1987 *The Flesh Made Word. Female Figures and Women's Bodies.* New York: Oxford University Press.

Miles, Margaret R.
  1985a The Virgin's One Bare Breast: Female Nudity and Religious Meaning in Tuscan Early Renaissance Culture. In Susan Suleiman, ed., *The Female Body in Western Culture. Contemporary Perspectives,* pp. 193-208. Cambridge: Harvard University Press.
  1985b *Image as Insight. Visual Understanding in Western Christianity and Secular Culture.* Boston: Beacon Press.
  1989 *Carnal Knowing. Female Nakedness and Religious Meaning in the Christian West.* Boston: Beacon Press.

Monastersky, Richard
  1993 Mysteries of the Orient. *Discover* 14(4):38-48.

Morgan, Elaine
  1972 *The Descent of Woman.* New York: Stein and Day.
  1982 *The Aquatic Ape.* New York: Stein and Day.

Morgan, Sandra, ed.

1989   *Gender and Anthropology. Critical Reviews for Research and Teaching.* Washington: American Anthropological Association.

Morris, Desmond

1967   *The Naked Ape: A Zoologist's Study of the Human Animal.* New York: McGraw-Hill.

Moser, Stephanie

1992   The Visual Language of Archeology: A Case Study of the Neanderthals. *Antiquity* 66: 831-44.

Nanda, Serena

1993   Neither Man nor Woman: The Hijras of India. In Caroline B. Brettell and Carolyn F. Sargent, eds., *Gender in Cross-Cultural Perspective*, pp. 175-79. Englewood Cliffs, NJ: Prentice Hall.

Nead, Linda

1988   *Myths of Sexuality. Representations of Women in Victorian Britain.* Oxford: Basil Blackwell.

1990   The Female Nude. *Signs* 15(2):323-35.

Newell, Norman D.

1974   Evolution Under Attack. *Natural History* 83(4):32-39.

Ortner, Sherry B.

1974   Is Female to Male as Nature Is to Culture? In Michelle Z. Rosaldo and Louise Lamphere, eds., *Women, Culture and Society*, pp. 67-88. Stanford: Stanford University Press.

Osborn, M.F.

1936   *Men of the Old Stone Age.* New York: Scribner. 1st Edition 1915.

Ostrom, John, and Theodore Delevoryas

1977   *A Guide to the Rudolph Zallinger Mural* The Age of the Reptiles in the Peabody Museum, Yale University. New Haven: Discovery Supplement Number 1, Peabody Museum of Natural History, Yale University.

Owen, Roger, James J. Deetz and A.D. Fisher, eds.

1967   *The North American Indians. A Sourcebook.* New York: MacMillan Publishing.

Pearce, Lynne

1991   *Woman Image Text. Readings in Pre-Raphaelite Art and Literature.* Toronto: University of Toronto Press.

Pelto, Perti, and Gretel Pelto

1978   *Anthropological Research: The Structure of Inquiry.* 2nd Edition. Cambridge: Cambridge University Press.

Pericot, Luis

    1961   The Social Life of the Spanish Paleolithic Hunters as Shown by Levantine Art. In S. L. Washburn, ed., *The Social Life of Early Man*, pp. 194-213. New York: Wenner-Gren Foundation for Anthropological Research and Chicago: Aldine Publishing.

Peterson, Jean T.

    1978a *The Ecology of Social Boundaries.* Chicago: University of Illinois Press.

    1978b Hunter-Gatherer/Farmer Exchange. *American Anthropologist* 80: 355-61.

Pfeiffer, John E.

    1972   *The Emergence of Man.* New York: Harper and Row.

    1978   *The Emergence of Man.* 3rd Edition. New York: Harper and Row.

Pilbeam, D.R.

    1980   Major Trends in Human Evolution. In L.K. Koenigsson, ed., *Current Argument on Early Man*, pp. 261-351. Oxford: Pergamon Press.

Poirier, Frank.

    1982   *An Introduction to Physical Anthropology and the Archaeological Record.* Minneapolis: Burgess Publishing.

Poirier, Frank, W.A. Stini and K.B. Wreden

    1994   *In Search of Ourselves. An Introduction to Physical Anthropology.* Englewood Cliffs, NJ: Prentice Hall.

Polanyi, Karl

    1968   The Economy as Instituted Process. In Edward E. LeClair, Jr. and Harold K. Schneider, eds., *Economic Anthropology.* New York: Holt, Rinehart and Winston. Reprinted from *Trade and Markets in the Early Empires,* pp. 122-43. Karl Polanyi, Conrad Arsenberg and Harry Pearson, eds., 1958. New York: The Free Press.

Reader's Digest

    1984   *Quest for the Past.* New York: Reader's Digest Association.

Rensberger, Boyce

    1981   Facing the Past. *Science* 81 (October):40-51.

    1994   Skull of Oldest Human Ancestor Is Found. *The Washington Post,* Thursday, March 31, 1994.

Richards, Graham
    1991   The Refutation That Never Was: The Reception of the Aquatic Ape Theory, 1972-1987. In Roede, Machteld et al., eds., *The Aquatic Ape: Fact or Fiction? The First Scientific Evaluation of a Controversial Theory of Human Evolution.* London: Souvenir Press.

Roede, Machteld, and Jan Wind, John M. Patrick and
Vernon Reynolds, eds.
    1991   *The Aquatic Ape: Fact or Fiction? The First Scientific Evaluation of a Controversial Theory of Human Evolution.* London: Souvenir Press.

Rose, Lisa, and Fiona Marshall
    1996   Meat Eating, Hominid Sociality, and Home Bases Revisited. *Current Anthropology* 37(2):307-38.

Rosser, Sue V.
    1990   *Female-Friendly Science. Applying Women's Studies Methods and Theories to Attract Students.* New York: Pergamon Press.

Rudwick, Martin
    1989   Encounters with Adam, or At Least the Hyaenas: Nineteenth-Century Visual Representations of the Deep Past. In James R. Moore, ed., *History, Humanity and Evolution,* pp. 231-51. Cambridge: Cambridge University Press.

Russell, Pamela
    1991   Men Only? The Myths about European Paleolithic Artists. In D. Walde and N.D. Willows, eds., *The Archeology of Gender,* pp. 346-51. Proceedings of the 22nd Annual Chacmool Conference. Calgary: The Archaeological Association of the University of Calgary.

Sacks, Karen
    1989   Toward a Unified Theory of Class, Race and Gender. *American Ethnologist* 16:534-50.

Sahlins, Marshall
    1982   The Original Affluent Society. In Johnnetta B. Cole, ed., *Anthropology for the Eighties. Introductory Readings,* pp. 219-40. New York: The Free Press. Reprinted from *Stone Age Economics,* 1972.

Said, Edward
    1978   *Orientalism.* New York: Pantheon.

Sarich, Vincent M.
   1968   The Origin of Hominids: An Immunological Approach.
          In S.L. Washburn and Phyllis C. Jay, eds., *Perspectives on Human
          Evolution*, pp. 94-121. New York: Holt, Rinehart and Winston.
Service, Elman R.
   1966   *The Hunters.* Englewood Cliffs, NJ: Prentice Hall.
Shelley, Cameron
   1996   Rhetorical and Demonstrative Modes of Visual Argument:
          Looking at Images of Human Evolution. *Argumentation and
          Advocacy* 33(2):53-68.
Shostak, Marjorie
   1981   *Nisa, the Life and Words of a !Kung Woman.* Cambridge:
          Harvard University Press.
Shreeve, James
   1992   As the Old World Turns. Human Origins. *Discover* 14(1):24-29.
   1995   *The Neandertal Enigma.* New York: William Morrow.
Solecki, Ralph S.
   1971   *Shanidar. The First Flower People.* New York: Alfred A. Knopf.
Solway, Jacqueline, and Richard B. Lee
   1990   Foragers, Genuine or Spurious? Situating the Kalahari San in
          History. *Current Anthropology* 31(2):109-22.
Sorrell, Mark, ed.
   1981   *Reconstructing the Past.* London: Batsford Academic and
          Educational.
Spector, Janet D., and Mary K. Whelan
   1989   Incorporating Gender into Archaeology Courses. In Sandra
          Morgen ed., *Gender and Anthropology. Critical Reviews for
          Research and Teaching*, pp. 65-94. Washington, DC: American
          Anthropological Association.
Sperling, Susan
   1991   Baboons with Briefcases vs. Langurs in Lipstick. In Micaela
          di Leonardo, ed., *Gender at the Crossroads of Knowledge.
          Feminist Anthropology in the Post Modern Era*, pp. 204-34.
          Berkeley: University of California Press.
Staski, Edward, and J. Marks
   1992   *Evolutionary Anthropology. An Introduction to Physical
          Anthropology and Archaeology.* New York: Harcourt Brace
          Jovanovich College Publishers.

Stern, J.T., Jr., and R.L. Susman
  1983   The Locomotor Anatomy of *Australopithecus afarensis.*
          American Journal of Physical Anthropology 60:279-317.
Stevens, William
  1994   The Tracks of Man in Mud and Fossil. *The Globe and Mail,*
          Saturday, January 22.
Stocking, George W.
  1968   *Race, Culture and Evolution. Essays in the History of Anthropology.*
          New York: The Free Press.
Strathern, Marilyn
  1980   No Nature, No Culture: The Hagen Case. In Carol
          MacCormack and Marilyn Strathern, eds., *Nature, Culture and
          Gender,* pp. 174-222. Cambridge: Cambridge University Press.
Stringer, Chrisopher, and Clive Gamble
  1993   *In Search of the Neanderthals. Solving the Puzzle of Human
          Origins.* London: Thames and Hudson.
Suleiman, Susan
  1985   *The Female Body in Western Culture. Contemporary Perspectives.*
          Cambridge: Harvard University Press.
Sydie, R.A.
  1992   The Female Body in Eighteenth-Century Art. In D.H. Currie
          and V. Raoul, eds., *Anatomy of Gender. Women's Struggle for the
          Body,* pp. 65-80. Ottawa: Carleton University Press.
Szwed, John F.
  1975   Race and the Embodiment of Culture. In Jonathan Benthall
          and Ted Polhemus, eds., *The Body as a Medium of Expression.*
          London: Allen Lane.
Tannen, D.
  1993   Wears Jumpsuit, Sensible Shoes, Uses Husband's Last
          Name. *New York Times Magazine,* June 20:18, 52, 54.
Tanner, Nancy
  1981   *On Becoming Human.* New York: Cambridge University Press.
  1987   The Chimpanzee Model Revisited and the Gathering
          Hypothesis. In Warren G. Kinzey, ed., *The Evolution of
          Human Behavior: Primate Models*, pp. 3-27. Albany:
          State University of New York Press.
Tanner, Nancy, and Adrienne L. Zihlman
  1976   Women in Evolution. Part I: Innovation and Selection in
          Human Origins. *Signs* 1(3, part 1):585-608.

Tattersall, Ian
  1993   *The Human Odyssey. Four Million Years of Human Evolution.*
          New York: Prentice Hall.
  1995   *The Fossil Trail. How We Know What We Think We Know About
          Human Evolution.* New York: Oxford University Press.
Taussig, Michael
  1992   *The Nervous System.* New York: Routledge.
Thomas, Elizabeth Marshall
  1958   *The Harmless People.* New York: Vintage Books.
Tiger, Lionel
  1969   *Men in Groups.* New York: Random House.
Tobias, Phillip V.
  1974   The Taung Skull Revisited. *Natural History* 83(10):38-43.
Tooby, John, and Irven DeVore
  1987   The Reconstruction of Hominid Behavioral Evolution
          through Strategic Modeling. In Warren Kinzey, ed.,
          The Evolution of Human Behavior: Primate Models, pp. 183-237.
          New York: State University of New York Press.
Treviño, Sergio
  1990   *Grain Collection. Humans' Natural Ecological Niche.* Translated
          by Rebeca San Martin-Feeney. New York: Vantage Press.
  1995   Victims of Our Own Intelligence. *American Anthropological
          Association Newsletter* 36(1):8.
Trinkaus, Erik, ed.
  1989   *The Emergence of Modern Humans. Biocultural Adaptations in the
          Later Pleistocene.* Cambridge: Cambridge University Press.
Trinkaus, Erik, and Pat Shipman
  1993   *The Neandertals: Changing the Image of Mankind.* New York:
          Knopf.
Tsing, Anna Lowenhaupt
  1993   *In the Realm of the Diamond Queen.* Princeton: Princeton
          University Press.
Tuttle, Russel H.
  1985   Ape Footprints and Laetoli Impressions: A Response to the
          SUNY Claims. In P.V. Tobias, ed., *Hominid Evolution: Past,
          Present and Future,* pp.129-33. New York: Liss.
  1988   What's New in African Paleoanthropology? *American Review
          of Anthropology* 17:391-426.

Unger, Rhoda, and Mary Crawford
  1992 *Women and Gender. A Feminist Psychology.* New York: McGraw Hill.
Valeri, Valerio
  1990 Both Nature and Culture. Reflections on Menstrual and Parturitional Taboos in Huaulu (Seram). In Jane M. Atkinson and Shelly Errington, eds., *Power and Difference. Gender in Island Southeast Asia,* pp. 235-72. Stanford, CA: Stanford University Press.
van Benthem van den Bergh, Godfried
  1986 The Improvement of Human Means of Orientation: Towards Synthesis in the Social Sciences. In Raymond Apthorpe and A. Krahl, eds., *Development Studies: Critique and Renewal,* pp. 109-35. Leiden: E.J. Brill.
Volback, Wolfgang Fritz
  1964 *Early Christian Art.* New York: Harry N. Abrams.
Vrba, Elisabeth S.
  1993 The Pulse That Produced Us. *Natural History* 102(5):47-51.
Warner, Marina
  1985 *Monuments and Maidens. The Allegory of the Female Form.* New York: Atheneum.
Washburn, Sherwood
  1961 *The Social Life of Early Man.* Sherwood Washburn, ed. Viking Fund Publications in Anthropology, No. 31. New York: Wenner-Gren Foundation for Anthropological Research and Chicago: Aldine Publishing.
  1962 The Analysis of Primate Evolution with Particular Reference to the Origin of Man. In W.W. Howells, ed., *Ideas on Evolution: Selected Essays 1949-61,* pp. 154-71. Cambridge: Harvard University Press. Original Publication 1951.
  1968 One Hundred Years of Biological Anthropology. In J. Brew, ed., *One Hundred Years of Anthropology,* pp. 97-115. Cambridge: Harvard University Press.
Washburn, S., and Virginia Avis
  1958 Evolution of Human Behavior. In Anne Roe and George Gaylord Simpson, eds., *Behavior and Evolution,* pp. 421-36. New Haven: Yale University Press.

Washburn, S., and Irven DeVore
    1961   Social Behavior of Baboons and Early Man. In S.L.
           Washburn, ed., *The Social Life of Early Man,* pp. 91-105. Viking
           Fund Publications in Anthropology, No. 31. New York:
           Wenner-Gren Foundation for Anthropological Research and
           Chicago: Aldine Publishing.
Washburn, S., and David A. Hamburg
    1965   The Study of Primate Behavior. In I. DeVore, ed., *Primate
           Behavior: Field Studies of Monkeys and Apes,* pp. 1-13. New
           York: Holt, Rinehart and Winston.
Washburn, Sherwood, and Phylis Jay, eds.
    1968   *Perspectives on Human Evolution,* Vol. 1. New York: Holt,
           Rinehart and Winston.
Washburn, Sherwood, Phylis Jay and Jane B. Lancaster
    1968   Field Studies of Old World Monkeys and Apes. In Sherwood
           Washburn and Phylis Jay, eds., *Perspectives on Human
           Evolution,* Vol. 1, pp. 196-212. New York: Holt, Rinehart and
           Winston.
Washburn, Sherwood, and C.S. Lancaster
    1968   The Evolution of Hunting. In Sherwood Washburn and Phylis
           Jay, eds., *Perspectives on Human Evolution,* Vol. 1., pp. 213-29.
           New York: Holt, Rinehart and Winston.
Washburn, Sherwood, and R. Moore
    1974   *Ape Into Man.* New York: Little, Brown Publishers.
Watson, Ernest W.
    1956   Stanley Meltzoff, Picture Maker for the Printing Press.
           American Artist 20:25-66.
Weaver, K.F.
    1985   Stones, Bones and Early Man. The Search for Our Ancestors.
           National Geographic 168(5):574-623.
Wheeler, P.E.
    1985   The Loss of Functional Body Hair in Man: The Influence of
           Thermal Environment, Body Form and Bipedality. *Journal of
           Human Evolution* 14:23-28.
White, T.D., Gen Suwa and Berhane Asfaw
    1994   *Australopithecus ramidus,* a new species of early hominid from
           Aramis, Ethiopia. *Nature* 371:306-12.

Whitehead, Harriet
    1981 The Bow and the Burden Strap: A New Look at Institutionalized Homosexuality in Native North America. In Sherry Ortner and Harriet Whitehead, eds., *Sexual Meanings,* pp. 80-115. Cambridge: Cambridge University Press.

Whitley, Richard
    1985 Knowledge Producers and Knowledge Acquirers. Popularization as a Relation Between Scientific Fields and Their Publics. In Terry Shin and R. Whitley, eds., *Expository Science: Forms and Functions of Popularization,* pp. 3-28. Dordrecht: D. Reidel Publishers.

Wiber, Melanie G.
    1994 Undulating Women and Erect Men: Visual Imagery of Gender and Progress in Illustrations of Human Evolution. *Visual Anthropology* 7:1-20.

Wilford, John Noble
    1994 Skull in Ethiopia Is Linked to Earliest Man. *The New York Times,* March 31, sec. A, p. 1, col. 3.

Wills, Christopher
    1993 Escape From Stupid World. *Discover* 14(8):54-59.

Wilmsen, Edwin N.
    1989 *Land Filled With Flies. A Political Economy of the Kalahari.* Chicago: University of Chicago Press.
    1993 On the Search for (Truth) and Authority: A Reply to Lee and Guenther. *Current Anthropology* 34(5):715-21.

WoldeGabriel, G., T.D. White, G. Suwa, P. Renne, J. de Heinzelln, W. Hart and G. Helken
    1994 Ecological and Temporal Placement of Early Pliocene Hominids at Aramis, Ethiopia. *Nature* 371:330-33.

Wolf, Eric
    1982 *Europe and the People Without History.* Berkeley: University of California Press.

Wolpoff, Milford H.
    1989 The Place of the Neandertals in Human Evolution. In Erik Trinkaus, ed., *The Emergence of Modern Humans,* pp. 97-141. Cambridge: Cambridge University Press.

Wright, Robert
    1994 Our Cheating Hearts. Devotion and Betrayal, Marriage
          and Divorce: How Evolution Shaped Human Love. *Time*
          144(7):28-36.
Young, Louise B., ed.
    1970 *Evolution of Man.* New York: Oxford University Press.
Zihlman, Adrienne L.
    1967 Human locomotion: A Reappraisal of the Functional and
          Anatomical Evidence. Ph.D. thesis, University of California,
          Berkeley.
    1978 Women and Evolution, Part II: Subsistence and Social
          Organization among Early Hominids. *Signs* 4(1):4-20.
    1981 Women as Shapers of the Human Adaptation. In Frances
          Dahlberg, ed., *Woman the Gatherer*, pp. 75-120. New Haven
          and London: Yale University Press.
    1985 *Australopithecus afarensis*: two sexes or two species? In P.V.
          Tobias, ed., *Hominid Evolution: Past, Present and Future,* pp. 213-
          20. New York: Liss.
    1989 Woman the Gatherer: The Role of Women in Early Hominid
          Evolution. In Morgan, ed., *Gender and Anthropology. Critical
          Reviews for Research and Teaching*, pp. 21-40. Washington:
          American Anthropological Association.
    1991 Gender: The View from Physical Anthropology. In D.
          Walde and N.D. Willows, eds., *The Archeology of Gender*, pp.
          4-10. Proceedings of the 22nd Annual Chacmool
          Conference. Calgary: The Archaeological Association of the
          University of Calgary.
    1994 Naked Truth: Letter to the Editor. *Discover* 15(2):10.
Zihlman, Adrienne, and Douglas Cramer
    1976 Human Locomotion. *Natural History* 85(1):64-69.

Index

Adam, 57, 85, 194. *See also* Biblical
   themes
adaptation, 179
   for cause, 153
adaptationism, 80, 149, 154, 159, 177,
   183
   evolutionary bush vs. ladder,
     153-54
   nuclear family, 180
   retrospective fallacy, 160
   sexual division of labour, 180
   utility
     current, 179
     future, 179, 182
aesthetic athleticism, 51, 82, 84, 100,
   231. *See also* male
aggression
   adaptive significance of, 79, 80
   as a masculine trait, 25, 92, 132
Agta, 145
American Museum of Natural History,
   68, 72, 114, 206, 213-14
analogy
   defined, 122-23
   foragers as, 108-109, 121, 128
   in origins research, 103, 123, 124-49
   Man the Hunter, 108-109
     baboon, 124, 131-34, 154
     langurs, 139-40
   scientific basis, 124
   Washburn's contribution to the use
     of, 122, 124, 128
   Woman the Gatherer, 109
     chimpanzee, 109-10, 136
anatomical reconstructions, 48
   Matternes, 72-73
androcentrism
   in origins illustrations, 81, 86, 232

in origins publications, 3, 190, 202,
   232
in origins research
   the feminist challenge, 34, 38,
     81, 106-107
   in science practice, 143
   Man the Hunter, 38, 137
   Sherwood Washburn, 138
anthropology
   and feminism, 76-78
   gender research, 76, 79
   nature/culture boundary, 77
   nature/nurture research, 79
   visual, 235
aquatic ape theory, 27, 34. *See also*
   Morgan, Elaine
art, 231
artists
   labour of, 205
   motives of, 3, 216
ascending anachronisms, 93
Auel, Jean M., 6
australopithecine, 7, 29. *See also*
   Australopithecus
   dates of, 172
   gender representation, 87-94, 196,
     202
   gender roles, 87, 222
   gracile form
     as ancestral species, 29-30, 92,
      114, 165
   importance of, 85, 86
   in illustrations, 86-94, 167, 168,
     191-99
     ape-like, 88, 91
     Negroid, 93, 113-14, 169
   nuclear family, 87, 170
   "of nature, not in nature," 167

robust form
    as evolutionary backwater, 30,
        90-91
Australopithecus, 24. *See also*
    australopithecine
    ancestral status, 165
    Australopithecus afarensis, 59
        adaptive stability, 181-82
        sexual dimorphism of, 39, 94
    Australopithecus boisei, 7, 32
        evolutionary dead end, 30
        extinction at the hands of *Homo
            habilis*, 7
        sexual dimorphism, 39, 94
    Australopithecus ramidus, 32
    in ladder of human evolution, 84
author motives, 207, 217-19

baboons
    in human origins analogy, 124, 154
    sexual infidelity among, 124-25
    social life, 132-34
Biblical themes
    Adam, 85, 194
    australopithecines and, 85, 89, 170,
        194
    Eve, 194, 196
    in illustrations, 86, 89, 169
        Eden convention, 169-70, 176
bipedality
    at the hominoid/hominid transition,
        42
    functionalist explanations, 42, 179,
        180-81
    origins of, 24-25, 31, 135, 161
    sign of modernity, 184
    Woman-the-Gatherer hypothesis
        and, 37, 135-36
    Zihlman's research and, 35, 135-36
blame orientation, 232
blind test, 9

bodily revision, 51-52
    of australopithecines, 86-87
    "brief," 210. *See also* "charge"
Burgess Shale, 163
    in evolutionary theory, 165
    Walcott's conservatism, 177
Burian, Zdeněk
    biography, 69
    illustrations, 70, 97, 98
        female mourner, 200
        first artist, 71, 116-17, 199-200
        Homo erectus in Java, 95, 115, 170
        Neandertal burial, 98, 118
        Neandertal rhino hunters, 97,
            116, 130, 172
    illustrative style, 70, 71, 129
    tracking copyright, 215
Bushmen, 40. *See also* Dobe San; !Kung
    as inspiration for illustrations, 93,
        121-22, 145
    Great Kalahari Debate, 141-49
    historicity, 144-46
    Harvard Bushmen (San) Project,
        127
    use in analogy, 109, 142-44

captions, 222
caricature, 60, 172, 175. *See also*
    grotesque; hybridization;
    inversion
cave art, 118
"charge," 210, 219. *See also* "brief"
chimpanzee
    and female centrality, 109, 136
    as origins analogy, 109-110, 136
Christian representation, 55-61
    books of the illiterate, 58, 82
    female, 56, 57, 58
        Eve codification, 56, 57, 82
        Virgin Mary (Madonna)
            codification, 56, 57, 82

male, 55-56, 58
    Christ, 56, 59
    nakedness, 57
    nudity, 57
    witchcraft, 59
commodification
    of images, 15, 203-206, 215, 235
commoditization
    consequences of, 223
commodity
    defined, 203
    value
        exchange, 203-204
        social use, 203-204
cone of increasing diversity, 164, 178.
    See also Darwin; evolution; Gould
conflation, 105
contested meanings, 21, 228-30. *See
    also* Haraway, Donna
copyright, 15, 215-16
    form of trademark, 217
Cro-Magnon illustrations, 94-95, 168
cultural studies, 11-12
culture, 146, 148-49
    high culture, 98

Darwin, Charles
    delay in publishing, 178
    on human evolution, 157, 158-59
deconstruction, of illustrative content,
    82, 234-35
    feminism and, 50
descending anachronisms, 93
DeVore, Irven
    baboon research, 109, 123, 124,
        132-34
    biography, 127
    genderism, 80, 139
    Harvard Bushman (San) Project,
        127
    on feminism, 148

dioramic representations, 48, 70, 97,
    206, 213, 223
division of labour, 79, 87, 102-103, 197
Dobe San. *See also* Bushmen; !Kung;
    Richard Lee
    as inspiration for illustrations, 93,
        121-22, 145
    Great Kalahari Debate, 141-49
    historicity, 144-45
    the Harvard Bushmen (San) Project,
        127
    use in analogy, 109, 142-44
dualism, 233

early transition
    from ape to hominid, 29
encephalization, 25
erasure, 206, 235
    of the artist, 205
    of the production process, 206,
        207-208
    within illustrations, 206
eroticism
    in female representation, 83, 190,
        194, 199-200, 202, 218-19, 232,
        237
    in male representation, 194
    nudity, 66
    recent trend, 15, 83, 236, 189-201
essentialism, 45, 178
    as a logical flaw, 14, 184-87
estrus
    evolutionary problems caused by,
        26
    sexual receptivity, 26
Euro-american, 6 n1
Eve. *See also* Biblical themes; Christian
    representation
    in female representation, 57, 194,
        200, 201, 237
    Gothic, 54

Lucy as, 194, 196
  made repellent, 59
  undulating, 57, 58
evolution. *See also* Darwin; Gould,
    Stephen Jay
  discourse, 153
    conservatism in, 176-78
  historical meaning, 157
  human, 14, 154-55, 159, 161
    biological change, 155
  phenotypical variation, 159
  theoretical paradigm in
      anthropology, 79
    flaws in, 178-88

family. *See also* nuclear family
  antiquity of, 7, 87
  cult of the nuclear, 98
  in illustrations, 87, 88, 98
  role in society, 211
  triangle, 63, 87, 89, 98
  Victorian representation of, 63
fashion. *See also* ghostly clothing; Anne
    Hollander; invisible clothing
  defined, 54
  influence on the European nude, 54
female
  atomism, 80
  black (body), 117
  centrality, 186-87, 191, 198, 220
  in ladder of human evolution, 85
  natural, 88, 228
  nutritional stresses, 37
  nude, 51, 53-54, 56
    as allegory for sin, 53, 56, 59,
        117, 189
    Gothic, 54-55
  passive, 62, 92
  representation in art
    caricature, 60
    cult of sensibility, 61

fetishism, 59, 189
  grotesque other, 171
  hybridization, 61
  inversion, 60-61
  modern, 66
  motherhood code, 90, 200, 222
  rococo, 61
  Victorian, 63
  reproductive demands on, 81, 106,
      136
  reproductive strategies, 81, 137, 139
  science skills, 186-87
  sexuality, 62, 236
  static, 97, 228
feminism, 76, 78, 139, 143, 148, 150,
    186, 228
  and anthropology, 76-78, 109, 178
fetishism, 59, 189
"First Family," 8, 31, 39, 88, 93. *See also*
    Lucy
foragers. *See also* gathering;
    hunter/gatherers; !Kung
  as origins analogy, 108-109, 121,
      128
  the original affluent society, 112
foraging, 142-43. *See also* gathering;
    hunter/gatherers
  importance in early transition
      period, 36
  symbiotic relationship, 145
functionalism
  bipedalism, 42, 135, 179, 180-81
  gender and survival, 79-80
  logical flaws, 14, 149, 178-84

Garden of Eden
  artistic convention, 169, 201
  as thematic content, 169
gatekeeping
  in publishing, 187, 209
  of images, 214-15

gathering, 36, 136, 138, 143, 183. *See also* foraging; hunter/gatherers

gaze

male active, 65, 195, 196, 202

seven gazes, 4

gender. *See also* sex role specialization

defined, 75

dimorphism, 31, 94, 229-39

gender attributes, 75, 79, 81, 83, 85, 90, 103, 196, 233

gender identity, 76

gender roles, 75, 79, 81, 83, 85, 197, 199, 201, 202, 233

Victorian, 62

in anthropological research, 77, 188

genderism, 234

in evolutionary research, 80, 154, 162, 187

in illustrations, 2, 81-100, 196, 199, 231-32

in physical anthropology, 80

ghostly clothing, 53, 193-94, 195, 196, 200. *See also* fashion; Hollander, Anne; invisible clothing

Gifford-Gonzalez, Diane, 4, 12, 94

"Drudge-on-a-Hide," 98

Goodall, Jane, 40, 109

influence on Zihlman, 136

Gould, Stephen Jay. *See also* evolution

adaptationism, 14, 179

Burgess Shale, 177-78

bush model of evolution, 158, 164

cone of increasing diversity, 164

human evolution, 161-62

intelligence feedback loop, 162

science popularization, 163

visual representation, 163-64

grandstanding, 218. *See also* popularization

Great Chain of Being, 28, 156, 171-72, 175

Great Kalahari Debate 13, 141-49. *See also* Richard Lee

historical revisionism, 144

Greco-Roman

artistic traditions, 51

nude, 51

grotesque, 60, 231. *See also* caricature; hybridization; inversion

Neandertal, 97, 98, 172, 175

women as grotesque other, 60, 96, 170, 171

guarantee of continuity, 130, 162, 185

Gurche, John

illustrations, 93, 194

Haraway, Donna. *See also* contested meanings

boundary sciences, 20-21, 160

culture/nature boundary, 106

feminism, 76-77, 237

Lucy as Barbie Doll, 196

neocolonial practices, 48, 107, 111, 117, 141

patriarchal conspiracy, 236-37

primatology, 127

science and culture, 148

sociobiology, 139-40

story field, 154-55, 187, 228-29

destabilizing, 237

hermeneutics, 148

Hollander, Anne, 53-55, 193. *See also* fashion; ghostly clothing; invisible clothing

erotic awareness, 55, 193, 201

hominids

gathering, 36

hominoids

foraging, 36

Homo erectus, 7, 24, 82, 160, 172

Homo erectus Boy, 32

in illustrations

cultural tropes, 170, 171
gender representation, 90, 94-97
Negroid, 114-15
Homo habilis, 24, 30, 59, 93, 115, 167
Homo sapiens sapiens, 24, 117, 160, 174
gender representation, 99-100
in illustrations, 99-100, 115, 165,
   167, 175-76
in nature, not of nature, 167, 176
hunter/gatherers. *See also* foraging;
   gathering
definition, 142-43
female contributions, 135, 143
Lee, Richard, 142-43
male hunting, 129, 141-42
origins analogy, 125, 142
hybridization, 60. *See also* caricature,
   grotesque; inversion
in female representation, 61, 96

iconography, 83, 207
idée fixe
gender in paleoanthropological
   illustrations, 81
in origins research, 128-35
illustrations
anatomical reconstructions, 48, 73
commodities, 204-205, 230
   market life of, 224
defined, 47
dioramic, 48, 70
narrative content, 82
popularization of science, 67-68
power of, 203
production of, 205
science and, 67-69, 73
uncritical consumption of, 47
in education, 82-83
illustrative outcome, 3-4, 5
illustrators
as artists, 67-74, 216

Burian, Zdeněk, 69, 70, 71
Forestier, 68, 70
Gurche, John, 93
Knight, Charles R., 68, 70, 71
Kupka, 68, 70
Matternes, Jay H., 69, 71, 72
Schlecht, Richard, 70
Wilson, Maurice, 68, 70, 71
Zallinger, Rudolph, 68-69
impressionistic vs. authoritative
   voices, 70-71
incident pictures, 64, 73
infanticide
among langurs, 139-40
infants
in illustrations, 89-90
inversion, 60. *See also* caricature,
   grotesque; hybridization
invisible clothing, 53, 193, 199, 202. *See
   also* fashion; ghostly clothing;
   Hollander, Anne
and eroticism, 54, 193

Johanson, Donald C., 38-39, 93
juveniles
in illustrations, 89, 90, 191, 198,
   199, 201

Knight, Charles R.
biography, 68
illustrations
early neolithic hunters, 99, 116,
   119
"Parade of Life," 71, 129, 163
illustrative style, 70, 71
!Kung, 40, 148. *See also* Dobe San;
   Bushmen; Great Kalahari Debate
hunter/gatherers, 142-43
inspiration for origins illustrations,
   93, 121-22, 208
use in analogy, 109-10, 142-45, 146

ladder of human evolution, 83-85,
  157-58, 166. *See also* march of
  progress
Laetoli footprints, 8, 31, 88-89
Landau, Misia, 17, 18
  morphology of folk tales, 17
  narrative constraints, 18, 238
landscape, 67-68, 156
Leakey, Mary, 29, 211
  interpretation of Laetoli footprints,
    8, 31, 88-89
Leakey, Richard, 30, 153
Lee, Richard, 109. *See also* Great
  Kalahari Debate
  Man the Hunter, 142
  contribution of female gathering,
    135
  Harvard Bushman (San) Project,
    127
  postmodernism, 147
  Wilmsen, 146
Lewin, Richard, 153-54
Linnaeus, 156
Looking practices, 209, 220, 222
Lovejoy, C. O., 39
Love-Joy Hypothesis, 19, 38-40, 139,
  175, 202. *See also* nuclear family;
  sexual dimorphism
  in Matternes illustrations, 87, 88, 92
Lucy, 30, 48. *See also* "First Family"
  ancestral form, 92
  as Barbie doll, 189, 196
  bipedality, 31
Lutz, Catherine, and Jane Collins, 210,
  212
  Africa in *National Geographic*, 209
  black bodies in *National Geographic*,
    112
  halo of green, 169
  lyrical fixative, 222

seven gazes in *National Geographic*, 4
women in *National Geographic*, 111

male
  active, 62, 92, 192
  aesthetic athleticism, 51, 82, 84,
    100, 231
  aggression, 25, 92, 132
    hypothesis, 79, 80
  bonding, 25
    hypothesis, 79, 80
  caricature, 60
  centrality in illustrations, 87, 95, 97,
    99, 172, 199, 200
  cultural accomplishments, 88, 98,
    117, 142, 175
  gaze, 65, 195, 196, 202
  in ladder of human evolution, 84
  leadership, 131
  nude, 52
    Gothic, 55
  reproductive strategies, 124-25,
    139-40
  strength hypothesis, 79, 80
    plow theory, 80
  technology, 2, 25, 96
  white (mind), 117, 228
Man the Hunter, 11, 19, 21, 22-27, 44,
  238
  analogy, 108-109
  androcentrism, 38
  conference, 127
  "march of progress," 84. *See also* ladder
    of human evolution
  marked bodies, 2, 100
Martin, Angel
  illustrations, 119
Marxism, 203
  masculine technology, 43
    origins of, 25
  mass culture, 12

mate selection, 38
materialism, 79
Matternes, Jay H.
    androcentrism, 86
    australopithecine illustrations, 86
    biography, 72-73
    eroticism, 192-96
    illustrations, 59, 191
        ancestral australopithecines, 92
        australopithecine family, 87-88,
            116
        australopithecine female digging
            for tubers, 195-96
        fleeing the volcano, 2, 5, 8, 49,
            88, 93, 169
        foraging for figs, 191-95
        Homo erectus and the prairie fire,
            114
        intra-species battle, 92, 197-98
        Johanson and Shreeve endpaper,
            202
        ladder of human evolution, 84,
            113, 167
        Neandertal preparing a kill, 130,
            198, 199, 220
        Paranthropus robustus, 114
        refined ancestral
            australopithecines, 93
        robust australopithecines
            (leaping male), 90, 114
        robust australopithecines
            (digging female), 91
        scavenging australopithecines,
            92, 113
    motives, 216, 217
    realism, 72, 192
    scientific reconstruction, 71, 72-73
Mead, Margaret, 76
meat. *See also* scavenging
    and cultural evolution, 42, 167, 170,
        229

and intelligence, 43
and tools, 43
Meltzoff, Stanley
    illustrations
        Homo erectus fireside scene, 94
    illustrative style, 70-71, 171
meta-narrative, 18
methodology, 9
    blind test, 9
    interviews, 10
Miocene, 23, 24, 37
monogamy, 26, 138. *See also* pair
    bonding
    and masculine provisioning 37-38,
        39, 87, 89, 92, 94, 95
Morgan, Elaine, 21, 23, 27. *See also*
    aquatic ape theory
    Descent of Women, 34
motives
    artist, 218-19
    author, 205, 216-18
    publisher, 208-16

naked, 50, 51-53, 189, 192, 199, 202,
    220. *See also* nudity
    code for primitive, 119
    in Western art conventions, 56-57
National Geographic, 4, 12, 47, 69, 70,
    71, 72, 169, 190, 191, 203
    Christian readership, 211-12
    gatekeeping on illustration
        republication, 214, 215
    human evolution illustrations, 7-8,
        48, 84, 86, 88, 93, 102, 103,
        113, 114, 163 189, 191-96
    production guidelines, 209-10,
        219-20
    representation of women, 111-12
Natural History Museum of London,
    68, 96, 213
natural selection, 154, 157

nature/culture
  boundary, 112, 131, 134, 172
  boundary sciences, 20
    contested meanings, 21
  female is to nature what male is to
    culture, 105-106
  human condition, 161
  low (juveniles, female, dirt), 2, 87, 98
nature/nurture debate, 6, 78-79, 85
Neandertals
  brain size, 173
  cannibalism, 98
  cultural stability, 173-74
  illustrations
    burial representation, 97-98, 118,
      220
    culture, 97-98
    gender representation, 97-99
    nuclear family, 98
    preparing a kill, 130, 198, 199
    revisions, 172, 198
  place in human evolution, 130,
    172-75
nuclear family. *See also* Love-Joy
  Hypothesis
  antiquity of, 7, 87, 88, 139, 211
  cult of the, 98
  in illustrations, 87, 88, 98
  Victorian representation of, 63
nudes, 50, 51-53, 201, 202
  lack of reality in art, 51
  Classical (Greco-Roman), 51
  Gothic, 54-55
nudity, 169, 192-93, 199, 201, 232.
  See also naked
  double meaning, 52, 200
  in public art, 65-66
nuditas virtualis, 52, 120, 169, 231

origins
  analogy, 13

bipedality, 24-25, 31, 135
images
  global marketing of, 230
  gendered behaviour, 78, 139, 180
  human behaviour, 78
  fiction, 5
  nuclear family, 87, 88, 139, 180
  political economy of, 161
  of reproductive behaviour, 78,
    139
  research, 11, 184, 238
  technology, 88
oversimplification, 235

pair bonding, 26, 37-38, 211. *See also*
  monogamy
paleoanthropology, 20
paleontology, 20, 163
  conservatism in, 176-77
Paranthropus, 91-92, 167, 197
patriarchal
  conspiracy, 232-33, 236-37
  Victorian family, 63
Peabody Museum of Natural History,
  69
Peterson, Jean, 145. *See also* Agta
physical anthropology, 20
political correctness
  resistance to, 3
  Women the Gatherer and, 38
popular culture, 12
popularization, 5, 218. *See also*
  grandstanding
  low academic status, 217-18
pornography, 63, 196, 200
postmodernism, 147
  and origins research, 147-48
presentism, 45, 178
  in history, 183-84
  logical flaw, 14, 183-84
primates

as origins analogy, 131-35, 139-40
genderism, 137, 139
primatology, 20, 135, 137
progress
    and evolution, 14, 120, 149, 157,
        166, 176
    in illustrations, 155, 167-76
    motif, 153
pubic hair, 53

"race," 105, 108
racial imagery, 12, 111-19
racism, 105, 110, 115-16, 121, 126. *See
    also* significant other
    Darwin, 158
    physiognomy and, 64
realism, 197, 207, 210
    as objective truth, 9
    role in scientific credibility, 4, 122
readerly autonomy, 3, 4
    conservative, 220, 221-22
    looking practices, 220
reprints
    fees, 206, 212
        barrier to illustrations, 213, 216
    gatekeeping, 214
    permissions, 213
reproductive politics, 78
road to progress, 13. *See also* ladder of
    human evolution; march of
    progress

scavenging, 42-43
    at the hominoid/hominid
        transition, 42, 138-39, 170
    in illustrations, 92
science
    exercise, 218
    popularization, 163, 203, 218, 236
semiotics, 228 n1
    defined, 148

illustrations as signs, 204-205
sex role specialization, 39, 86. *See also*
    gender
sexism. *See also* genderism
    in human evolution research, 39
    in illustrations, 2
sexual dimorphism, 25, 39, 94. *See also*
    Love-Joy Hypothesis
    pelvic differences, 39
    relation to specialized sex roles, 40,
        154
Shanidar Cave, 98
significant other, 107-12, 231-32, 150
    sanitizing the, 210, 223
Smithsonian Institution, 213
sociobiology
    gender, 79, 80, 139
    langur infanticide, 140
    primatology, 139-41
stone tools, 25, 43. *See also* masculine
    technology
story field, 17, 154-55, 187, 228-29,
    237
student responses, 99, 101, 116, 117,
    197-99, 220-21
structural-functionalism
    in anthropology, 79-80
    in primatology, 137, 139
    Sherwood Washburn and, 130
survival of the fittest, 164, 181. *See also*
    Darwin; evolution; Gould,
    Stephen Jay
    functionalism, 179
    natural selection and, 157, 178
    progress through evolution, 92, 177

Tanner, Nancy, 35. *See also* Woman
    the Gatherer; Zihlman, Adrienne
    adaptationism, 182-83
    australopithecine illustration, 196,
        197, 221

!Kung/chimpanzee conflation, 109-10

On Becoming Human, 35

Tarzan theory, 21 n1

Taung Child, 29, 48, 85

Taussig, Michael, 204

taxonomic classification, 156

terrestriality, 131

tool making, 184

trademarks, 214

    legal control, 122, 215

    nation building tool, 230

tropes (visual), 170

undulating women, 51-52, 54-55, 81, 191, 200. *See also* women

universalism, 178

    gender research, 79, 103, 187

    illustrations, 190

    logical flaw, 14, 185-86

Victorian

    cult of motherhood, 63-64

    cult of sensibility, 61

    educational art, 64-65

        history, 65

        social pathology, 64

    family triangle, 63, 87, 89, 98

    female representation, 61

    incident picture, 64, 73

    physiognomy, 8-9, 64

    sexuality, 61-62

    voluminous hair, 62, 100, 200, 201

Virgin Mary (Madonna), 56, 57, 82, 237. *See also* Christian representation

Walcott, C.D., 176-78

Washburn, Sherwood

    anti-racist, 126

    baboon research, 123, 124, 132-34

biography, 126-27

genderism, 80, 125

influence on origins research, 122, 124, 126-27, 129-35

progress and, 131

support for Man the Hunter, 24, 125, 133, 138

use of analogy, 123, 124, 125

Western, 6 n1

whiteness, 105, 117

Wilmsen, Edwin, 144-45. *See also* Great Kalahari Debate

    cultural cohesion, 145

Wilson, Maurice

    biography, 68

    illustrations

        Homo erectus in cave, 90, 95, 115, 170, 206, 235

        Neandertal family, 98

        Swanscombe Man, 100

    illustrative style, 70, 71, 72

witchcraft, 59, 189

women

    as fertile earth, 196

    childbearing hypothesis, 79, 81

    undulating, 51-52, 54-55, 81, 191, 200

    Eve, 57

Woman the Gatherer, 11. *See also* Zihlman, Adrienne; Tanner, Nancy

    academic response, 138

    adaptationism, 182-83

    alternative to Man the Hunter, 19, 21-22, 33-38

    central premise, 138-39

    illustrative response, 189-90

    lack of popularity, 38, 196

    truth value, 237

    use of analogy, 109

Zallinger, Rudolph, 214
    biography, 68-69
    illustrations
        ladder of human evolution, 83,
            113, 167
    illustrative style, 70
Zihlman, Adrienne, 1, 34, 198, 229. *See
    also* Women the Gatherer;
    Tanner, Nancy
    bipedality, 35, 135
    chimpanzee as origins analogy, 40,
        136
    early transition period, 35
        food getting activities, 36, 135
    Natural History publication, 208-209
    positive trends in illustrations,
        189-91
    teaching gender, 1, 189
        origins illustrations in, 190
Zinjanthropos boisei (Zinj), 29